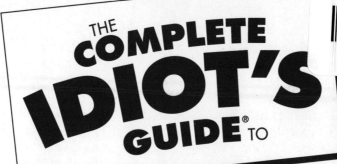

THE COMPLETE IDIOT'S GUIDE® TO

Handwriting Analysis

Second Edition

by Sheila Lowe

ALPHA

A member of Penguin Group (USA) Inc.

This book is dedicated to my brother, Rick Taylor. He's been my inspiration on so many levels, and I'm forever grateful for his presence in my life.

ALPHA BOOKS

Published by the Penguin Group

Penguin Group (USA) Inc., 375 Hudson Street, New York, New York 10014, U.S.A.

Penguin Group (Canada), 10 Alcorn Avenue, Toronto, Ontario, Canada M4V 3B2 (a division of Pearson Penguin Canada Inc.)

Penguin Books Ltd, 80 Strand, London WC2R 0RL, England

Penguin Ireland, 25 St Stephen's Green, Dublin 2, Ireland (a division of Penguin Books Ltd)

Penguin Group (Australia), 250 Camberwell Road, Camberwell, Victoria 3124, Australia (a division of Pearson Australia Group Pty Ltd)

Penguin Books India Pvt Ltd, 11 Community Centre, Panchsheel Park, New Delhi—110 017, India

Penguin Group (NZ), cnr Airborne and Rosedale Roads, Albany, Auckland 1310, New Zealand (a division of Pearson New Zealand Ltd)

Penguin Books (South Africa) (Pty) Ltd, 24 Sturdee Avenue, Rosebank, Johannesburg 2196, South Africa

Penguin Books Ltd, Registered Offices: 80 Strand, London WC2R 0RL, England

International Standard Book Number: 978-1-59257-601-2
Library of Congress Catalog Card Number: 2006932992

09   08   07   8   7   6   5   4   3   2   1

Interpretation of the printing code: The rightmost number of the first series of numbers is the year of the book's printing; the rightmost number of the second series of numbers is the number of the book's printing. For example, a printing code of 07-1 shows that the first printing occurred in 2007.

Printed in the United States of America

Note: This publication contains the opinions and ideas of its author. It is intended to provide helpful and informative material on the subject matter covered. It is sold with the understanding that the author and publisher are not engaged in rendering professional services in the book. If the reader requires personal assistance or advice, a competent professional should be consulted.

The author and publisher specifically disclaim any responsibility for any liability, loss, or risk, personal or otherwise, which is incurred as a consequence, directly or indirectly, of the use and application of any of the contents of this book.

Most Alpha books are available at special quantity discounts for bulk purchases for sales promotions, premiums, fund-raising, or educational use. Special books, or book excerpts, can also be created to fit specific needs.

For details, write: Special Markets, Alpha Books, 375 Hudson Street, New York, NY 10014.

Publisher: *Marie Butler-Knight*
Editorial Director: *Mike Sanders*
Managing Editor: *Billy Fields*
Acquisitions Editor: *Paul Dinas*
Development Editor: *Michael Thomas*
Production Editor: *Kayla Dugger*
Copy Editor: *Amy Borrelli*

Cartoonist: *Richard King*
Cover Designer: *Bill Thomas*
Book Designers: *Trina Wurst/Kurt Owens*
Indexer: *Brad Herriman*
Layout: *Brian Massey*
Proofreader: *Aaron Black*

Contents at a Glance

Contents

Appendixes

Introduction

Is something blocking you from getting what you want, socially, financially, in your marriage? Your career? Sometimes we don't know the answer ourselves, but the causes appear in our handwriting. The fact that you've picked up this book shows that you are interested in learning more about yourself or someone you care about.

Handwriting analysis can provide the kind of information you need to improve your self-image and all your relationships. Like a mirror image of who you really are inside, your handwriting reflects your strengths and potentials, fears and dreams, thinking style and social style, and helps identify areas you might like to develop further.

When I began studying handwriting in 1967, I felt frustrated by the vagueness in the explanations for different parts of handwriting. Even worse were the contradictory definitions between books. How do you know which one to believe?

Graphology is about the way *strokes* are made, not about interpreting particular letters. *The Complete Idiot's Guide to Handwriting Analysis, Second Edition*, teaches the *theory* behind handwriting analysis. Thus, rather than making lists of what each letter supposedly means, you will learn why strokes are formed the way they are and how that is reflected in behavior. By understanding the theory behind the strokes, you'll be able to analyze any handwriting in any language.

Maybe you've studied handwriting analysis before, but found that the method you learned didn't quite "click" for you; or maybe this is your very first exposure. Either way, you're about to get an entirely different perspective on those squiggles and lines we leave on paper. So get ready to change the way you look at other people, yourself, and, most assuredly, handwriting!

How to Use This Book

An old Chinese proverb says a journey of a thousand miles begins with the first step. Learning to analyze handwriting may seem like an impossible task, but if we break it into manageable parts, you'll be surprised at how easy it can be. This book has six parts, each one designed to lead you step-by-step though the process.

Part 1, "Read My Loops," lays a foundation of solid research. We'll discuss what you can learn from handwriting, and the tools you'll need.

Part 2, "This Is Your Life: The Page," shows a whole new way to look at handwriting and the paper it's written on. You'll learn about time and space in handwriting before dipping your toes into the complexities of personality development.

Part 3, "Let's Dance: Movement," introduces the more advanced concepts of rhythm, speed, and pressure. Then we'll learn how connections between letters and slant reveal emotional responsiveness.

Part 4, "Just My Style: Form," moves into the outer self, and explores the masks people wear in public.

Part 5, "Sweating the Small Stuff," gets into some of the finer details of individual letter forms, and beginning and ending strokes. You'll also learn about red flags for some very nasty behavior, including substance abuse.

Part 6, "The Last Word," teaches you how to write a handwriting analysis and shows how to make your education pay off. Finally, we'll discuss the role computers play.

Scattered throughout each chapter are boxes of useful and interesting "extra" information.

def•i•ni•tion

Graphology has some words you've probably never heard of before. Here's where you'll find out what they mean.

Fine Points

These are the nitty-gritty, down-and-dirty tips and tricks that give you that little something extra.

Tales from the Quill

Graphologists have some fascinating stories to tell. Here's where you'll find them.

Chicken Scratch

Pay attention to these warnings. They'll help you avoid the mistakes and pitfalls that could end up hurting the people you want to help.

Acknowledgments

Thank you to all whose handwritings have enhanced this work, whether they knew they were contributing or not! An extra-special thanks is due to the following people for generously contributing celebrity handwriting samples to the second edition of this book (in alphabetical order):

Hazel Dixon Cooper, Christopher Darden, Leslie Klinger, and Sheldon Siegel for agreeing to allow me to use their own handwritings.

Steve Hodel for a sample of his own handwriting and samples of his father, George Hodel, prime suspect in the Black Dahlia murder (http://blackdahliaavenger.com).

Louis M. Jason for several samples from his book, *Literary Celebrity Doodles* (http://mysterypierbooks.com).

Richard Kokochak for Donna Yost.

Edda Manley for Margaret Atwood.

Raul Melendez for samples from his collection of autographed books (http://raulmelendez.com).

Lena Rivkin for obtaining several samples.

Roger Rubin for several important samples.

Lionel Strutt for sharing many of his famous autographs from http://mayflowerstudios.com.

Lawrence Totaro for Bobby Fischer's sample from his book, *Fisching for Forgeries*.

Some samples came from my second book, *Handwriting of the Famous and Infamous* (Metro Books), and from my personal collection.

My apologies to anyone I've overlooked, and I am conscious that there are some.

I have learned something from every handwriting I've ever analyzed, and am grateful to anyone who ever picked up a pen and revealed themselves to me in ink.

Sheila Lowe

Trademarks

All terms mentioned in this book that are known to be or are suspected of being trademarks or service marks have been appropriately capitalized. Alpha Books and Penguin Group (USA) Inc. cannot attest to the accuracy of this information. Use of a term in this book should not be regarded as affecting the validity of any trademark or service mark.

Part 1

Read My Loops

Before you get started studying for your new career or hobby as a handwriting analyst, there are a few things you'll need to know—such as where it all got started, who the masters were, and the feud that's been waged between the two main schools of thought for most of this century.

Then there's the stuff you'll need to outfit your graphologist's toolkit. It's not a lot, but it is important. I'll also get you prepared to head out in search of those all-important handwriting samples. Suitably outfitted, you'll soon be on your way to looking at handwriting up close and personal.

Chapter 1

Your Handwriting Is You

In This Chapter

- ◆ Who is this person, anyway?
- ◆ Historically speaking
- ◆ How the French and Germans see it
- ◆ Everybody else gets into the act

Have you ever looked at your doctor and wondered if the sloppy, illegible handwriting on his prescription pad reflects the way he diagnoses and treats his patients? Or have you noticed a neat, pretty handwriting and thought, "That looks like a friendly person"? If you're reading this book, you've probably looked at many handwritings and connected what you saw with some personality trait that you know fits the writer to a T.

The study of personality is as intriguing as a garden maze—just when you think you've got it figured out, another curve emerges to mystify and confound you. Long before Sigmund Freud, who brought new meaning to the word "complex," people sought answers to the question of why we feel and act in the ways that we do. This chapter will tell you a bit about where graphology started and how it can help you in your life.

Researchers in the field of psychology have developed an astounding array of personality tests to help psychologists understand what makes people tick. If you've ever been faced with a psychological test battery, you know how intimidating they can be. There you are, sweating the 550 items on the widely used MMPI (Minnesota Multiphasic Personality Inventory), wondering whether you've given the "correct" answers. Or you're trying to decide whether that ink blot is a sheep in wolf's clothing or merely a flower. Or you're madly making up stories that you hope will properly fit the TAT (Thematic Apperception Test), all the while wondering if the results will make you look like an axe murderer. And by the time you've finished, you're beginning to actually *feel* like an axe murderer!

There's an easier way to learn the truth about who someone really is on the inside: handwriting analysis. And that person doesn't have to answer even one test question. Handwriting itself is a projection of personality, and like a movie projected onto the silver screen, the trail of ink you leave behind on a sheet of paper vividly tells your story for you.

Behind Every Handwriting Is a Human Being

From the moment of birth, your brain begins to record every experience, every sight, every sound. Millions of life events are stored in that miraculous computer in your head, waiting for just the right moment, the right stimulus, to recall them. No number of terabytes or RAM could match the memory functions of this computer as its highly complex system of programming keeps track of every single piece of information that comes your way.

> **Tales from the Quill**
>
> Legend has it that when Thomas Gainsborough painted a portrait, he would place the handwriting of his subject on his easel next to the painting. By studying the way the person wrote, it was as if he could glimpse her soul and "know" the sitter at a depth not otherwise possible.

Of course, most experiences are not going to be important enough to keep in the foreground of our daily life, and some are just too embarrassing or too painful to *want* to remember. Recognizing that most memories are stored in the unconscious mind, Freud described the human psyche as being like an iceberg with most of its mass hidden below the surface. Thus, when a particular event, sight, scent, or sound jogs your memory, something that happened when you were only 3 years old pops back into consciousness, clear as day.

Handwriting as Body Language

Think of handwriting as a "psychic photograph" of the hidden part of the iceberg, or perhaps as a sort of EEG (brain wave recording) of personality. In fact, some handwriting analysts say "brainwriting" is a more descriptive term than handwriting. Why is that?

When you pick up a pen and begin to write, it's as if everything that ever happened to you comes together and travels down the nerves from your brain, through your arm, into your hand, and out onto the paper.

Body language, tone of voice, and facial expressions reveal a lot about a person, and handwriting is also an important piece of the personality puzzle that reveals information about how the writer functions. But whether a handwriting sample represents a sweet-natured, generous person, or an uptight, angry one, it is important never to forget that there is a human being behind *every* handwriting, and to always apply the age-old Golden Rule: treat others as you want to be treated.

The generic term for handwriting analysis is *graphology*, which comes from two Greek words that mean to learn about writing (if you're a Greek scholar, please don't write to me with the "real" definitions, I'm just paraphrasing here!).

It's a good idea to begin your study of graphology by having your own handwriting professionally analyzed. Giving a stranger the power to know so much about you is a humbling experience and may leave you feeling vulnerable. It's a feeling that I hope you will remember every time you pick up a new handwriting sample and begin an analysis, because it will remind you to treat the writer with kindness, the way *you* would want to be treated.

def·i·ni·tion

graph-o-lo-gy, n. The study of handwriting, and the inferring of character or aptitude from it [fr. Gk *graphein*, writing, + *logos*, discourse]. *The New Lexicon Webster's Dictionary.*

Chicken Scratch

Along with his handwriting sample, you hold the writer's psyche in your hands. The power this gives you may be wielded delicately like a surgeon's scalpel, or carelessly, like a chainsaw. Here's a good maxim from Stan Lee for the beginning handwriting analyst: *"With great power comes great responsibility."*

Serious Fun

It's fun to discover what your handwriting says about you, but it's also important to realize that graphology is a serious business with many and varied applications. Helping someone gain greater self-knowledge is one important use. We already know our personal faults and foibles, so it can be a nice surprise to learn from an objective third party about all the *good* qualities that we've taken for granted.

Couples can learn more about each other's needs and motivations through graphology, and teachers often find they can bring out better behavior in problem students. A career change to one's dream job might be facilitated by handwriting analysis.

People studying genealogy have used the services of graphologists to help them better understand their ancestors through an analysis of their handwriting. Therapists can track clients' progress in therapy, and some law enforcement agencies use handwriting analysis to determine dangerousness in suspects, as well as truthfulness of victim and witness statements.

One of the most popular uses of graphology is by employers. By having the handwritings of employees analyzed, they are able to build a more productive team whose members will work better together. New applicants are analyzed, too, to make sure they are a good fit for the team.

Tales from the Quill

In *United States v. Mara.* 410 U.S. 19, 41 LW 4185 (1973), the Supreme Court stated: "Handwriting, like speech, is repeatedly shown to the public and there is no more expectation of privacy in the physical characteristics of a person's script than there is in the tone of his voice." Although this case dealt with whether or not a person can be compelled to produce an example of their own handwriting for examination, it is important to graphology because it demonstrates that the courts consider handwriting to be an individual characteristic.

In the Beginning: The Origins of Graphology

Where did it all begin? The first recorded remarks about handwriting being related to personality are attributed to Aristotle in 330 B.C.E. He wrote (the italics are mine):

> Speech is the expression of ideas or thoughts or desires. *Handwriting is the visible form of speech.* Just as speech can have inflections of emotions, somewhere in handwriting is an expression of the emotions underlying the writer's thoughts, ideas, or desires.

Since Aristotle's time, graphology has had a long history of university research, beginning in France and branching out to other countries, continuing to the present.

While it was generally accepted as a serious practice in Europe before WWII, Hitler outlawed handwriting analysis under the fortune-telling act, and it went underground for many years. Today, graphology is back, full-force, all around the world. In Italy, the prestigious University of Lumsa offers a graphology program for credit.

Of all the important names in the history of graphology, first and foremost is Jean Hippolyte Michon, a French monk, who is considered to be the grandfather of modern graphology. Michon devised a classification system of handwriting called the study of fixed signs. His was the first formal system to study handwriting, and all modern graphological thought has its foundations in his research. It was Michon who coined the French term *graphologie.*

Abbé Michon's student, Jules Crepieux-Jamin, recognized the need to view handwriting as a whole, rather than simply as a collection of individual fixed signs. He taught that the "study of the school of fixed signs is to graphology as the study of alphabet is to reading prose."

Later, the German philosopher Ludwig Klages became a proponent of a more intuitive method of analysis, called the gestalt method, which is a forerunner of the method you will learn from this book.

Another name to remember is Dr. Max Pulver, a Swiss graphologist who applied the principles of Klages's system to the field of psychoanalysis and Jung's depth psychology. Perhaps Pulver's greatest contribution to the field was in his identification of three zones in handwriting, which parallel Freud's concept of personality structure: id, ego, and superego.

It wasn't until the turn of the 20th century that graphology made its way to the United States. Louise Rice, an American newspaperwoman, learned about it while on assignment in Europe. Her 1927 book, *Character Reading from Handwriting* (Newcastle Publishing Co., Inc., 1996), is available again after being out of print for many years.

There are many more greats to learn about, each of whom made his or her own valuable contributions to the scientific study of handwriting. From their research, two major methods of analysis emerged: the French and the German. (You can read a brief history of graphological research on my website: www.sheilalowe.com/support.html.)

In the next section, we'll look at the basics of the French and German methods of graphology.

Mais Oui! The French Approach

Besides being a priest, Abbé Michon was a philosopher, botanist, geologist, archae-ologist, architect, historian, and more. According to the late Edward B. O'Neill, translator of many French graphological works, Michon made some mistakes in his method, but "he gave us the very basis of the science and the art of graphology." O'Neill goes on to quote the eminent modern graphologist, Dr. Jean-Charles Gille:

> Michon believed in fixed signs but not in *isolated* signs, as one sometimes unjustly reproaches him for. Indeed, he mentions a "theory of the complex sign" and explicitly indicates that therein lies an immense field for investigation and the germ of future progress in graphological science.

Fine Points

The French method of graphol-ogy is also called atomistic (consisting of many separate, often disparate elements). Using Crepieux-Jamin's system of cat-egories, the handwriting is bro-ken into its various components and examined separately, as if through a microscope.

Here is what Michon himself said, which speaks volumes about the man and the way he saw hand-writing:

> The slightest movement of the pen is a vibration of the soul in one direction or another. As soon as the graphic sign is known, it is, in application, a game of stating what the soul has produced, what it has felt, what it has wanted, etc.; more artfully still, what the nuance was in each manner of pro-ducing, feeling, wanting.

Although what follows is an oversimplification, it will give you an idea of how French graphologists divide handwriting into several categories for analysis. The main ones are as follows:

1. *Layout:* how the writing is organized on the page

2. *Dimension:* how much space the writing takes up (size of letters)

3. *Pressure:* the depth component

4. *Form:* writing style

5. *Speed:* writing tempo

6. *Continuity:* types and degree of connections within and between letters

7. *Direction:* which way the writing is moving

In 1930s Chicago, a man named Milton Bunker founded a school based on Abbé Michon's method (Michon was not credited), and coined the term "graphoanalysis." Only graduates of Bunker's school, the International Graphoanalysis Society (IGAS— now under different ownership) can legally use the trademarked name. The IGAS system is known as the trait-stroke approach because it assigns a personality trait name to each writing stroke. IGAS students often quote the maxim, "A stroke is a stroke, wherever you find it."

Achtung! The German School

The German method, which came later, is known as holistic or *gestalt* graphology, which means that the whole is greater than the sum of its parts. In other words, no single element of handwriting means anything outside the context of a given handwriting sample. In gestalt analysis, there is no "this means that" answer. Meanings can change and are dependent upon the context in which a particular feature appears.

In gestalt graphology, handwriting is composed of three big pictures, each of which relates to an aspect of behavior:

def•i•ni•tion

Gestalt is a pattern of unified elements that cannot be interpreted outside of the whole. The sum is greater than its parts.

1. *The picture of space:* how the writer sees the world

2. *The picture of movement:* how the writer acts in the world

3. *The picture of form:* how the writer sees himself

The way these three pictures fit together forms the basis for understanding the core personality. Disturbances in one or more of the big pictures tell the graphologist where problems originate. This idea will begin to make more sense as we delve further into each of the three pictures.

Although both the atomistic and the gestalt methods are successfully used around the world, the emphasis in this book will be on the gestalt. Without a good grasp of the whole picture (which is what gestalt really is), all that remains is a list of personality traits that mean little without a context in which to place them. Neither the trait-stroke nor the holistic method are the "one and only way," however. A good foundation in gestalt graphology, augmented by an understanding of atomistic graphology, seems to provide the most complete picture of personality.

Okay, so there are different ways of analyzing handwriting. So what? What can we really learn about people from their handwriting?

Symbols Etched in Ink

Everyone living has needs—from the most basic biological, instinctual needs for food, safety, and reproduction, to the need for belonging and love, to the need to express one's creative urges. All humans share similar needs, but not all of us express them in exactly the same way.

Unless the most basic needs of life are met, one doesn't progress to the next level. Someone who is literally starving generally doesn't care about meeting their creative needs or going to a movie. All you can think about is meeting that most basic need for food. If you don't eat, you'll die. And when one is stuck at such a basic level, it's extremely difficult to progress to the next stage of emotional growth.

Handwriting reveals the level of need at which the writer is operating. If, early in life, he had difficulty getting his most basic needs taken care of (food, water, warmth, safety), his handwriting will be stuck at a very undeveloped stage.

If he has moved up a few rungs on the needs ladder, but hasn't gotten his need for love properly satisfied, it will be seen in the overly rounded forms of one who depends on others for emotional nurturing and love because he hasn't learned to love himself.

Fine Points

Viennese psychiatrist Carl Jung said, "A true symbol appears only when there is a need to express what thought cannot think or what is only divined or felt."

While the lower-level needs, the physiological ones, are innate and unconscious, other needs are conscious, such as the need for intellectual stimulation. Handwriting is a demonstration, a manifest symbol, of whatever needs the writer feels compelled to express at the time he is writing.

Symbols in handwriting:
O. J. Simpson.

The following handwriting is that of Christine Falling, a woman in her early 30s who was convicted of killing several children for whom she babysat. Unattractive, abused as a child, and mentally slow, Falling became jealous when she had to share her cousin's attention with the cousin's new baby. One day when she was left in the car with the infant for a few minutes, she smothered the baby. When the crime was successfully covered up as an incidence of crib death, she repeated her bad act several times with people who employed her, until finally someone began to connect the dots and she was arrested.

Falling became eligible for parole in 2007. Can you guess her answer to what she would like to do if released? When interviewed in a CNN documentary film titled *Murder by Numbers*, Christine Falling declared that she would like to babysit again: "I love kids to death."

Christine Falling, serial killer.

Was just thinking about I thought I would sit c and write you a letter. I enjoyed the interview w and anytime you want another with me just be to let me know and

Through these pages, you will learn how Christine Falling's handwriting reveals clear red flags for pathological behavior. If only they had known what her handwriting said about her, the parents who hired her to care for their children might have been able to avoid the tragic losses that followed wherever Falling went.

Learning to measure and weigh the written line in all its many expressions is the key that unlocks the door to personality. The forms created in ink and the spaces around them reveal to the trained eye what motivates a particular type of behavior.

The Least You Need to Know

◆ Graphology tells the truth about what is inside the writer.

◆ A vast body of formal research has been done in the field of graphology, which supports its validity and reliability.

◆ All graphology methods begin with Abbé Michon's system, but they don't end there.

◆ It is important to always remember to be kind to the writer when analyzing handwriting.

Dead Men Tell No Tales, but Handwriting Does

In This Chapter

- Handwriting shows your style
- Signatures can be symbolic
- Handwriting can't tell everything
- Tools you'll need
- Why school models are important

The written forms created in ink and the spaces around them reveal to the trained eye just what motivates a particular style of behavior. Similar to the way an artist uses line, color, and texture in her brush strokes, every movement of the pen uncovers something of the writer's temperament and style.

French impressionist Claude Monet often painted outdoor scenes. Daubing vivid colors on the canvas in thick, sensuous brush strokes, his slightly blurred style suggests a love of natural beauty, color, and texture. Now contrast Monet with a stark scene by Dalí, whose sharp edges, strong colors, and clearly defined objects often depict disturbing subject matter.

Artists and their works evoke distinct and very different sensations, because each creation was produced by a very different type of personality. Not surprisingly, the handwritings of artists—and musicians, too—are often similar to the works they produce.

Tales from the Quill

One's handwriting is such a personal thing that when someone discovers that her script reveals her true personality, she immediately either feels defensive or wants to share herself with you. About 95 percent of people who learn about your graphology skills will offer one of four stock responses: 1) "I should let you see my handwriting!" 2) "You don't want to see my handwriting!" 3) "I wouldn't want to know what you would find out!" 4) "I hate my handwriting."

In handwriting, as in art, even subtle changes in the line of ink demonstrate different aspects of the writer's character. As she guides the pen across the page, it is as if the writer is drawing the observer a picture of what is going on inside him from moment to moment. In this chapter, we'll begin to explore some of what handwriting can tell about the writer. By observing someone's facial expressions, body language, and tone of voice, you can usually figure out how she is feeling. An unhappy or depressed person's shoulders tend to droop, the spring goes out of her step, her eyes are lackluster. On the other hand, when things are going well and the same person is having a good day, she'll throw her shoulders back, and put a smile on her face and a lilt in her voice.

Handwriting changes to some degree to reflect mood. However, the basic personality doesn't change. So, while momentary excitement, anger, or other strong emotions will be reflected in the size of the writing, the direction in which it slants, and the baseline, the more basic character of the writing will stay the same.

Sometimes, when someone identifies very strongly with her profession, she creates a symbol that represents what she does. Liberace drew a little piano in his signature; football hero Joe Theismann draws a football on a tee. Golfer Greg Norman, known as "the Great White Shark," clearly draws—guess what?—yes, a shark in his signature, as you can see below.

Symbolic signature of golfer Greg Norman.

Whether symbols are added to a signature or not, handwriting is as individual as a fingerprint, and in many subtle ways is unique to the writer. If parts of one's personality were not manifest in handwriting, everyone would write alike, just the way they learned in school.

But personality *is* manifest in handwriting and we *don't* all write alike. So, when a letter arrives in the mail, the handwriting on the envelope can usually be readily identified as Cousin Ted, or Jenny's boyfriend Mark, or Mom because the familiar script symbolizes the individual personality of the writer. Yet, while handwriting provides a great deal of important information about behavior, there are some things a graphologist cannot conclusively identify.

What Handwriting Can and Can't Tell

Knowing what handwriting cannot reveal is just as important as knowing what it can. By recognizing your limitations as a graphologist, you can avoid creating unrealistic expectations in yourself and your clients. What information is not conclusively available in handwriting?

- ◆ Gender: You may be surprised if you assume that a pretty, rounded script was written by a woman, only to discover that the author was a 45-year-old man. The reverse is also true. Rather than gender, we can only infer the degree of masculinity/femininity (yin/yang) in the script. Sexual preference cannot be determined, either.

- ◆ Age: Chronological age cannot be determined from handwriting, but emotional maturity can. That's why it's important to get at least a ballpark idea of the writer's chronological age before you begin the analysis. The handwriting below, of Nicole Brown Simpson, is a good illustration.

The handwriting of Nicole Brown Simpson looks like that of a 16-year-old, but she was in her 30s when she wrote it.

◆ Writing hand: Another "can't do" is handedness. Nongraphologists believe it's possible to tell writing hand by checking the slant. Contrary to popular belief, however, left-slanted writing is not preferred by left-handed people.

Fine Points _____

Marie Bernard's book, *Sexual Deviations as Seen in Handwriting* (The Whitston Publishing Company, 1985), contains many interesting handwriting samples of famous people, including Oscar Wilde. What she labels as "deviations" includes homosexuality, which is no longer considered abnormal by psychologists, but the samples are worth the price of the book.

Finally, handwriting does not conclusively reveal race, religion, or the future, which makes it completely nondiscriminatory as a personnel selection tool.

What handwriting does reveal are the writer's potentials at the time of writing. Whether the writer will act on those potentials is a question the graphologist cannot answer. We'd have to be God to do that, and that's one responsibility most of us can do without. Anyone who brags, "I can tell you *everything* about you from your handwriting," is either lying or psychic. People are far too complex for one tool—even handwriting analysis—to reveal 100 percent about them.

Here are some of the aspects of personality that handwriting reveals:

◆ Social style: How does the writer relate to other people? Is she friendly or reserved, sociable or antisocial, aggressive or submissive?

◆ Thinking style: How does the writer think? Is she logical or intuitive? Does she create entirely new ideas or is she stuck in the mud of convention, afraid to move out and generate her own ideas?

◆ Ego strength: Is the writer's ego strong and well-developed, or weak and battered?

Tales from the Quill

I once asked a client how she felt about her handwriting analysis report. She said, "I thought it was great! It was really me!" Then she hesitated. "But it wasn't *all* of me." This was a humbling reminder of my own limitations as an analyst: handwriting does not reveal *everything* about the writer.

◆ Use of energy: How does the writer use her energy? Does she conserve it carefully or spread it around with wild abandon? Does she tire easily, with low vitality and stamina, or can she work all day and party all night without feeling the strain?

◆ Fears and inhibitions: How does the writer use what she has learned from past experiences?

◆ Locus of control: Where do the writer's controls come from—conscious self-discipline, painful experiences, or "old messages" from childhood conditioning?

As we continue our discussion of what handwriting can show us, you'll need to start collecting samples. Never throw away a sample, as you might want to study a particular characteristic at some later date. After nearly 40 years of collecting, I estimate there are about 10,000 samples in my personal collection. You might not want to go to that extreme, but once you get hooked, it's hard to part with a sample.

Where can you get handwriting samples? Start with your friends and relatives, your kids' teachers, your dry cleaner, the UPS guy who delivers the stuff you ordered from eBay … in other words, anyone who is willing to share her inner self with you. If you have trouble coming up with enough good samples to practice on, there's a nonprofit organization called Human Graphics that sells packages of handwriting samples for a nominal fee. You can contact them through their website: www.huvista.com.

While you won't always get the "ideal sample," there are some minimum requirements a sample must possess if you are to make an accurate report, especially if you're a beginner.

Getting the Perfect Handwriting Sample

It makes sense that the best analysis is made from the best handwriting sample. And even when you aren't able to get the perfect sample, you should know what it consists of. So, when asking someone to provide a sample of her handwriting, keep the following in mind:

- ◆ Ask for a full page or more of original writing on unlined paper. Photocopies, faxes, or scans distort some important aspects of handwriting, and a newbie could make some serious mistakes by working with anything less than an original. A sheet of photocopy paper is ideal.

- ◆ The subject matter of the sample is the writer's choice, but it should be free-flowing like a letter, not copied and not lyrics or poetry.

- ◆ If the writer says, "I only print," let her print. Forcing someone to write in a way that is unnatural can skew the results of the analysis. In such a case, ask for a sample of both printing and cursive. Similarly, if the person learned to write in a foreign country, ask for a sample of writing in her natural language, as well as one in English.

- ◆ Any pen will do, according to the writer's preference. The choice of pen can tell a lot about the person. Only accept a sample written in pencil if there is no other choice, as some nuances may be lost.

◆ Get the writer's age (approximate age is good enough), gender, and which hand she uses to write with. Also, ask whether she uses medications or drugs, or whether she has suffered any recent physical or emotional trauma that might affect her handwriting.

◆ The sample should be written on a smooth surface, while the writer is relaxed. She should not have consumed any alcohol, as even one beer could potentially affect the handwriting.

◆ If you are asked to do a *third-party analysis*, make sure there is a good reason for the third party to request it. Graphology is not a party gag or parlor game, so only someone with a genuine need to know should be privy to the information you can uncover. Only an experienced graphologist should handle such cases. Who might have such a need to know? Parents who suspect their teen might be in trouble with drugs, for example; someone concerned about her spouse's truthfulness; an employer investigating a sexual harassment matter.

def•i•ni•tion

It's called a **third-party analysis** when you are requested to analyze the handwriting of someone who hasn't been asked permission.

In the next section, we'll discuss what tools you will need to begin your hobby or career as a graphologist.

The Absolute Necessities

A basic understanding of personality development is integral to being a good graphologist. Without it, you won't be able to coherently put all of the various indicators and traits that you find into a meaningful report. After all, handwriting analysis is, first and foremost, about understanding and describing personality.

Besides understanding normal personality development, a smattering of abnormal psychology is also important. You have to know what's not normal to know what is! There are enough examples of pathology in handwriting to keep you busy. Learn to recognize it when you see it.

So, get out your Psych 101 college textbook and brush up on the main schools of thought—psychoanalytic, neo-Freudian, humanistic, behaviorism, and learning theories. If you didn't go to college, this would be a good time to take some psychology courses. If you don't have time to add external courses to your schedule, there are some good ones available online.

Okay, now let's talk about tools.

The Tools of the Trade

Back in 1967, when I began reading books on graphology, I was confused by references to "long lower loops" or "tall upper loops." How am I supposed to know what's long or short or tall, I wondered. I just had to guess. Ten long years later, I discovered the *Roman-Staempfli Psychogram* chart and other instruments that had been invented to quantify handwriting. I learned to plot 40 handwriting factors on the Psychogram, which led to a pictorial view of the personality that looked rather like a Rorschach ink blot.

def•i•ni•tion

The **Roman-Staempfli Psychogram** is a scientifically based circular graph that was created by Klara Roman for the Hungarian government in the 1930s.

As a beginner, it will be important for you to learn how to measure certain aspects of handwriting. However, once your eyeball is trained, in most cases, absolute measurements are not necessary. Left-brain learners are the analysts who feel lost without a ruler and a protractor. Right-brainers are less enamored of numbers and measurements, preferring a more conceptual approach. But either way you do it, once you're secure in knowing what the measurements mean, you can experiment until you find the style of analysis that works best for you.

The actual tools of the trade are few. You'll want to have a ruler for measuring baselines and margins (millimeters are the best scale for measuring handwriting), and a protractor to measure slant (wood, metal, or plastic will do). Most important, though, is to have a good magnifying glass.

Why magnify handwriting? Under magnification, otherwise hidden features may be exposed that could affect the analysis. Little dots or "blebs" in the writing line that are unseen by the naked eye, for example, may point to a physiological problem.

You can find an adequate magnifying glass in the drafting section of your favorite office supply or camera store. It doesn't have to be expensive—usually well under $20. As for the shape, as long as you can see through it clearly, it doesn't matter whether the lens is round, square, or rectangular.

The degree of magnification should be between 2x and 5x. That's quite strong enough for our purposes. It's really not necessary to see the fibers of the paper, which is what you'll get with much stronger power. Some magnifiers have a small inset with a higher magnification than the main part of the lens for getting up close and personal. Some have a long, flexible neck and attach to a desk. These have a wide viewing area and a ring light, at a cost of about $50.

A photographer's loupe makes an excellent magnifier for the graphologist. eBay advertises them starting at under a buck.

Chicken Scratch

Measurements provide a good frame of reference for beginners, but don't get so caught up in taking exact measurements that you forget to keep the whole picture in mind.

So, if magnification is good, what about a microscope? Unless you plan to branch out into the field of handwriting authentication, don't bother. That's a whole different story with an entirely different focus (if you'll forgive the pun). Handwriting authentication work (also called document examination) takes additional specialized training and equipment that go beyond the scope of this book.

Books for the Budding Graphologist

Most of the graphology books on the market are trait-stroke oriented. They often promise quick and easy shortcuts to learning your friends' and neighbors' secrets. Some even claim to be able to turn you into a graphologist in 10 minutes! If only it were that easy. Wouldn't it be nice if you could just check off a list of traits and know that every time you saw a particular characteristic it always meant the same thing? Well, it doesn't work that way. There are no shortcuts to good analysis.

Mostly Books in Tucson, Arizona, carries many graphology texts that you won't find elsewhere because Tricia Clapp, one of the owners, is herself a graphologist. When graphologists retire or go to that great inkwell in the sky, their libraries often end up for sale there. Check out www.mostlybooks.biz or order toll-free by phone at 1-877-39BOOKS. Mostly Books also sells some excellent privately published monographs that may not be available anywhere else.

School Models You Should Know

When you measure handwriting, there has to be a basis for what is small-medium-large, long-short-wide-narrow, etc. The school copybook is the standard that graphologists use for comparison. Most American Baby Boomers learned to write using the Palmer or Zaner Bloser methods, which were commonly used prior to 1980. Since then, the more simplified D'Nealian method has come into widespread use.

By using the writer's original copybook or school model as a frame of reference, you can determine how much and in what ways she has deviated from the norm. The writing may be larger or smaller than the copybook, more simplified or more complicated, or different in dozens of other ways.

As a general rule, few adults write exactly the way they were taught in school, and those who do tend to work in administrative-type jobs where they have a specific structure to follow, such as nurses, school teachers, and secretaries. Most people do their own thing, altering the copybook they learned to suit their own style. It is those alterations that tell us about the writer's unique personality.

If the writer first learned to write in a foreign country, you will want to look up the copybook she learned from, as there is a lot of variation from one nationality to another. Below are the Palmer and D'Nealian copybooks, which are most likely to have been taught to people who were raised in the United States.

Several copybooks from other countries are posted on my website and you're welcome to download them: www.sheilalowe.com/gestalt.html.

Palmer copybook.

D'Nealian copybook.

Many people feel ashamed that their handwriting is not as "beautiful" as the copybook model. What they need to know is, sticking to exactly the way you were taught isn't necessarily a positive thing. Those who adhere to the copybook model all their lives need a high degree of structure and order. Nothing wrong with that—we need people who can provide an orderly framework within which to operate. But the downside is, they are often afraid to be original, to step out of their mold and do something different. Luckily, there is room for all types in the world.

The Least You Need to Know

- ◆ Handwriting is symbolic of behavior and attitudes.
- ◆ You can learn a lot from handwriting, but it doesn't reveal *everything* about you.
- ◆ Handwriting cannot reveal the future, but it tells a lot about the past.
- ◆ Handwriting tells a lot about how the writer thinks, feels, and behaves.

Looking at the Big Picture

In This Chapter

- ◆ Looking at handwriting in a whole new way
- ◆ What environment means in handwriting
- ◆ How to find a balance between writing and paper
- ◆ Putting yourself in someone else's space

Handwriting is rich with symbolism that is not readily apparent to the untrained eye. For the graphologist, an empty sheet of paper waiting to be filled with writing takes on a special significance that might surprise the casual observer.

The way the handwriting is arranged on the page is a metaphor for how the writer organizes his daily affairs, his perspective on life, how he expresses his emotions, and much more. Handwriting clearly demonstrates the writer's behavior within his environment, and you are about to learn how to unravel the mysteries found there. In this chapter, we'll learn what balance means in handwriting and why it's so important to achieve.

First, though, let's clarify what *environment* means in this context. To the average person the word "environment" means something quite different from what it means to the handwriting analyst. It might be your living room, the office, or your car. Essentially, it is wherever you are at the moment.

An environment may be natural or unnatural. A lion's natural environment is the jungle where he can roam free, doing what lions do best. The zoo is an unnatural environment for a lion. Yet, while he is probably not as happy in the zoo as he would be in the jungle, he can live a long life there.

Humans, too, have natural and unnatural environments. Someone raised in the inner city, or a sophisticated cosmopolite, might feel strange and uncomfortable if he was suddenly transported to the Appalachian Mountains. But just like the lion, a human can adapt to the new environment and learn to live in it if necessary.

def•i•ni•tion

According to *Webster's Revised Unabridged Dictionary,* **environment** means that which environs or surrounds; or refers to surrounding conditions, influences, or forces by which living forms are influenced and modified in their growth and development.

By now you're probably scratching your head wondering, "What does all this have to do with handwriting?" The answer is, everything, because your handwriting depicts how you behave within your environment, natural or unnatural, physical or emotional. And handwriting analysis helps us determine how well you have made the necessary adaptations to your environment.

A Room with a View

The sheet of paper on which you write represents your personal environment. The handwriting you place upon it illustrates how you behave there. It doesn't matter whether you use a piece of lowly notebook paper or expensive watermarked vellum. You can turn it into a jungle, a desert, a cozy den, or a sophisticated drawing room. It's entirely up to you.

Let's visualize a piece of paper as a room. Until you begin laying ink on the paper, the "room" remains empty, a background waiting to be filled with the furnishings you choose. Begin to mentally plan the decor of your imaginary room. Pick out the color and style of carpeting and paint or wallpaper that appeals to you, the type of furniture you prefer; consider where you might hang the artwork, the personal knick-knacks and ornaments that make it yours and no one else's. You can have whatever you want in this room. After all, it's just a mental exercise, so live a little! Be as extravagant as you like.

Just as your personal style and tastes determine the design and final look of a literal room, so your past experiences and relationships will influence how your handwriting appears in your symbolic room.

It's All in How You See It

Analyzing handwriting is a way of exploring someone else's reality. Doing it successfully is a matter of learning how to see handwriting in an entirely new way, and that requires a change in your frame of reference. This section is all about *eye training*, or how to change your frame of reference.

Changing your frame of reference can be as easy as turning out a light. Things look very different in the dark, even though the same objects you saw with the lights on are still there. Or you could look at an object from a different perspective. As a kid you may have laid on your back and hung your head off the end of your bed to find that the floor and ceiling look completely different from that angle.

Changing one's frame of reference means scrapping what you think you know about something and looking at it from a different point of view. Let's see how.

Fine Points

Betty Edwards's book, *Drawing on the Artist Within* (J.P. Tarcher, Inc., 1979), offers some exercises to help get in touch with your creative side and change your frame of reference. These are helpful in training your eyes to look at handwriting in a new way.

Eye Training: Your First How-To Exercise

To get you looking at handwriting in a new way—that is, as a whole entity, rather than as a collection of individual words—we'll apply a very simple technique. Before we begin, it will help if you can activate your right brain. Automatically switching over from the left-brain to right-brain functioning can be accomplished with a simple handwriting movement. Take a sheet of lined paper and make several rows of infinity signs, turned on their sides. Focus on the movement until you feel the perceptual shift. You'll know it when you feel sort of dreamy, which means your conceptual self—the right brain—has taken over. You can even use your nondominant writing hand if you like!

Okay, having accomplished the shift, let's now begin your eye training. You'll need a full-size sheet of paper covered with writing, your own or someone else's—any old page of writing will do. Take a good look at it. What do you see? At this point it's still just a bunch of words. Now let's change your perspective. Prop the paper up on a stand, or tape it to the wall and stand far enough away that you cannot clearly read the content. Stare at it for a while. Try to see the page as if it were a painting, your own personal Picasso or Rembrandt.

Force yourself to look past what you *think* you know about handwriting and see just the lines produced by the ink. See the shapes, the colors produced by the flow of ink, the textures, the area between the shapes, the white space that creates a border around the whole picture.

Let your eyes relax and become unfocussed. There is an "Aha!" moment where the marks on the paper seem to shift and change. They are no longer distinct words; they are elements of a whole picture, which may be somewhat different from your original impression.

Now turn the page of writing upside down and once again step away. What happened? You lost your original frame of reference and were forced to see the writing as a whole object instead of as single words, letters, and parts. Even if you wanted to, you could not identify individual elements of the writing. And that is our goal—to force you to look at the page as a whole object.

Fine Points

If you studied the stroke method of handwriting analysis and consequently can't resist picking out individual strokes, try turning the writing upside down. It's an effective way of tricking your brain into seeing the whole picture.

When you analyze someone's handwriting, you can actually experience the emotions that the writer experienced as he drew the trail of ink across the paper. Once you are able to see the writing as a whole, you will get an instinctive feeling about it that has nothing to do with logic. It takes practice, but if you allow your intuitive sense to take over, you will learn to perceive the patterns of the writing, the rhythms, the way the writing moves on the page, the symbols—slashing knives, hearts, whirling tornadoes.

The "Ground" Work

We're about to dive into a concept that may at first seem strange—gestalt psychology as it relates to handwriting analysis—but I hope that by the end of this chapter, you will understand why I've borrowed the gestalt terms "figure" and "ground" to explain the basic principles of gestalt graphology.

Gestalt psychology is a school of thought that has its roots in 1930s Germany, and grew popular in the United States around World War II. The most famous names associated with it are its originators: Kurt Koffka, Max Wertheimer, Wolfgang Kohler, and Fritz Perls. It is based on the concept that nothing exists in a vacuum. In other words, when something affects one part of an organism, it affects all of the other parts in some way, too.

In gestalt psychology, there is no meaning without a context in which to put all the elements. Applying this idea to handwriting, it is possible to comprehend the essence of the personality only by viewing an adequate-sized sample of writing within the context of the whole page. Picking out a single letter or stroke, or analyzing just a scrap of writing and trying to reach a conclusion about the whole person, makes little sense. According to gestalt psychology, we tend to see things as solid objects (a figure) against a background (the ground). For example, you see your friend John as a whole person against the background of his house; he's not just an inventory of body parts. A computer is made up of CPU, cables, monitor, keyboard, mouse, and many other parts, but most people view all those parts simply as "the computer." Likewise, handwriting is made up of many different parts: strokes, letters, words, sentences, and paragraphs, but we see it as a whole object—handwriting.

In handwriting, the ground (the background) is the paper on which you prepare to write. The ink is the figure (the object). Thus, in a sense, we see the trail of ink as an object against the background of the paper. Singling out individual letters or strokes contributes some superficial information about the writer, but the sum is always greater than its parts: outside the context of the whole writing, individual bits and pieces of writing reveal little of the whole person.

Let's take the letter *t* for example. You might examine a handwriting where the *t*'s are crossed very high on the stem. In the trait-stroke handwriting analysis system, the small letter *t* relates to one's work and goals. The height of the crossbar indicates how high the writer sets her goals. If the *t* is crossed high on the stem, theoretically, the writer sets his goals at high levels. A well-trained stroke handwriting analyst will add and weigh many other factors against the *t*-crossing in order to reach a conclusion, but beginners often base their judgment on individual strokes alone.

The problem with this approach is that a lot of important information is left out. We don't know whether the writer has the energy to follow through on his goals and see them to completion. We don't know what types of goals he might have, or how firmly he is committed to his goals. Only by examining the entire handwriting can we get the answers to those questions.

Look at it this way: in order for a human to live and breathe, he needs a circulatory system, nervous system, respiratory system, skeletal system, and all the other systems working together as a whole entity. If a few parts of a system are missing or not working properly, it affects the way all the other parts work. Remember Frankenstein's monster?

But at what point can we say we have a whole person? When the heart is pumping blood? When the lungs are sucking in air? When synapses are sparking in the brain?

There is no such point. None of the individual organs or other parts by themselves, or even one or two together, are representative of the whole, living human being. Not until all the pieces are working together can we say, "It's a person."

Handwriting is like a microcosm of the human body: the strokes that make up the letters, the letters that make up the words, and the words that make up the paragraphs are analogous to the various organs and systems that make the body work. Just as the various organs must all function together within the framework of the body, all the parts of handwriting must be seen as working together as a whole entity within the context of the paper.

A Fine Balance

Handwritings are as varied as the individuals who write them. The first glance at a writing sample speaks volumes to the handwriting analyst, even before he gets started on the analysis. Doubtless, you've heard it said that when meeting someone, "You never get a second chance to make a good first impression." When looking at a handwriting sample, you are meeting the writer for the first time. That first impression is a very important one.

Pay attention to your gut reaction. When you first pick up a handwriting sample, ask yourself, how well balanced is this page? Is the figure/ground relationship (the amount of writing compared to the white space on the paper) fairly even, or does one overpower the other so much so that viewing it is disturbing?

What does a well-balanced page look like? It "feels" organized, with a pleasant harmony between the writing and the paper on which it is written. The writing is framed by even, balanced margins on all sides; the lines are clearly spaced, without loops hanging down from one line, interfering with the next one. If you look at a writing and your first response is "yuck!" there's probably a lack of balance somewhere. When there is a lack of balance you may feel uncomfortable, as if you need to fill in the blank spaces with something, or erase some parts because there is too much writing and too little white space.

The "yuck" factor might not sound like a very scientific approach, but don't forget, handwriting analysis is partly an art that requires eye training and intuition. The intuitive part will be more difficult for those who need strict rules to follow. Still, the handwriting analyst must learn to be objective when it comes to interpreting what he sees, not allowing his own personal biases to affect the outcome. Looking for balance in handwriting involves seeing not only the writing itself, but also the *negative space*.

Huh? The blank spaces in and around the writing can be just as significant as the writing itself.

Pressed In

When the page is unbalanced because of a problem with the writing (the figure), you will know it because you'll see very little of the paper. The writing overtakes the entire sheet; words and lines are pressed in, compacted, crowded together, leaving little breathing space.

What type of person uses up all the space on the paper? Someone who feels the need to dominate and control the space in his environment. His literal living area may be just as cluttered with furniture and other objects as the written page he produced. The writer may be a collector of fine art or a greedy hoarder. Other aspects of the writing that we will cover later will reveal which is more likely to be the case.

Spaced Out

If an imbalance is caused by too much white space, it's because the paper (ground) has overwhelmed the figure (the writing). There will be too little writing with large *lakes* of space between words that draw your eye; or the appearance of a *river* is created by a pattern of wide spaces that moves down the page. Or maybe one of the margins is extremely wide and the other extremely narrow, making the page look lopsided. All of these create a lack of balance.

def•i•ni•tion

The **negative space** (the spaces around words) helps define the relationship of figure and ground. **Lakes** are extremely large spaces between words. **Rivers** are wide word spaces that create a pattern that looks like rivers flowing down the page.

What type of person leaves big holes of space in their writing? Someone who needs an abundance of space in his day-to-day life. The writer tends to arrange his personal space with an aesthetic eye. His house may be sparsely furnished, or he may isolate himself and avoid contact with other people. The whole handwriting will tell us which is true.

Exaggerations of any kind disturb the whole picture. Your eye should not be drawn to any one particular element on the page. A balanced picture is pleasant to look at with nothing jumping out at you to jar the symmetry.

Test yourself with the handwriting samples presented next. You probably already know much more about handwriting than you think you do. Which sample is balanced? Which is too spaced out? Which is too pressed in? Check the amount of white space on the paper against the dark area of the writing to see if there is a balance.

It's Time to Take Up a Collection

Handwriting provides important information about the person who wrote it. Begin the process of analysis by collecting as many handwriting samples as you can, using the guidelines in Chapter 2. With each one, do the exercise described earlier in this chapter, where you looked at your own handwriting from a distance. Train yourself to look at the writing as a picture and decide whether the picture is well balanced or not. The answer will tell you how well the writer organizes his life.

Without exercise, muscles get weak and atrophy. Strengthen your graphology muscles by continually looking for ways to exercise your perception and eye training. Ask everyone you know to get their friends and acquaintances to volunteer handwriting samples for you to use for practice. Collect samples of as many different writing styles as you can.

Take a look at the following three handwritings. Which are balanced and which are unbalanced?

> **Chicken Scratch**
>
> Remember, as a beginning graphologist, you are supposed to look at the whole page as if it were a picture. *At this point, don't try to analyze the handwriting or decide why it looks the way it does.* Such analysis takes lots of practice and eye training, and that means observing many handwriting samples before you can expect to "get it."

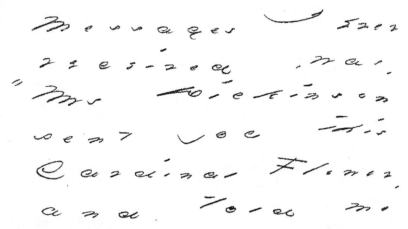

Sample A: Emily Dickinson, poet.

you still have your coca-cola bottle cover in your apartment – I still have my red hat plus bell and I suppose I always will have. Who knows I

Sample B: Dame Maggie Smith, actress.

But I really appreciate the sweet letter you have sent me — love + kisses forever to yn. I wish I could see you in the

Sample C: Jimi Hendrix, musician.

It's not too difficult to recognize which are the samples that lack balance, is it? If you picked Sample B as the balanced one, you were correct. If you picked Sample A or C, you need to do some extra homework!

The following table gives you some pairs of opposites to help you decide how to describe the writing you want to analyze.

Harmonious	Inharmonious
Orderly	Disorderly
Clear	Confused
Light	Heavy
Lively	Sluggish
Elegant	Crude
Simplified	Complicated
Regular	Irregular
Original	Commonplace

It's time to begin thinking of handwriting in terms of the words in the table. As we progress through the coming chapters, you will learn how each element of handwriting builds upon the others and blends into a totality that helps determine its final appearance.

When we analyze handwriting, we take on the awe-inspiring task of putting ourselves into someone else's space, that person's reality. In a very real sense, we must "become" that person by becoming one with his handwriting, and hearing the story it wants to impart. The person who examines handwriting and imposes on it what he wants to hear is likely to get the wrong message.

Let's say you and I just met for the first time and I remind you of someone you don't like. If you project what you feel about that other person onto me without letting me show you by my actions who I am, you may form a wrong impression of the real me. The analyst must put his "self" aside and ask the writing questions, then be ready to receive the right answers. Allowing the writing to speak to you lets you connect naturally with the personality behind it.

Returning to the opening concept of this chapter, look at your handwriting and ask yourself, "How do I act within my environment?" Picture yourself in a crowded room at a party where you don't know anyone. The guests seem to be having a good time, eating hors d'oeuvres and dancing, enjoying their conversations. What do you do? Make a grand entrance, jump right in, and introduce yourself? Or do you feel awkward and sit shyly in a corner on your own, waiting for others to introduce themselves? How about when you're alone? How do you use your environment then? Or when you're at work, at school, on the road in your car, or in the supermarket?

Handwriting is the body language of the mind. It reflects in a very real way how people act within their environment. I haven't seen Italian film star Roberto Benigni's handwriting, but the way he clambered over the seats, nearly trampling Steven Spielberg, on his way to the stage to accept his 1999 Oscar, suggests the exuberance of a large, right-slanted writing with loose rhythm, splashing across the page with abandon. Someone who timidly retires to a corner all by himself, on the other hand, is likely to have small, sober writing, crammed up against the left side of the page.

People come in all shapes, sizes, and types, and their handwriting shows it. A one-dimensional handwriting analyst who understands only someone who is just like him makes a bad graphologist. The greater the variety of personalities you can find to study, the faster you will grow into a good graphologist. You can have fun along the way, too, because you'll be helping people, and they'll think you're terrific for doing it. And they'll be right!

Tales from the Quill

Tam Deachman, a retired advertising executive and graphologist on the side, sat down with his companion at the counter of a small bistro. The daily specials were handwritten on a chalkboard in a flamboyant script with an obvious flourish, as well as many embellishments and ornamentations. His companion issued a challenge: "Who wrote it?" Tam looked around the restaurant at the various employees. Just then, the kitchen door was flung open and into the dining room stepped a man dressed like a French chef, complete with floppy hat and curled moustache. "There's your writer!" Tam declared. He was right.

The Least You Need to Know

- Handwriting symbolizes how you behave in your environment.

- Looking at handwriting as a whole picture is more important than identifying individual strokes.

- Balance between the writing and the paper is the first item to check when making your analysis.

- Collecting as many different types of samples as you can will start you on the road to being a good graphologist.

Part 2

This Is Your Life: The Page

Okay, you've got a handwriting sample in front of you—what now? What do all those squiggles and lines mean, anyway? Part 2 takes you through the basic principles of handwriting analysis, and shows you how to see handwriting differently.

We'll go to the very heart of handwriting—space, form, and movement— and learn how each aspect affects all the rest. This part is like no other book you'll read on this subject, anywhere.

Chapter 4

Space: The First Frontier

In This Chapter

- ◆ Economy or extravagance—it's in the space
- ◆ Relationship to the environment
- ◆ Relationship with self
- ◆ Relationships with others

In handwriting, space is the empty area around the writing on a page (the margins), as well as the areas between words and between lines. It symbolizes the invisible boundaries we set between ourselves and others.

Space also reveals our perspective on life, how clearly we see the relationships between ourselves and others, and how we arrange our environment. In this chapter, we'll learn why interpreting the meaning of the empty spaces is just as important as understanding the writing movement itself.

A Space Odyssey: Your Environment and How You Use It

The way we use space is the most unconscious element of handwriting. We don't take the time to stop and measure the distance between each letter, word, and line—that would make communication impossible. Still, there is a surprising consistency in the spatial arrangement, which continues throughout the writing, particularly in the spaces between words.

def•i•ni•tion

Perspective is the ability to judge relationships between ideas or distances.

To get a clear *perspective* of an object, you have to stand away from it, but not too far back. Imagine standing 2 feet away from the Sears Tower and looking up. Would you be able to tell how tall it was? No. Neither could you properly tell its height if you drove 50 miles away and tried to gauge it from there. Too close or too far, and your perspective would be skewed.

Setting Boundaries

Handwriting is limited by two physical factors: the available space bounded by the edges of the paper, and the energy you invest when writing on the paper. A small sheet of paper creates artificial boundaries that are tighter than those of a larger sheet, forcing the writer to limit herself.

A small amount of writing space constricts the writing movement. That's why it is important to give the writer an ample sheet of paper. If she crams a few words into the top left-hand corner of an 8½×11-inch page, it will say something quite different about her than if she takes up every bit of white space on the paper.

The writer's actions within the boundaries of paper size provide clues about how she views time, space, and money. Is she generous or stingy? Is she a profligate time waster, or one who jealously guards every minute of the day, the way Scrooge hoarded pennies?

Don't Fence Me In: Line Spacing

There are no rules about how much space should be left between lines of writing. Not even a school model provides guidelines on that issue. So, the choice of line spacing is a very personal one that provides the graphologist with several pieces of information about the writer:

- How she uses time
- How she uses her material resources
- How orderly her thinking processes are

Line spacing is one indicator of self-control. The amount of space left between one line and the next establishes how well the writer recognizes the need for order in her environment and how well she organizes her life. Because writing is a form of communication, clarity should be a high priority. Someone who communicates clearly wants to make sure she is properly understood by leaving a reasonable distance between the lines of writing. Each line should be clear, with no loops hanging down to interfere with the next line. When the lines are too close together, it's like being in a crowd with someone whispering in your ear.

At the end of each line of writing, you must decide where you will place your pen to begin the next line. If you are relaxed and know you have plenty of time, you may feel free to use up more space. The writer who feels pressured for time is more likely to start writing the new line closer to the previous one.

Fine Points

Balance is always the key. The interpretation changes when the line spacing becomes *too* wide.

Clear Line Spacing

Clear line spacing indicates mental clarity and a sense of order. The person who leaves moderate distances between the lines is able to plan ahead and organize her life and time effectively. She knows the importance of contingency planning—that is, leaving enough time and space in which to handle the various emergencies of daily life without leaving herself in a pinch. When a writer feels free to leave ample white space between the lines, it shows that she's not afraid to use her environment to her advantage and implies self-assurance.

Clear line spacing demonstrates an ability to assimilate the impressions and experiences one accumulates from day to day and to express them appropriately. The writer is objective when dealing with a situation or problem, and considers a variety of potential responses and how they might affect the outcome. She reasons well and uses good old-fashioned horse sense to help her make decisions.

Narrow Line Spacing

When the spacing between the lines of writing is narrow, the writer's perspective becomes somewhat impaired. It indicates an impulsive person who goes with her gut reactions, rushing ahead too quickly without taking time to reason things out. A subjective viewpoint allows her to see things only in terms of how she feels about them and how they affect her, rather than keep the bigger picture in mind.

Narrow line spacing also tells us something about the writer's spending habits. Jammed-together writing suggests compulsive caution in spending. That's a nice way of saying "cheap." Just how careful she is with her resources depends on how closely the writing is packed. When there is little or no white space to be seen, one of several options will be true:

- The writer has a "poverty consciousness," which means she expects to be poor, so fears spending.

- The writer is a stingy cheapskate.

- The writer is genuinely conscious of the need to use her resources very carefully.

Narrow line spacing: Herb Brenk, convicted of killing his wife and sawing her body in half.

Crowded Line Spacing

The writer of extremely narrow, crowded line spacing is driven by impulse and lack of ability for abstract thinking and objectivity. She may be more imaginative than one who chooses wider line spacing. She's certainly less interested in taking time to reason things out than going with her instincts. She tends to live in the moment. Even in speech, her words are more impulsive and less discreet, and she has plenty to say! The trouble is, she doesn't think far enough ahead to measure her words. She gets so caught up in her own ideas that when the words come tumbling out, she isn't always clear and the meaning is obscured.

Please note: although I've used the handwriting of a killer to illustrate narrow line spacing, you must not interpret this as meaning that narrow line spacing all by itself is a sign of psychopathology. Remember, *no single element means anything outside the context of that particular handwriting.* Herb Brenk's handwriting has many other danger signs, too.

Tangled Lines

When lines are written so close together that loops and/or parts of letters hang down and collide with writing on the next line (or several lines), the writer suffers from a loss of perspective. She's too busy acting on her instincts and emotions to take the time to keep things in their proper place. Thoughts and ideas, feelings and actions are all jumbled together.

There is always so much to do and she doesn't plan very far ahead, so the tangled writer's activities spill over into each other. She's at the hairdresser when she should be at a meeting, or she's playing golf when she was supposed to have lunch with Mother. Without a strict schedule (which she hates), the tangled writer spins her wheels, doing what feels good at the moment. The vital but mundane routines that keep life running smoothly, like paying bills or doing laundry, are delayed or ignored entirely.

Life with this type of person can get pretty chaotic. Continually involving herself in situations that have nothing to do with her, she doesn't always use the best judgment and may allow her prejudices to overrule her common sense. She may mean well, but you can't always count on her to be where she said she would be, when she was supposed to be there. That's because she's rushing around, trying to fit in more activities than humanly possible! Her motto might be, "You only go around once." Don't expect the tangled writer to listen if you try to offer constructive advice on how to better organize her life, however. She simply doesn't hear you. Oh, she may nod and say, "M'hm," but her eyes will be all over the room instead of on you. As always, the whole picture will help you decide whether to interpret this characteristic positively or negatively. The handwriting of Nora Roberts is overall positive, for example.

Tangled lines: Nora Roberts, author.

Moderately Wide Line Spacing

The writer who leaves wide spaces between the lines of writing has a logical, orderly mind and a preference for keeping things clear. She is good at analyzing situations and concepts, and always plans ahead. This is not someone who acts spontaneously or on impulse. Her thinking is measured and orderly, and she considers the consequences before acting.

Her tastes tend to be elegant and refined, with a strong sense of aesthetics, a love of beauty. She might be more at home at the Met than the local wrestling arena.

Whether or not they actually have money, some people who leave wide spaces between their lines tend to be extravagant. They may feel less constrained to hold on to their resources, so they spend more freely.

The key to a positive interpretation for wide line spacing is that it should not be *excessively* wide. When spaces between the lines become so wide that you notice the white spaces between the lines more than the writing, we look at it differently.

Moderately wide line spacing: Jacqueline Kennedy.

Please thank all the
help at W.H who stay up till
dawn at these parties + never
Complain & tell them how much we

Extremely Wide Line Spacing

Line spacing that is far too wide suggests someone who has lost the capacity to act spontaneously. This person isn't an active joiner. She stands back and observes rather than participates. Permanently anxious, she feels isolated, separated from her fellow human beings and the world at large.

Fine Points

The writer who leaves *excessively* large spaces between the lines may be trying to bring order to her inner world, which is falling apart. The wide spaces are an attempt to create some kind of structure and order.

Don't expect her to do anything on the spur of the moment, because she quickly puts the kibosh on any spontaneous act. She wants time to consider how any future action might affect her before making a move.

This might be the absent-minded professor who goes around with her head in the clouds, forgetting to take a lunch break because she is too busy working out a formula in her head. She tends to see things more in discrete pieces than as whole concepts or, to put it another way, she sees only individual trees rather than the whole forest. She's not particularly considerate of other people, because she's more concerned with maintaining her own space.

Extremely wide line spacing: Jeremy Irons, actor.

Irregular Line Spacing

The writer who writes sometimes with wide line spacing and sometimes narrow, who sometimes lets her loops get tangled and at others keeps them separate, is inconsistent in how she uses her time, money, or other resources. Her reactions depend on the circumstances and how she feels at the moment.

She may start out with the best of intentions (clear line spacing), but soon gets carried away with what she's talking about or the project she's involved in (her writing gets more crowded). If the line spacing is wide at the top of the page and narrow at the bottom, the more she gets swept up in her daily activities, the more difficult it is for her to maintain a clear perspective. She wavers between organized, abstract thinking and the need to go with her gut.

She wants to be generous, but that conflicts with a resolve to be conservative and thrifty. In any case, the writer lacks good self-discipline and is unsure of herself. She engages in a continuing struggle between the limitations of time and resources and what she wants to accomplish.

Extremely Regular Line Spacing

Extremely regular line spacing is made by the inflexible, obsessive person who feels compelled to follow a strict routine. She finds it impossible to vary from the daily rituals she has established to help her get through life. If you come across someone who writes this way, refer her to a counseling professional. You'll know this type of writing by its machinelike look.

Tales from the Quill

The handwriting of one of America's best-loved poets, Emily Dickinson (seen in Chapter 3), is an excellent example of extremes in spatial arrangement. She isolated herself, and during her 30s saw few people but her family. Even those closest to her sometimes had to communicate with her through a closed door. The excessively wide spaces between letters, words, and lines reflect her isolation.

Outer Space: Word Spacing

Inhale. Exhale. Inhale. Exhale. We speak and we pause to breathe at the end of a thought. Some people speak quickly with less breathing space between their words than others do. Some speak so fast that their words run into one another. The spaces between words have been compared to taking a breath in speech and reveal one's need for social distance. How much space do *you* need in order to feel comfortable around other people?

The amount of space a writer leaves between words is a good indication of how much personal space she demands from others and the degree of self-restraint she uses in social situations. What is a "normal" amount of space between words? A good rule of thumb is to use the width of a letter *m* in the writing you are analyzing (this is not an absolute measure).

Balanced Word Spacing

The writer whose word spacing is well balanced is comfortable asserting her need for space. She expects other people to respect her privacy and is willing to give others the space they deserve. She is comfortable around other people but, when appropriate, can spend time alone. She is conventional when it comes to social interaction and likes to feel that her behavior conforms to her social group.

Balanced word spacing: Microsoft magnate Bill Gates.

To my fellow Capitalist!
Thanks for coming?
Bill Gates

Wide Word Spacing

Moderately wide spaces between words (slightly wider than the letter *m* in that writing sample) tell us that the writer is a clear thinker who likes to step back and pause for reflection. That willingness to pause for a breath shows also that she is considerate of others, because she takes the time to see if her listener understands her.

As in wide line spacing, wide spaces between words have an effect on the writer's ability to act spontaneously. She may be charming and sophisticated, but she is also reserved and keeps her distance. This is probably not someone you should run up to and give a big sloppy kiss in public. She's not easy to get to know, because her objective outlook keeps her from becoming involved on an intimate level. She views relationships more in the abstract than the personal, and you can expect her social circle to consist of a carefully chosen few.

Fine Points _____

Teenagers who choose a wide spatial arrangement often suffer from feelings of loneliness and isolation, which they try to cover with indifference.

Wide word spacing: Sir Michael Caine, actor.

Extremely Wide Word Spacing

Extremely large spaces between words disrupt the flow of communication. This indicates problems in the writer's ability to string ideas together in a logical progression. She is socially isolated and has difficulty getting her thoughts across. Although she may have some wonderful concepts in her head, they may not make it out of her mouth, because she gets lost in the unimportant details and forgets to keep the big picture in mind.

When words become islands in oceans of space, it implies a profound inability of the writer to connect with other people on their level. This is not a voluntary condition. The writer may have a deep desire to make contact but her fear of intimacy is stronger. The long pauses between words, rather than taken as a moment to reflect, become social crevasses. Awkward and insecure around people, she is uncomfortable in crowds and withdraws into a shell of shyness.

In extreme cases, the writer may not even be aware of appropriate social relationships. All she knows is the need to protect and defend her ego, which to her means shunning physical and social contact.

Extra-large word spaces are sometimes found in the handwritings of developmentally delayed people. They feel isolated and cut off from the rest of the world, unable to communicate what they want to say and helpless to express their inner needs.

Extremely wide word spacing: Princess Grace Kelly, actress.

we spend every possible minute out doors - we were beginning to forget what sunshine was like

Narrow Word Spacing

As in narrow word spacing, narrow spaces *between* words signify an impulsive, spontaneous person who doesn't take the time to reason things out. She acts and reacts as the mood takes her. So many impressions bombard her all the time that it is hard for her to sort them out. Step back and take an objective look before making a decision? I don't think so! The word "rational" isn't in her vocabulary.

She is driven by a strong need for involvement and socializing, so don't expect her to keep her distance. This is an in-your-face, touchy-feely person who expresses herself through physical contact. She may pat you on the shoulder, hug you, or put her face close to yours when speaking. Her conversation is stream of consciousness—whatever pops into her head one minute comes out of her mouth the next.

Because she's insecure, she looks outside herself to get her needs met. She can't stand to be alone for very long and will soon be looking for ways to make contact with someone, anyone. Unfortunately, she's not always very choosy about who she calls her friends.

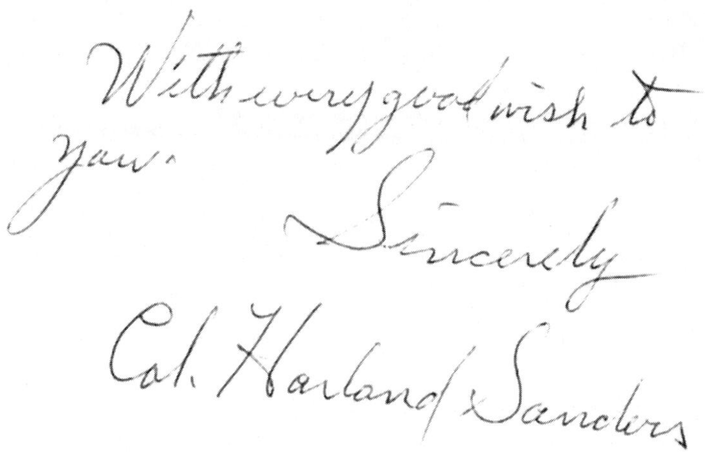

(handwritten signature)

Narrow word spacing: Colonel Harland Sanders, founder of KFC.

Extremely Narrow Word Spacing

The purpose of spaces between words is to create proper boundaries. The letters form groups that are framed by the spaces between them. When a writer disregards the proper boundaries, she is behaving like the gal on the subway who stands so close that you can hear her breathing in your ear, even though the train isn't all that crowded. You want to elbow her out of your way!

Words so close together that they almost (or do) touch suggest a writer with an extreme need to surround herself with other people. She leaves no space for self-exploration and, since she requires no space for herself, she also has no regard for the space of others. Her social boundaries—her sense of what is appropriate—are blurred.

Like a puppy always on the heels of whoever walks into the room, she needs constant attention and approval to feel good about herself. She acts purely on instinct. Without continual reassurance from others she gets anxious, and the moment she's not getting attention, her self-esteem plunges. The problem is, when it comes to the need for approval, the writer of very close word spacing is a bottomless pit.

A murderer of three little boys, Westley Dodd, whose handwriting follows, had such a need to talk to the media (and anyone else who would listen) about his crimes that during his trial, the judge took away his telephone and mail privileges.

Chicken Scratch

Extremely narrow word spacing, especially when combined with narrow letters, can be one sign of obsessive thinking. Stalkers may adopt this type of spacing (though not everyone with extremely narrow word spacing is a stalker!).

Extremely narrow word spacing: killer Westley Dodd, who asked to be executed, and was in 1993.

Irregular Word Spacing

Irregular spaces between words suggest behavior that changes unpredictably from moment to moment. You can't count on this writer to act consistently. Filled with inner conflicts, she's unsure of how to behave, either in the company of others or when she's alone.

Always on the move, she can't sit still for long (especially when irregular word spacing is combined with extremely long lower loops), though her movements may not have any particular purpose. When her letters spill over their proper boundaries she doesn't mean to be impulsive, but the confusion that drives her is more compelling than her ability to control herself.

Inner Space: Letter Spacing

Spaces between the letters give us clues about the degree of freedom the writer allows herself internally and her receptiveness to others. They show her gut reactions to emotional situations and her ability to act on them appropriately.

The ideal amount of space between the letters (intraletter spacing) should be about the width of the letter *n*. In "ideal" writing, this amount of space would indicate adaptability, a capacity for give-and-take relationships. The writer is spontaneous and friendly, with the appropriate amount of warmth in relationships. She has the capacity to learn new ideas and is open to changing her mind when she finds a better way of doing things.

Wide Letter Spacing

If the letters themselves are also wide, the writer is talkative, spontaneous, and out-going. She is open to everything and does whatever comes naturally without a lot of restraint. She doesn't take the time to analyze a situation using logic, but "lets it all hang out," responding according to what's happening from moment to moment.

Do NOT

Remove under

Pain of

dismemberment

Wide letter spacing: Sam Donaldson, ABC News correspondent.

Narrow Letter Spacing

Letters crammed together reveal an impetuous person who rushes to judgment and overreacts. Impulsive and often confused about what she feels and what others feel, her need to fit in with a social group can push her to behaving inappropriately. She desperately wants acceptance, so she'll do anything she thinks will help her fit in. This is the type of person who will give in to either internal emotional pressures or external peer pressure. The letters in the handwriting of Susan Smith are so close that they actually bump up against each other.

When I left my home on Tuesday, was very emotionally distraught. I didn

Very narrow letter spacing: "Killer Mom" Susan Smith.

Inconsistent Letter Spacing

Inconsistency in any area of writing symbolizes ambivalence. In letter spacing, the ambivalence is about whether the writer should move forward or stay back in the shadows. She's uncertain and worried about what to do. An internal tug of war keeps her unsettled most of the time.

Secondary Expansion

A special situation called secondary expansion is where the letters themselves are narrow but the spaces in between them are wide. On the surface the writer appears to be outgoing, but inside she shrinks away from social contact. Yet despite her insecurity and shyness, she pushes herself to interact, at least in groups where she knows the people. We call this type of person a "converted introvert" because while it isn't natural to her, she's learned how to behave as an extrovert in social situations. Prince Charles's handwriting is a good example of secondary expansion.

Secondary Expansion:
Britain's Prince Charles.

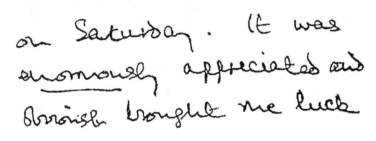

The Least You Need to Know

- ◆ Spatial arrangement is the most unconscious aspect of handwriting.
- ◆ Clear line spacing suggests clear thinking.
- ◆ Word spacing shows how close you need to be to other people.
- ◆ Letter spacing shows how much space you give yourself.

Chapter 5

Margins: Back to the Future

In This Chapter

- ◆ It's about time—past, present, future
- ◆ More about balance
- ◆ Have you left the past behind?
- ◆ How you approach the future
- ◆ What margins have to do with respect for authority

When you think back over your childhood, are the memories mostly happy, with a few experiences you'd rather forget? Or do you recall what should have been a carefree time but was instead filled with sadness and pain? The margins on the page reveal whether you have moved on from the past or it holds you back from emotional growth.

In this chapter, we'll look at the margins that frame handwriting. We'll find out about the writer's emotions and mental outlook as they relate to time and space. We'll also discover how he feels about the past and his outlook on the future, as well as his social behavior.

Somewhere in Time

Are you punishing yourself for the past? Raring to race into the future? Ambivalent about what lies ahead? *Margins* reveal how you perceive time.

def•i•ni•tion

> The **margin** is the perimeter area bordering a page of handwriting.

The margin on the right side of the page shows how we view the future, whether we look forward to it with a hopeful, optimistic outlook or as something to delay facing as long as possible.

Handwriting in English and other Western-style languages begins on the left side of the page and progresses across to the right side. The margins are created when the writer consciously makes a decision about where initially to place the pen. As he moves across toward the right side of the page, two new decisions are called for—where to end that line and where to start the next. These decisions form a pattern of blank space—the margins—as the writing progresses down the page.

The average margin consists of about 1 inch of blank space all around the paper. Yet, as a handwriting analyst, you will be confronted by many samples with virtually or literally *no* margins at all, or others with margins so wide that they form a huge frame of space around a small amount of handwriting. The left side of the paper, where the writing effort begins, symbolizes the past. After moving across the page toward a goal, the writer ends up on the right side of the page, which represents the future. What goes on in the middle, therefore, represents the present.

The left margin also represents the self ("me"); the right margin, other people ("you"). As the writer moves from "me" to "you," he reveals whether he faces the future and other people with hopeful optimism or fear and trepidation. Additionally, the top third of the paper represents the past, the middle third represents the present, and the bottom third represents the future. Thus, you will be able to see where in a project—beginning, middle, or later—the writer begins to lose or gain confidence. Just look for the point where the writing either pulls away from or toward the margins.

Fine Points

> Margins are not handwriting, but blank spaces. This is a reminder that blank spaces on a page can be just as revealing as the writing that rests between them.

Well-Balanced Margins

A handwriting that is well framed by nicely balanced margins (they shouldn't be absolutely perfect) on all sides looks like a picture in a frame. Balanced margins reveal a careful planner with a good sense of timing. The writer creates structure and order in his environment and doesn't appreciate it when disruptions threaten to mess things up. He prefers to carry out his activities according to a plan. He isn't stingy, but neither is he likely to spend lavishly. He uses common sense to budget his resources (time, energy, and money).

The nicely balanced (not perfect) margins of novelist Dean Koontz.

His social manners are slightly formal and reserved, and while he's polite and courteous, he probably won't go beyond the boundaries of convention because he feels most comfortable within familiar limits.

When the margins are too exact, too careful, appearances mean more to the writer than substance. His home is likely to be just as orderly as his handwriting. In fact, his motto might be, "A place for everything and everything in its place." When things get out of place or unexpected events happen, the writer's anxiety skyrockets. He can't stand for anyone to see him at less than his absolute best.

Extremely Wide Margins All Around the Page

The person who places a small amount of handwriting in the middle of a vast desert of space is terrified of getting involved with life. He feels inadequate, and so keeps himself apart from others in an effort to hide what he thinks are his deficiencies. His limits are self-imposed, but that doesn't make it any easier for him to reach out and make connections.

Extremely wide margins in an undeveloped or immature script may simply be a writer who is showing off and attempting to pass himself off as sophisticated and cultured when in reality he is not at all.

Extremely wide margins all around.

Physical contact is especially difficult for the writer of extremely wide margins. The only way he will allow physical touching is when he initiates it. If you reach out for a hug or to pat him on the back, he'll shrink away from your touch. He might even take a step backward to put more distance between himself and the other person— a greater *margin* of distance, that is.

Narrow Margins All Around the Page

Looking for someone to take on that tedious project? Ask the person with no margins. Running a few bucks short for the rent? No problem, ask the guy with no margins (unless his letters are narrow). He may not have the time or money, but he gets involved in anything and everything, whether he can afford to or not.

He doesn't know when to say no, which means he's often overextended. This habit can become problematic when his time and energy are wasted on trivia that doesn't get him anywhere. Not only does he waste his own time, he'll make demands on yours, as well. This person is the juggler of innumerable activities and tries to keep so many balls in the air at the same time that it would be a miracle if he could complete half of what he takes on.

Narrow margins all around: Diane Downs, convicted of attempting to kill her children. She still claims a bushy-haired stranger shot them.

The writer with no margins usually crowds other parts of writing, too, such as lines and words. If that's the case, he feels compelled to control "all space," which includes other people's space. He gets involved in others' lives to the point of intrusiveness.

If handwriting without margins is also large in its overall size, money probably burns a hole in the writer's pocket. No matter what resources he has at his disposal, he feels obliged to use them up.

Ghosts of Christmas Past: The Left Margin

Let's begin at the beginning. *All* the way back, as far as you can go. Life experiences begin with birth, and the initial placement of the pen symbolizes that magic moment. The left margin represents how the writer feels about the past.

Narrow Left Margin with Wide Right Margin

A narrow left margin combined with a wide right margin suggests that the writer finds the past a more comfortable place than the present or the future. Safety and security are very important to him, and he is afraid to spend his resources. The need to economize nags at the back of his mind.

Going into unfamiliar places and situations or trying new things is stressful for him, so in order to keep the stress at bay he limits himself to whom and what he already knows. He looks to old friends and family for support. The downside is, he may miss out on opportunities for growth when they threaten to take him out of his depth.

Chicken Scratch

The writer of small or narrow writing with no margins hoards everything. This is the person about whom it can be said, "He still has the first nickel he ever made."

Narrow left margin with wide right margin.

Wide Left Margin

A moderately wide left margin shows a strong desire to move forward and leave the past behind. Willing to get involved with life, the writer welcomes opportunities to meet other people and quickly takes hold of new ideas and projects. That he doesn't cover all the space he reasonably could indicates some degree of extravagance. He is not overly concerned about utilizing all his resources, but will spend the time and money it takes to get where he wants to go.

Especially when the right margin is narrow, courage is evident in the way the writer forges ahead into new territory and charts new goals. He is more interested in what is coming up in the future rather than worrying about the past, and doesn't overly concern himself about conforming to convention or doing things the way they were always done before.

An extremely wide left margin suggests that the writer may be running away from something in the past—something so upsetting that he can't bear to think about it. The painful event could be in the distant past or it might be something that happened recently. You'd have to examine a series of samples written over a period of time to determine whether this was habitual or situational.

Wide left margin.

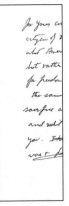

Shrinking Left Margin

When the left margin starts out wide but shrinks toward the left edge of the paper as it progresses down the page, the writer begins with plenty of enthusiasm, but doubts soon begin to creep in. He starts backing off, wondering whether he is doing the right thing, or whether that new project was a good idea.

He begins to look for ways to return to the safety of the past, which could mean going home, or calling old buddies, or following some ritual that makes him feel secure. His misgivings will have to be put to rest before he'll return to his original plans.

Shrinking left margin.

Growing Left Margin

As you might guess, a left margin that gets wider as it moves down the page represents the opposite of the shrinking left margin. The writer is a slow starter but his enthusiasm grows by leaps and bounds the more he gets involved with a new situation or project.

If the handwriting is also large, there is a tendency toward extravagance. The writer may not show the appropriate restraint when it comes to spending his time, energy, and money.

Growing left margin.

Concave or Convex Left Margin

You're in a department store with your girlfriend, and she's about to splurge on a $75 black lace teddy but changes her mind at the last minute because it's just too extravagant. Check her left margin for the concave pattern.

A left margin that starts at one point, gets wider, then somewhere down the page begins to get narrower again is called a *concave* margin. We find it in the basically thrifty person who fights a desire for extravagance and pulls himself back before he gets completely carried away.

def•i•ni•tion

A **concave** margin dips inward toward the middle or "caves in." A **convex** margin bulges outward and away from the middle.

Convex is the opposite of concave. Something convex pushes outward, like a contact lens. The left margin starts at one point and moves further to the left for a while, then starts back toward the right again.

You've probably already figured it out—the writer continually puts the brakes on his behavior, which tends to be a bit more openhanded than he can afford. He recognizes his tendency to be extravagant and tries to control it. Yet, because the end result is movement toward the right, we know that he can't always resist the temptation for a more freewheeling lifestyle.

Right concave margin.

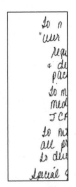
Left concave margin.

Right convex margin.

Rigid Left Margin

The left margin is consciously chosen, whereas there is less control over the right margin—we're not always sure of how much space will be left as we move across the page. The left margin represents the ideal self, or who the writer would really like to be. The right margin is more symbolic of his real self—who he actually is.

Strong self-discipline and will power are needed to begin every new line in exactly the same place under the previous one. It also takes longer to maintain a strict left margin, suggesting someone who doesn't make decisions without first taking his time to consider all potential outcomes.

A rigidly straight left margin is made by a writer who is highly conscious of appearances and who doesn't allow himself or others any slack. Just as his margin is inflexible and premeditated, so are his attitudes and behaviors. Someone this rigid is not easy to live or work with.

Chicken Scratch

A rigid margin is interpreted the same as *any* element of writing that is rigid: fear and inflexibility.

Rigid left margin.

Irregular Left Margin

A left margin that has a different starting point with practically each new line signifies conflict about what to do next. The writer doesn't care about society's convention and standards, but prefers to make things up as he goes along. He is a poor manager of his resources and probably runs out of money long before payday.

If the writing is done on lined paper with a printed left margin but the writer begins to the left of the ruled line, he literally makes up his own rules. Among the writers who ignore the left margin are juvenile offenders who refuse to follow the standards and rules of polite society. Yet, at the same time, they may be easily influenced by their peers.

Irregular left margin.

Future Perfect: Right Margin

Courtesy of the left margin, our virtual time machine has taken us on a voyage through the past. Now we move forward in time and explore the writer's attitudes about the future. The right margin tells us how ready he is to face what's ahead, as well as more about how he handles his time, energy, and money, and how he feels about making contact with other people.

Wide Right Margin

Leaving an extra-wide right margin is like stopping your car about 15 feet behind the stop sign. It's just a little too soon. The person who stops so far back is telling us that he is being cautious, very cautious. He wants time to see what's coming before deciding how to proceed.

Past experience has taught him to view the future as an unfriendly place where he can get hurt if he's not careful. He feels overwhelmed by life and fears he won't be able to cope with any additional stress. Staying away from the right margin allows him to avoid reality for a while. He creates a safe framework for himself and rarely extends his reach beyond those self-imposed limits. A wide right margin may be temporary and related to a particular situation, such as a job loss. An out-of-work single mom, worried about how she's going to feed her kids next week, may show her concern by pulling back from the right margin (the future). When she's bringing home a regular paycheck again, the right margin will return to a more normal width.

Wide right margin.

Narrow Right Margin

The spontaneous, action-oriented person makes a narrow right margin. Eager to set new goals and work on them, he cares about progress and is constantly looking ahead to see what he should do next. He is outgoing and at ease meeting new people and trying out new things. If a wide left margin is balanced with a moderately narrow right margin, the writer is poised, ready to jump at the chance to move forward on his goals.

When the right margin is overly narrow, almost to the edge of the page, it can be a sign of an eager beaver who lacks self-discipline. His impulses take over and he doesn't consider the consequences before acting.

When the words actually careen off the edge of the paper, the writer is rushing headlong into the future. At the extreme end of the future is death. The writer whose words fall downward and crash right into the edge of the paper may be having thoughts of suicide. Or, he may be suffering from temporary financial embarrassment because he has spent beyond his means. Be careful how you interpret this characteristic and always look at the whole picture.

Narrow right margin.

Expanding Right Margin

What if, as the writing proceeds down the page, the right margin begins to pull back, so it is wider at the end of the writing than at the beginning? Although he may jump in with enthusiasm, the writer needs encouragement to keep on going. He reverts to behavior that has proved safe and effective in the past rather than travel into uncharted waters. Completing new projects may be a bigger challenge than he can comfortably handle, unless he receives a lot of encouragement from the people he loves or respects.

Expanding right margin.

Shrinking Right Margin

When the right margin moves ever closer to the right edge of the paper, the writer welcomes new challenges. The more he gets swept up in his interests, the more his excitement grows. He is progressive and goal-directed, involving himself in things he's never done before without a second thought.

He may be shy on a first introduction, but his reticence soon disappears. In a group he watches everyone until he understands the power structure, then he'll put in his two cents.

Shrinking right margin.

Extremely Straight Right Margin

Making a straight right margin is much harder than making a straight left margin. The writer has to hyphenate words and take great care to line up last words of lines.

Someone who goes to this much trouble has lots of self-control. He also needs a tremendous amount of structure to function comfortably.

Whatever this person does, it's going to be something he's done before and will be done strictly by the book. Don't expect him to act independently or quickly. He's self-protective and has trouble adapting, so he needs time to adjust to new situations and people. He can't trust others because he doesn't trust himself. In an effort to safeguard his ego he creates the most predictable environment possible.

Extremely straight right margin.

Extremely Irregular Right Margin

Some variability is expected on the right margin because it's not always possible to predict how the line will end. However, when the irregularity is extreme, the writer is guaranteed to be emotionally unreliable.

Extremely irregular right margin: JonBenét Ramsey ransom letter.

A poor planner, he's unsure of how he feels about other people or the future. An adventurer who is content with the turbulent life he creates, he'll take whatever comes next, and the more exciting the better. Pressured by a strong need for variety (especially when combined with very long lower loops), he vacillates from one position to another, unable to stick with a steady point of view about anything or anyone.

Greetings, Your Majesty: Upper and Lower Margins

In bygone days it was customary to leave a very wide upper margin when addressing a letter to an important personage, such as royalty. It was as if the writer were putting a respectful distance between himself and the recipient of the message. Although that rule doesn't seem to apply so strictly in modern times, it is still appropriate to leave a respectful margin at the top of the page.

As a gauge of personal space, a narrow upper margin is like starting the conversation in the middle—the writer doesn't care whether you understand what's going on or not. This inconsiderate kind of behavior may show a lack of discretion and appropriateness, especially if there are other supporting factors, such as narrow word and line spacing.

Because there is no set standard, the lower margin is less significant. A narrow margin at the bottom of the page indicates enthusiasm and spontaneity. The writer is so wrapped up in the message that he doesn't want to take the time to stop and turn over the paper or start a new sheet.

A lower margin that is too wide for the message, on the other hand, may indicate that the writer is more concerned about appearances than what he has to say. He doesn't reveal much about himself, and may not be telling the whole story.

The Least You Need to Know

- Margins reveal where you are in time and space.
- The left margin reveals how you feel about the past.
- The right margin shows how eager you are to meet the future.
- Upper margins indicate your respect for the reader.
- Lower margins reveal enthusiasm.

Chapter 6

From Here to Eternity: Baseline

In This Chapter

- The ground rules, or standing on the baseline
- To rule or not to rule—writing on the line
- How to measure a baseline
- Going for the goal—the right margin
- The ups and downs of baselines
- Your health plays a part

The *baseline* of handwriting represents the ground we stand on. The question is, how steady is the ground as you move from one place to another? Is it solid concrete, asphalt, loamy soil, or quicksand?

Solid ground, not trembling and shaking ground, offers a measure of security. If you've ever been caught in an earthquake or tornado, you know that when terra isn't so firma, you feel insecure and anxious. Keeping your balance or finding something substantial to hold on to or hide under for

def•i•ni•tion

The **baseline** is the invisible or printed line on which handwriting rests and is created by the bottoms of the individual letters and their connections.

protection, are all you can think of. When the earth stops moving, you breathe a sigh of relief.

The graphologist examines the baseline of writing to see how much it fluctuates. The direction the line runs is also important: does it move uphill, downhill, or straight across? In this chapter, we'll cover how to measure the baseline and what baseline direction really means.

The Invisible Line

When kids begin learning to write, the teacher supplies paper with ruled lines printed on it. This provides a road map of where to go and how to get there. Without that printed line, and left to their own devices, there's no telling where the little writers would travel. After all, the empty page offers an unlimited playground where anything goes!

Later, after the child understands the rules (literally and figuratively), she is able to form a mental picture of the baseline she needs to follow and is not so dependent on the ruled line.

When Is No Line a Line?

The baseline of writing may be an actual ruled line on the paper or it may be invisible. The bottoms of letters and the connections between them (also called ligatures) form an imaginary line that moves across the page.

The position of the paper on the writing surface (desk, table, or other) affects the direction and shape of the baseline, as does the position of the writer's body.

Some people turn the paper at an angle to the writing surface, which tends to push the writing uphill and also produces a rightward slant. It may also force the body to turn to the left, which affects the tension/release pattern. This position allows the right-hander more freedom of motion, which in turn means a greater release of tension. The same is true of the left-hander, but from the opposite direction.

The person who places her paper square to the edge of the desk and sits very straight generally produces writing that is upright or left-slanted. Here's an experiment you can try:

Sit straight, facing the table or desk on which you are preparing to write. Put both feet flat on the floor and the writing paper square in front of you. If you're right-handed, you'll find that your writing arm is pulled leftward, while your hand is slightly torqued to the right, producing tension in the writing movement.

The Underground Is Not Just the Subway

Whether invisible or on ruled paper, the baseline separates the handwriting into two parts: above the baseline and below the baseline. In handwriting symbolism, the baseline represents the actual ground, so it follows that the area below the baseline represents *under the ground*.

Remember, we're talking in symbols. Plants that feed and nourish the body grow under the ground, an area we normally don't see. In handwriting, the area below the baseline corresponds to the subconscious, where *unseen* forces motivate behavior and either stimulate personality growth or stunt it. The baseline is also the dividing line between reality (the conscious) and fantasy (the unconscious).

Logically then, it follows that the area above the baseline represents *above the ground*, where the fruits of the underground growth are visible. In terms of the writer's personality, this area represents the conscious aspects or expressed behavior.

Following the Rules

The response to a request for a handwriting sample on unlined paper is often unmitigated horror—"You want me to do *what?*" The person who must have a ruled line has a strong need for direction, for specific rules, structure, and a pattern to follow.

More compulsive still, though fairly rare, is the person who chooses to write on ruled paper, *and* places a ruler on the ruled line to boot. In nearly 40 years as a graphologist, I've probably witnessed this phenomenon only about a dozen times.

The "ruler writer" is an example of extreme insecurity. Think of how it feels to enter an unfamiliar room in the dark. You cautiously feel your way around the perimeter, afraid to step out into what might be empty space or a space filled with unfamiliar objects that might trip you. That's how the ruler writer experiences life. She doesn't know what might be waiting for her in that empty room, and that is intolerable to her. Thus, she sticks like glue to what is familiar—the baseline.

The ruler writer often has unresolved, difficult sexual issues and uses the ruler to separate the middle and lower zone (the lower zone is the area of sexuality). In some cases, she puts entire lower zone letters into the middle zone. In others, she will make lower zone letters in two segments. Jittery and high-strung, the ruler writer lives with the continual threat that her internal chaos will overwhelm her. She fears that if she lets go for an instant, her life will spin out of control. Returning to the baseline—something familiar and safe—is like a ritual that gives her a point of reference she can count on. Knowing what to expect allays her anxiety to some degree.

Fine Points

The closer the handwriting sticks to the baseline, the more realistic and less imaginative the writer is.

How About a Hug?

Among other things, the baseline tells the graphologist how much stability and security the writer needs. The degree to which the writing clings to the baseline tells us how firmly she needs her feet planted on the ground.

When the bottoms of letters look very even and always return to the baseline, they are said to *hug the baseline*. This type of writing usually shows strong regularity with little variation.

The writer believes only what she sees. She's not particularly imaginative, but has a pragmatic outlook, and because she takes things so literally often misses the irony in subtle humor. She is motivated by a need for security.

The baseline hugger makes sure the basic essentials are handled before attending to anything else: putting plenty of food in the fridge, getting insurance coverage, and depositing money in the bank. Yet, no matter how much she stockpiles the material goods and money it never seems to be quite enough to make her feel really secure.

Pretending to Follow the Rules

Then there are those who choose ruled paper but fail to follow the ruled lines, writing above or below the line. This type of writer wants us to *believe* she is going to follow the rules, but the truth is, she prefers to be independent. Writing that hovers above the ruled line suggests enthusiasm and a spirit of adventure. What the future might hold intrigues this writer. She focuses more on the possibilities and what might be, rather than what already exists. She doesn't need to see something to believe in it.

The person whose writing falls below the ruled line focuses almost entirely on the tangible, material realities of life. There is little or no energy left over for spiritual matters, as she exhausts herself pursuing her most basic needs. Depression or illness may be a factor in this case, as psychic heaviness drags her down.

Charting Your Goals

The baseline is a major indicator of how goal-oriented the writer is. The beginning of a writing line symbolizes the beginning of an effort, starting out toward a goal. The end of the line stands for the end of the effort, or completion of the goal. What happens in the middle reveals how the writer sets about attaining her objectives.

The steadier the baseline, the more focused the writer is on achieving her goals. At the same time, don't forget that balance is always important—a compulsively straight baseline (i.e., ruler writing) is too much of a good thing.

When you decide to take a road trip, how much preplanning do you do? Do you decide on a destination, call your auto club for a map, check a weather cable channel to make sure you have the appropriate dress, pack a cooler with snacks and drinks, fill up the car with gasoline, plan each stop carefully to make sure you have the proper amount of fuel, and let those who are expecting you know exactly what time you'll arrive?

If so, your baseline is probably very straight. You are highly goal-oriented. You focus on what you want, making certain that you won't run out of resources before reaching your goal. But at the same time, unplanned events are difficult for you to deal with. If you run into a roadblock and have to make a detour, or traffic is unexpectedly heavy and delays your arrival time, you may overreact with anger and frustration.

Tales from the Quill
Sally, who uses lined paper but writes well above the line, *seemed* like a pretty conventional lady. She dressed conservatively, held a respectable job as a secretary, and her manner was quiet and reserved. It was in her "other life" that her individuality bloomed. Sally's night job was acting! On stage, she was flamboyant, ebullient, and totally outrageous. Like her handwriting, she outwardly followed the rules, but only to a point.

Or, are you the type who suddenly decides you want to go somewhere, though you're not at all sure where; you just grab a jacket, jump in the car, and head out on the road? You don't bother to check the gas gauge, and might end up sleeping in the car because you have no hotel reservation.

As a result, you might find your unknown destination is somewhere exciting and wonderful, or you might discover the less attractive side of society in a yucky part of town. But it doesn't matter because, for you, the action is more important than the goal. Your baseline probably wavers quite a bit.

How to Measure a Baseline

There are two ways to measure baselines. Each provides a different type of information. The first is to find which direction the line is going, and the second is to determine how well the writer adheres to the baseline. (See the following illustrations.)

Measuring Line Direction

Place a ruler or any straightedge on a page of writing. Slide the ruler until its left edge rests on the bottom of the first letter on the line. Measure across to the last letter on the line and draw a line between the two points. (*Don't do this on the original—make a photocopy.*) This technique tells you the direction of the baseline, whether it is straight across, rising, or falling.

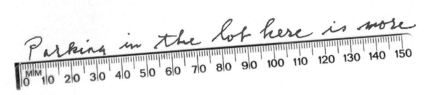

Measuring line direction using the handwriting of comedian Shelly Berman.

Measuring Across the Baseline

Now place the ruler on the page of writing so that the end of the ruler touches both the left and right edges of the paper. Place the ruler at the bottom of the first letter of a line and then lay it straight across the page. Draw a line to see if the words stay on the baseline, rise above it, or fall below it.

Measuring across the baseline.

Ruler writing.

can have both his & m
Hopefully, they're ao
Please return his to me
Hoping to see you next (

Moderately Straight Baseline

A moderately straight baseline varies to some degree. Overall, though, it proceeds directly from one side of the page to the other. It goes where it is supposed to go (from left to right), but is reasonably flexible about how it gets there. The writer has good willpower and can be relied upon to pursue her goals persistently, using common sense. She handles unexpected events without getting too distracted, finds a way around obstacles, and quickly gets back on track.

Researchers have found that blood-sugar levels have an effect on the baseline. When blood sugar is low, as in hypoglycemia, the person's mood plunges and her baseline becomes erratic. Blood pressure and muscle tension likewise affect the straightness of the line.

If nothing unfavourable happens
in the next ten days r so & at

The moderately straight baseline of former First Lady Eleanor Roosevelt.

Slightly Wavy Baseline

The writer whose baseline meanders casually across the page is easily distracted. She doesn't have a problem stopping what she's doing to handle something else. In fact, she probably welcomes interruptions. Will she return to finish the original project? Maybe. Maybe not.

Sensitive to what is going on around her, the wavy baseline writer easily adapts to people and circumstances. She is emotionally responsive and her feelings are suddenly aroused and quickly expressed. You can expect her to laugh and cry easily, because she experiences more emotional ups and downs than the writer of a straighter line.

Slightly wavy baseline of British Prime Minister Tony Blair.

time it takes to get persistent juvenile offenders to court.

7. we will help build strong families and strong communities and lay the foundations of a modern welfare state pensions and community care.

Extremely Wavy Baseline

A snakelike baseline is formed by one who can't make up her mind on even the smallest detail. She doesn't know whether to go east or west; to go to the movies or play video games; wear green or pink, wool socks or cotton. And it doesn't matter what she chooses anyway because the moment she decides, she'll probably change her mind. She's afraid that something better might come along as soon as she makes a choice, and then what would she do!

> **Chicken Scratch**
>
> The excessively wavy baseline is sometimes seen in the writings of criminals (but never judge criminal behavior or any other type based on only one sign!). One thing is certain—the writer is unreliable and not to be trusted with important decisions.

Don't expect her to take a firm stand on anything, even when her point of view is challenged, as she avoids conflict at all cost. She's as aimless as a little boat adrift on stormy seas, tossed here and there by the waves of emotion that threaten to capsize her. The writer of an extremely wavy baseline is an opportunist, always willing to quit what she's doing if something else looks like it might be more fun or more profitable, and it doesn't matter who was counting on her to meet the original goal. You have to wonder about her ability to plan coherently, not to mention her sincerity.

Extremely wavy baseline of a teenage boy.

we are planning to go to vic when he gets home I'll try to call us

Ready, Set, Goal!

The direction of the baseline (does the baseline as a whole move up, down, stay even across the page?) has something to do with enthusiasm and optimism, but other factors also affect it. The direction of the baseline is strongly affected by mood or emotional state. A sudden welling up of emotion may cause a change.

If you see something unusual in the direction of a baseline, ask for other samples of writing done over a period of time. Then you can better determine whether it's related to a specific issue or it's the writer's normal state of mind.

Uphill Baseline

Most graphology books claim that an uphill baseline means the writer is optimistic. In my experience, *this is not necessarily true.* Much depends on the degree of the uphill slope. A baseline with an exaggerated (but not extreme) uphill slope is more likely to be made by someone fighting depression rather than an optimist.

Remember the story of Sisyphus in the Greek myth? As a punishment for offending the gods, Sisyphus was doomed to push a massive boulder uphill. Once he reached the top of the hill, the boulder would roll back down to the bottom and he had to begin all over again, forever. That's how the person who creates an exaggeratedly uphill slope feels: as if life was an unending uphill battle. However, she works hard at keeping a positive mental outlook. Her attitude is "If I just keep on pushing, things are bound to get better tomorrow."

Uphill baseline: novelist Dean Koontz.

When the uphill slope is moderate, we interpret it as eagerness, ambition, and hopefulness. To interpret optimism there must also be self-confidence and self-assurance. The writer is not unduly influenced by her emotional state.

An extreme uphill baseline rises at about 45 degrees from the edge of the paper, which suggests impulsiveness. The writer is excitable and driven by her urges and emotions. It takes a certain amount of forcefulness and aggressiveness to produce this type of baseline, so it's a good guess that she pushes to get her own way.

Falling Baseline

Generally, a falling baseline is a sign of fatigue or illness, or it could indicate a generally pessimistic outlook on life. Again, only by examining a series of handwriting samples done over a period of time will you know which is true.

The bottom line, however, is that the writer is suffering from weakness for some reason, and she lacks the energy and enthusiasm needed to pursue her goals effectively. Assuming the writer is reasonably healthy, you can infer that she's probably easily discouraged and feels worn down by external events.

Fine Points _____

When a word falls below the baseline or jumps up above it, note what the word is. It may have a strong emotional association for the writer and provide an important clue to her personality.

Falling baseline: Adolph Hitler.

Convex Baseline

Earlier, we discussed convex margins, which bow outward. There are also convex baselines. This baseline rises in the middle and then falls back down by the end. It signals someone who starts out with passion about a new thing, but her interest and enthusiasm quickly die out. In other words, she's a better starter than a finisher.

I'm sorry THAT IT HAS
TAKEN ME So long TO GET BACK
TO YOU. I've JUST BEEN So BUSY
I Hope You AGENT IS STILL

Convex baseline: Erik Menendez (younger Menendez brother, convicted of murdering his parents).

Concave Baseline

We have also discussed concave margins—the kind that cave in. The concave baseline writer is a slow starter who bellyaches about how much she has to do, and how put-upon she is, but who nevertheless finishes what she starts. Bit by bit, as her enthusiasm and confidence grow, she pulls herself up out of her negative attitude and does all she can to meet her goal.

I'm Excited about my New
Book Justice which is a

Concave baseline: TV personality and author Dominick Dunne.

The Step-Up and Step-Down Baselines

Neither the step-up or step-down baselines will usually appear over an entire page of writing—they'll show up more or less sporadically. Think of them as the baseline of individual words. Note which words slant up or down, because they may be emotionally charged words that will help you understand the writer's emotional state at the time of writing.

The step-up baseline is created when the baseline of each word rises, producing a tiled effect. In this case, the writer struggles to keep her emotions and enthusiasm under control.

The step-down baseline is made by one who experiences life as a constant struggle. She expects things to go badly and must pull herself out of depression on a daily basis. No matter how much she fights the tendency toward discouragement, and no matter how many times she picks herself up, she just seems to fall back down into a dark pit of despair.

Chicken Scratch _____

Be careful of how you interpret the falling baseline. Before deciding that the writer is a pessimist or has a generally negative outlook, ask whether she has been ill recently, or has experienced a major life event, such as becoming unemployed, which might have a temporary effect on the direction of her baseline.

Step-up (above) and step-down (below) baselines: convicted of killing his wife, Herb Brenk makes a new baseline for almost every word.

Sometimes a baseline will be reasonably straight, but plunges downward at the end of the line. This indicates a lack of planning on the writer's part—she didn't see the end of the page coming. She's often unrealistic and extravagant and gets into financial hot water. She spends beyond her limits and has to pinch pennies to make ends meet. By using up most of her resources at the beginning of a project, she soon exceeds her budget and is forced to skimp later.

The Least You Need to Know

◆ The baseline of writing is the invisible line that you write on.

◆ A super-straight baseline isn't a good thing, but neither is a super-wavy one. Balance is the key.

◆ Slight variations in the baseline mean flexibility.

◆ An uphill baseline doesn't necessarily mean optimism.

7

Calling Dr. Freud: The Zones

In This Chapter

- Three isn't always a crowd when it comes to zones
- The middle zone—it's your daily life
- The upper zone—imagine that! The intellect
- The lower zone—a trip into the subconscious
- Sex and the single loop

Many cultures around the world divide things into threes. Many religions, both Western and Eastern, have trinities. There are the concepts of heaven, earth, and hell; mind, body, and spirit; and so on. Likewise, handwriting is divided into three individual zones: upper, middle, and lower. In this chapter, we look at the writing zones and learn how they represent the various parts of personality. We'll also see how the zones interact with each other. Although each zone serves its own function, none acts independently of the others. When one or two zones are either overdeveloped or underdeveloped, the effects span the entire handwriting and thus, the entire personality.

In the Zone

Everything passes through the middle zone to get to where it's going, and the letters connect there. We've already talked about the baseline as the dividing line between conscious reality and the unconscious (see Chapter 6). The middle zone sits right on this dividing line. But what is "reality"? The reality defined by the middle zone includes the following:

- The self
- Day-to-day life
- Interactions with other people
- Communication

- Expression or control of emotions
- Acting out moral principles
- Ego needs and ability to satisfy them
- Ability to adapt

Middle-zone letters include the vowels *a, e, i, o, u*, and other small letters that have no upper or lower extensions. They are *c, m, n, r, s, v, w*, and *x*. Some letters have upper and lower extensions, but parts of the letters fall into the middle zone. They are the circle parts of *b, d*, and *g*, and the hump on *h* and *y*. Really, any stroke passing through the middle zone counts.

Fine Points

Although handwriting is split into three zones, which represent different areas of personality, there is always an overlap. What affects one zone will have a corresponding effect in the other zones.

Like the middle zone, the upper zone is part of the conscious area of personality. The movement the hand makes going into the upper zone is up and away from the middle zone, away from the body, then back down to the baseline. When we go into the upper zone, the upward movement of the pen symbolizes reaching up into the mental sphere, where our minds are free to wander, unfettered by the material world. The mental sphere of the upper zone includes these elements:

- Mental processes
- Spirituality
- Standards, principles, conscience
- Abstract reasoning

- Ambition
- Intellectual pursuits
- Imagination
- View of authority figures, such as one's father, boss, or God

Upper-zone letters have extensions rising out of the middle zone: *b, d, f, h, k, l*, and *t*. Letters or parts of letters from other zones that wander into the upper zone where they don't belong are given special attention.

We're taught to write lower-zone letters by making a downstroke from the baseline into the lower zone, then a smooth turn to the left that forms a loop, then an upstroke that ends to the right for a return to the line of reality (the baseline). The unconscious, hidden, instinctual aspects of personality, as well as our attitudes toward work and productivity, are stored in the lower zone:

- Biological imperatives: food, sex, money, physical activity

- The past, including experiences and memories that influence our behavior in the present

- View of mother or other close female, and nurturing

- Dreams and fantasy

- Release or repression of anger

- Susceptibility to stimulation

- The energy of the personality

- Productivity

Lower-zone letters have extensions that reach down under the baseline: *f, g, j, p, q, y,* and *z*. Letters or parts of letters that don't normally belong in the lower zone but appear there are a sign of unresolved pain and frustration.

Back to School with Freud

Good graphologists understand personality development. Without a basic foundation in developmental and abnormal psychology, the best you'll be able to do is make a list of unconnected personality traits, and that won't help you or your client. Knowing how those traits work together as a dynamic system will allow you to create meaningful, helpful analyses.

Freud's *psychoanalytic model of personality* fits nicely with the concept of handwriting zones. While Freud's ideas may have been hotly contested over the years, it's generally accepted that most systems of personality development have their roots, at least partially, in his time-tested concepts of id, ego, and superego.

def•i•ni•tion

Freud's **psychoanalytic model of personality** development includes the id, ego, and superego.

The Id Did It

Every living organism uses psychic energy (basic life force) to meet its needs in the physical, emotional, and spiritual areas of life. Although energy cannot be destroyed, it can be transformed for different uses and distributed where needed.

When part of a lake is dammed, some of the water gets redirected into another area. The same amount of water is still there, but it isn't all available at the same time for the same purpose. Likewise in the human organism. We might expend some mental energy at work, then go to the gym and use some for physical exertion, and an entirely different kind in socializing when we go out for dinner with friends. Our energy is transformed for use in different parts of the personality at different times.

Freud called human energy the id, and identified it as the earliest part of personality to appear after birth. The id serves only one purpose: to reduce tension and produce pleasure. The id doesn't think or reason, it simply seeks ways to provide relief from discomfort and it doesn't matter what form the relief takes. If the source of discomfort is hunger, cold, sadness, or sexual tension, it makes no difference. The id's sole function is to make you feel good. That's why the id is called the pleasure principle.

The id knows only that it wants what it wants, and it wants it *now!* "Wait" is not a word the id understands. Like an infant who can't delay the urge to eat, the need to have its diaper changed, or the desire to be cuddled, the id demands instant gratification. Hungry, wet, or frightened, a baby will scream to get relief, and that's appropriate for a baby. But the same behavior in an adult draws stares of disgust.

We've all seen adults who, when they don't get their own way, have a tantrum. They'll yell and pound the desk and jump up and down, making unreasonable demands. We say to ourselves, "What a baby!" Such people act like babies because their emotional development never progressed past the infant stage. Their id impulses drive them, rather than the more mature adult quality of self-control.

Chicken Scratch

Unusual forms in the lower zone (the unconscious), which might include hooks, knots, twists, and angles, indicate an unhappy id. The writer's drives are not being satisfied in the usual, standard ways.

The distribution of id energy in the personality is seen throughout the zones of handwriting, but we look first at the lower zone. Some other zones may have a little more emphasis than others, but overall, in a mature personality, the energy is distributed throughout the writing, producing symmetry and balance.

When the personality is stuck in the id stage, the writing runs wild. There is unevenness and variability in practically every area: size, style, baseline, slant. Loops may balloon as the energy bursts into places where it doesn't belong. Id writing explodes into impulsive action. Life is all about having fun and doing what comes naturally without restraint.

★★
BRYAN MILLER, The New York Times
January 10, 1992

"...the endurance award has to go to Cafe Luxembourg, the 10-year-old Art Deco bistro that has remained vital, vibrant and as sturdy as Pavorotti's dressing-room chair."

Id writing: Singer Marianne Faithfull's uninhibited script.

For the id energy to be used effectively, it must be properly channeled. That is the job of the ego, the next area of personality to develop.

Ergo, the Ego

The ego is the "traffic cop" of the personality. It directs energy where needed and helps the individual make appropriate choices based on common sense and reasoning. The ego is called the reality principle.

A healthy ego uses self-discipline and self-control to ensure the appropriate amount of energy is available as and where needed. If you're playing racquetball, you need more energy for the physical than for the intellectual area. In the handwriting analysis class you are attending, you need more intellectual energy than emotional energy. When you and a couple of classmates go out for a latté after class, the ego channels the energy into the social area.

Let's say you're walking by a bakery and you smell warm bread. Your stomach grumbles longingly and your conscious mind starts a debate with your biological urge to eat: "You're on a diet and need to cut down on carbs," the mind says. "But it smells so good," argues the id. Hmmm, what to do? A well-developed ego gains the upper hand and says, "Not now, wait until you've lost 5 more pounds. Eat a salad instead."

A handwriting with good overall balance says the writer has developed common sense and self-discipline. He is even-tempered and has learned to delay gratification until the time is right.

Although its effects are imprinted on the entire handwriting, the ego is specifically found in the middle zone. That's where the day-to-day routines and social interactions are revealed, and where the traffic cop directs the energy where it needs to go. If a handwriting looks fairly neat and well organized and nothing pops out to hit you in the eye, chances are the writer has a healthy ego and the ability to get his needs met in socially acceptable ways.

San Francisco attorney Sheldon Siegel is the author of five critically-acclaimed best-sellers: Special Circumstances, Incriminating Evidence, Criminal Intent, Final Verdict and The Confession Mr. Siegel's novels feature criminal defense attorney Mike Daley, an ex-priest, ex-public defender and ex-partner in a prominent San Francisco law firm. Daley practices law with

Healthy ego writing: Sheldon Siegel, author of the Mike Daley & Rosie Fernandez mystery series.

Note: *excessively* organized writing, like any other extreme, is out of balance. In fact, excessive organization and rigidity indicates an overly active superego, the last part of personality to develop.

Tales from the Quill

Many teenage girls write only in the middle zone. (Their upper and lower extensions are so short they're practically nonexistent.) Interested solely in what is happening from moment to moment, they live for today. A large middle zone does not signify a strong ego, but a weak one. Overemphasis in the middle zone of an adult handwriting is generally a sign of immaturity.

Superego to the Rescue!

As the superego evolves and the child learns to live by the rules of society, his conscience begins to develop. The function of the superego is both to reward and punish, and it acts like a parent who peers over your shoulder when you want to do something and says, "Don't do that!" If you constantly hear a little voice in your head whispering "shoulds" and "shouldn'ts," it's a sure sign of a strong superego. This is called the morality principle.

A super-strong superego is like a strict dean of discipline mixed with Santa Claus. It punishes you with guilty feelings when you don't do what you're supposed to—you give in to the id's temptations and overspend your credit limit, for example. If, however, you are good and fend off the naughty urge, the superego might reward you with pride and self-satisfaction.

Handwriting of the person with a too strict superego looks rigid and overcontrolled. It is brittle and stiff, with tall upper loops. The writer's internal parent is a stern taskmaster that never relaxes and rarely allows the writer to experience anything that might be enjoyable. The superego writer is usually very serious and has a hard time allowing himself to have fun, unlike the id writer, who wants *only* to have fun.

Superego writing: radio personality and author Dr. Laura Schlessinger.

Welcome to My World: The Middle Zone

The middle zone, where the ego resides, shows how the writer acts around other people, how well adjusted he is, and whether all the parts of his personality are working together harmoniously.

In the middle zone, we act on the goals that were conceived in the lower zone (unconscious) and planned out in the upper zone (conscious). When one zone is much larger or smaller than the others—for example, a tiny middle zone with an extremely tall upper zone, or a large middle zone and stunted lower zone—the writer's goals conflict with his ability to meet them.

How uniform the size of middle-zone letters is tells something about the writer's sensitivity to the needs of others. The middle zone represents where we interact socially, so some variability in size shows ability to deal with various types of people. But

Chicken Scratch

Handwritings with middle-zone letters that suddenly flare up over other letters paint a picture of sudden outbursts. This phenomenon is known as jump-up or pop-up letters. The writer may normally be mild-mannered and low-key, but without warning, comes on strong.

while some fluctuation is normal and expected, when letter size (height and/or width) varies too much, the writer lacks confidence; his ego is in a constant state of flux.

How much variation is too much? When the middle zone looks very uneven, with letters randomly jumping up and squishing down, it's too much. Are the words "look for balance" becoming your mantra yet?

Middle-zone letters of more or less the same height indicate a degree of self-confidence and ego strength. But too much regularity is no better than too much variation. The writer is so fixed on his own ego needs that he can't understand or isn't interested in what others need. Machinelike handwriting means overcontrol. Because the writer represses his emotions, at some point they are likely to burst out in some unexpected behavior.

Overcontrolled handwriting.

The middle zone.

aeioucmnrsvwx

Soul Survivor: The Upper Zone

The upper zone is where the writer can expand his knowledge, let his imagination run wild, explore various philosophies, and satisfy his intellectual curiosity. To effectively use the ideas of the upper zone, the writer must bring them back into the middle zone. Otherwise, he is just building castles in the air. When too much emphasis is placed on the upper zone, either by making the loops extra tall or extra wide, the writer may have difficulty functioning in the real world (the middle zone), and is compensating for problems in the realm of the ego. Maybe because he feels socially inferior, he escapes into the upper-zone world of the intellect where he can create his own reality, which feels safer.

Let's look at some of the possibilities in different types of upper zones. Always keep in mind that no one element of handwriting means anything outside the context of the writing you are examining. Therefore, you'll need to confirm the interpretation of the upper zone with the rest of the sample.

- An extra-tall upper zone is like someone standing proud, as if he has just achieved some wonderful goal. Whether or not the pride is deserved and based in reality depends on how well developed the other zones are. If the upper-zone height is too tall in proportion to the other zones, the writer may be an intellectual dilettante who lacks the ability to manifest his ideas in middle-zone reality.

- A very narrow upper zone allows little room for the writer to expand his ideas. In a very real sense, he is narrow-minded and may be afraid to explore philosophies that threaten to draw him outside the realm of his own experience.

- A tall, narrow upper zone suggests that the writer may have been raised in a strict or authoritarian household. One's attitude toward authority figures (father, boss, minister, superior officer, etc.) is found in the upper zone, and the writer of tall, narrow loops views authority figures as extremely powerful, towering over him. Feeling inferior to those in authority, he compensates by dominating others over whom he feels superior.

- Those who expend too much time and energy thinking about things rather than doing them often make overly wide upper loops. The imagination is given free rein. The writer is also hypersensitive and imagines others are talking about him in a critical way. The wider the loops, the more unrealistic he is.

- Without the balance of a well-formed middle and lower zone, an overemphasized upper zone means the writer is unable to properly meet the demands of everyday life. Everything is filtered through the intellect, so his reality testing is poor.

- A short upper zone indicates a writer who generally doesn't have strong religious or spiritual beliefs, and who isn't interested in questioning his values. More materialistic than intellectual, he is interested in people and things that he can see and touch, not what he views as "airy-fairy" abstract ideas and philosophies.

The upper zone.

→ *bdfhklt*

What Dreams May Come: The Lower Zone

Keeper of secrets, gateway to the unconscious, the lower zone holds the mysteries of the psyche. The lower zone begins under the baseline and descends into the darkness of the past.

The lower zone.

→ *gyjpq*

The writer's expression of sexual and material desires is found in the lower zone. Whether he is inhibited, moderate, or freewheeling, whether he feels inferior or powerful when it comes to sex, the lower zone tells at least part of the story.

It also reveals whether the writer is apt to be a sensitive, considerate lover, or one who prefers to use brute force to subdue his partner. Of course, sex is more than just a physical expression, so different aspects of sexuality will be seen throughout the handwriting, not just in the lower zone.

Now we'll look at some types of lowers zones. As above, always keep the whole picture in mind.

◆ Moderately full lower loops balanced with the other zones signify the writer's ability to satisfy sexual and other biological urges adequately. He has the ability to plan (upper zone), call on past experience and draw on the necessary energy (lower zone), and effectively act on his plans (middle zone).

◆ Good pressure on the downstroke shows vitality. Check to see whether the loop is weakly falling into the lower zone or is thrust into the lower zone with a strong, purposeful movement. Is the writer easily led, or does he do the leading?

◆ The downstroke that moves decisively from the baseline into the lower zone is going underground, into the basement, where we explore all the stuff stored in the unconscious. There's a lot of old junk down there, but some bona fide treasures, too. What we bring "back upstairs" in the upstroke, to use in the reality of daily life, is our own choice.

- What if your particular basement is a dank and dirty dungeon, and there's nothing there that you want to use? What if, in fact, you have a strong aversion to going there at all? You might decide to rush back upstairs as fast as you can, pretending you never visited. That's what the writer does who, in the middle of a word, makes a straight downstroke with no return loop. Note: when a straight downstroke with no loop occurs only at the ends of words it is a form of simplifying the letter and does not have the same meaning as when it appears consistently in the middle of words.

- The writer of extremely long lower loops has a basement deep under the ground. He likes to delve into the past and is very interested in learning about his heritage, his roots, and even the skeletons in his closet.

- Very short loops suggest someone who's uncomfortable in his basement or just not interested in exploring the past, and quickly returns to the middle zone. Consequently, he is unlikely to learn from past mistakes. His mind is on what he's going to have for dinner, or whether the mail has arrived yet. Last year, last month, or even yesterday is all in the past. And he certainly doesn't want to bother with what might or might not happen tomorrow. All that counts is in the present.

Off the Beaten Path

The copybook lower loop returns directly to the baseline. When the loop veers off in another direction, chances are the writer has suffered sexual abuse, probably (though not always) in childhood. As a result, the emotions attached to sex are not always expressed in the usual, standard ways. What should be a natural expression of the basic drives turns into something self-conscious, shameful, and humiliating.

There is an almost unlimited variety of lower-loop formations. Suffice it to say that any habitually twisted or unusual forms in the lower zone suggest that the writer has been unable to resolve the past painful events, whatever the cause.

- Extremely wide lower loops that look like inflated balloons are made by writers with an overblown fantasy life. They'll talk ad nauseum about their sexual interest and prowess, but when it comes down to it, they're full of hot air. The writer feels sexually inadequate, and the extra wide loops help him put up a big bluff.

- Lower loops ending in a short, sharp hook suggest a cranky, short-tempered nitpicker. When found in combination with other negative signs, such as very heavy pressure, he may also be a bully.

Tales from the Quill

Claw-shaped lower-zone forms symbolize unconscious feelings of guilt that the writer has been unable to release. He unconsciously sets himself up for punishment because he believes he deserves it. One writer of hooked lower loops had a habit of gossiping about a particular friend to others. She did it in such a way that the talk would inevitably get back to the friend, which would lead to an angry confrontation that made her feel guilty.

Claw-shaped lower zone (sometimes poorly named "the felon's claw").

interests and, of course, I just a thoughtful, kind, and emotionally who is open-minded and creative

Examples of some unconventional lower zones.

and being company.

going

incredibly

really is—

DING YOUR

journey

my marriage my relationships

gave

utting

very wrong

autograph

already

love you

forgetting you

years ago,

When the lower zone pulls strongly to the left (more often seen in men's writing) it signifies a strong attachment to one's mother or a need for mothering that was not satisfied in childhood. Lower loops that pull to the right (more often seen in women's writing) are usually made by those who rebel against male authority.

Mom Always Gets the Blame!

Here are some examples of lower zone forms that are a bit out of the ordinary:

◆ A triangular-shaped lower zone that has sharp corners pointing to the left (mother, nurturing, the past) indicates unresolved issues—possibly with one's mother—that spill over onto other women in the writer's life. There is hidden aggression or hostility in this formation because it is below the baseline, the line of reality, in the lower zone, the area of the unconscious. The aggression may take the form of nagging and constant criticism. When the angles have soft edges, it mitigates the implication somewhat.

President Bill Clinton's two terms in office were marred by accusations of sexual misconduct. What does his handwriting reveal? A combination of hard and soft triangles in the lower zone.

Former President Bill Clinton.

◆ Large, rounded lower extensions that look like cradles don't return to the baseline but hang in the lower zone. The stroke ends in a leftward movement, toward the past and one's mother. The writer may have missed the nurturing, loving care that she would like to have had, and continually seeks it out in relationships with men (mostly it's women who adopt this form, but not always). She might be quite competent in her career world, but emotionally is as vulnerable as a kitten.

◆ Loops that curl inward like a snail's shell show strong self-involvement. They are made by the egocentric, insincere person who cannot be trusted to tell the truth. In relationships, this writer only has room for himself.

♦ When the upstroke crosses the downstroke too soon (before the baseline), it may indicate a lack of the proper emotional release in sex, resulting in frustration.

A well-developed lower zone, balanced with the other zones, shows good coordination, self-confidence, and an ability to relate effectively with other people. As in every aspect of handwriting, no zone should be interpreted separately from the others.

The Least You Need to Know

♦ Handwriting is divided into three zones—upper, middle, and lower—which correspond to areas of personality.

♦ The middle zone is the most important because all parts of handwriting pass through it.

♦ The upper zone represents conscious thought (how you think).

♦ The middle zone represents where you live (how you feel).

♦ The lower zone represents the unconscious (how you act).

♦ Although each zone has its own significance, all work together and affect each other.

Chapter 8

Size Does Matter: Writing Size

In This Chapter

- What does "size" really mean?
- From me to you—width and social skills
- Aspiring to visions of greatness—tall writing
- The material girl and boy—middle-zone emphasis

Now that we know the general areas symbolized by each zone, we need to talk about how writing size affects the writer's activities. First, though, we need to define what "size" means. Absolute size encompasses the entire scope of writing, from the tops of the upper loops to the bottoms of the lower loops. More important, however, is relative size, which refers to the ratio of the height of middle-zone letters to the height of upper-zone and length of lower-zone letters. In this chapter, we'll discuss how to measure size in handwriting, and what overall size and relative size mean.

The middle-zone measurement is the most important because several other measurements are based on it. But don't worry about making your measurements exact; a ballpark figure is good enough. We'll be measuring the height and width of the letters in each zone.

Leggo My Ego

The zone of the ego, the middle zone answers the question, "How tall does the writer feel?" Someone who isn't very tall in a literal sense but has a healthy ego can seem like a giant. What counts is how tall you feel *inside*. The middle-zone height (MZH) is an indicator for how tall the writer feels and how much recognition she needs. We're measuring *ego needs*.

def•i•ni•tion

Ego needs are what it takes to make an individual feel good about herself. Ego strength is the ability to get one's needs satisfied.

Middle-zone width (MZW) involves the movement from left to right (from me to you), and tells us how free the writer feels to move out into the world and satisfy her ego needs. One who is not afraid to ask for what she needs has a wider middle zone than the one who is shy and shrinks back. So, MZW is a measurement of *ego strength*.

Small, Medium, Large—As Opposed to What?

The American Palmer school copybook (CB) is the standard we'll use as a measure of small-medium-large. For the MZH, choose the letters *o*, *a*, and *e* (these are the easiest) from several parts of the handwriting sample and measure them with a metric rule from top to bottom.

Measuring the middle-zone height.

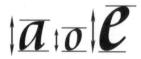

Fine Points

Someone who wants to seem taller than she really is may put on high-heeled shoes or pouf up her hair. In handwriting, she writes a tall middle zone. But if the writer doesn't also have sufficient self-confidence, the middle zone will be narrow.

If most of the middle-zone letters measure 3 millimeters, as in the Palmer copybook, the middle-zone height is medium. If they're taller than 3 millimeters, they are tall. If they're shorter than 3 millimeters, the middle zone is small. A wide variety of measurements means that the middle-zone height is variable.

Next, using the letters *o* and *a*, measure the MZW. Copybook dictates that MZW should be about the same as MZH or slightly less. That makes the ratio 1:1. If the letters measure less than 3 millimeters wide, the middle zone is narrow. If they measure more, the middle zone is wide. If there is a wide variety of measurements, the MZW is variable.

Measuring the middle-zone width.

Following is a list of abbreviations for commonly used graphological terms.

Abbreviation	Meaning
CB	Copybook
LZ	Lower zone
LZL	Lower-zone elaboration
LZW	Lower-zone width
MZ	Middle zone
MZH	Middle-zone height
MZW	Middle-zone width
UZ	Upper zone
UZH	Upper-zone height
UZE	Upper-zone elaboration
UZW	Upper-zone width

How About Those Loops?

In CB, the upper-zone height (UZH) is one-and-one-half times as tall as the MZH, which means the upper loops measure 4½ mm from the baseline to the top of the loops. Using the letters *l*, *b*, or *h*, measure several of the tallest ones. To be considered medium, the *width* of the upper loops (UZW) should be only about one-half as wide as the middle zone height.

Now, let's turn to the lower zone. Measure the longest loops on *g* or *y* from the baseline to the bottom of the lower-zone loops (LZL). The LZL should be twice as long as the middle zone is high, and the lower-zone width (LZW) should be half as wide as the middle zone height. That means loops measuring 6 millimeters long and 1½ millimeters wide are medium. Measure lower loops at their widest point.

Measuring upper and lower loops.

Bigger Than Small, Smaller Than Big

A middle zone that is medium in height and width suggests a writer who is well adjusted, realistic, and generally conventional. She is able to focus on what she wants to do and gets it done with adequate self-confidence. Socially, she knows her place and does what is expected within her chosen social group. She follows instructions well, so it bothers her when others break the rules or step too far out of line.

Chicken Scratch

Describing the middle-of-the road, average writer is one of the biggest challenges for the graphologist. It's like giving a description of a man in his mid-20s, with a medium build, brown hair, and brown eyes. There are no distinguishing characteristics!

When the middle zone is fairly uniform in height and width, it implies a degree of inner security, so that wherever she is, the external environment doesn't seem to affect the writer much. There is give and take in her relationships with others, and she feels comfortable in her own skin. A moderate degree of fluctuation in the middle zone is expected and indicates that the writer is responsive and reacts to emotional events around her. If there is little or no fluctuation, check the writer for a pulse!

Slightly larger than medium middle zone: author and television personality Dominick Dunne.

and trial pieces in Vanity Fair. They tell me I get too personally involved in my stories. So what I say. Dominick Dunne

The wider the middle zone, the more important it is to the writer to be accepted by others. An MZ much wider than it is tall is made by someone who tends to be indiscriminate in relationships. Quantity becomes more important than quality. Such an exaggerated need for acknowledgment and approval sets the writer up for disappointment.

Wide middle zone: Supreme Court Justice Sandra Day O'Connor.

It's the Little Things That Count

The writer of a small MZH with medium width doesn't much care what others think. She's more intellectual than social and is content to spend long periods alone, concentrating on the things that interest her. She works well under pressure, especially when small details are important. She recognizes her limits in social situations and her manner is restrained around other people. This writer is comfortable being an introvert, so don't try to talk her into being more sociable.

Small middle zone: actor Jeremy Irons.

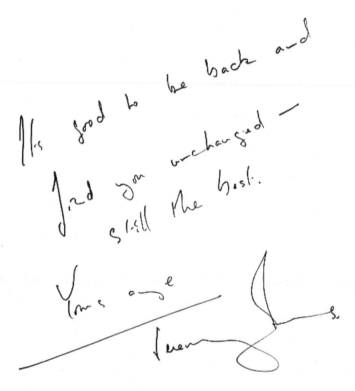

Small and Narrow

The narrower the MZ letters are, the greater the insecurity. When the writer refrains from moving toward the right, the letters become ovals instead of circles and "from me to you" becomes "from me to me." A lack of confidence restricts the writer so she feels tense and apprehensive in an unfamiliar environment. That short MZH says her self-concept may already not be so hot (she feels she doesn't deserve to command much space in the world). Add narrowness, and her emotional world becomes limited to what and who she knows. She may have few great passions or strong emotions. In fact, others may see her as impassive or even apathetic.

Very Small

A tiny middle zone is the sign of a shrinking violet. Rarely will anything get her to venture out of her confined space. She prefers her own company to that of others. She's afraid that others will see her for what she believes she is—nothing. When forced into the company of others, she'll be picking nits and generally being petty toward them. This is the porcupine defense—I'll attack you before you get a chance to attack me. As soon as she possibly can, she'll retreat to the security of her safe little shell.

Tiny middle zone: author William Faulkner.

An extremely small middle zone may be a sign of mental illness if the letters are so simplified that they become skeletal.

Big Is Beautiful

The large-middle-zone writer is less realistic than the smaller writer. The tallness of her strokes take her away from the baseline (the line of reality) so she sees things less pragmatically. She thinks *big*, and, because she doesn't believe she can fail, she happily takes on jobs that others might feel are beyond them. If there is also adequate width, she has the confidence to carry through her plans. With proportional width, this is the extrovert who wants to act upon the world, rather than have the world act upon her. She is determined to stand out in a crowd and behaves in ways that will put her at center stage with the spotlight directly on her. Her large ego, as reflected in her large MZ, reveals a need for approval and admiration.

Large (variable width) middle zone: actress Theresa Russell.

Large but Narrow

This ebullient personality can be more show than go. The tallness in the middle zone is a compensation for the feelings of anxiety demonstrated by the narrowness. The writer may talk about things she wants to do, but when it comes to performing, she is afraid to try, unless she knows with certainty that she will succeed. Note, the sample below has other redeeming factors, namely, energy and enthusiasm that pushes him forward.

Large, somewhat narrow middle zone: actor Robbie Coltrane (Harry Potter's Hagrid).

Too Much of a Good Thing

An extremely large middle zone (larger than 5 millimeters high) doesn't mean an extremely healthy ego. Quite the opposite, in fact. The writer believes the world revolves around her and that she's better than others. She's a know-it-all who behaves as if anything that doesn't serve her ego doesn't exist. She believes she can do anything she wants, even though a vague nagging voice reminds her that her bragging isn't based on truth. She makes mountains out of molehills—nothing is too small for her to turn into a major issue. When she fails, don't expect her to accept responsibility. It's always someone else's fault (especially when the spatial arrangement is crowded).

Decisions, Decisions—I Can't Make Up My Mind

Variable middle-zone height shows a wide range of emotions on a continuum from sensitivity to touchiness. Whether the writer is emotionally lively or simply unstable depends on the degree of variability. Some variability shows the capacity for adapting to the needs of the moment, but when the variability becomes extreme, the writer is a victim of her own moods.

Chicken Scratch

If the middle zone is much larger than the upper and lower zone, the writer is avoiding the intellectual and material areas of life in favor of social relationships and emotional concerns.

Typically, a variable middle-zone height ranges from 2 to 4½ millimeters. When the MZH fluctuates too much, you'll know that the writer's confidence level is changeable. She feels sure of herself now, but in 5 minutes she'll be berating herself for being inadequate. If she's feeling good, she might get involved in a project, then suddenly fear she won't be able to handle it and want to back out. Life is certainly never dull around this type.

Variable middle zone: Ludwig Von Beethoven.

The writer of changeable MZW is likewise unpredictable. You never know what she's going to do next because *she* doesn't know either. She might act friendly and welcoming one moment, then withdrawn and aloof the next.

Up, Up, and Away

If you want to know about someone's values, check the state of their upper zone (UZ). The upper loops show how interested the writer is in ideas, philosophy, and spirituality. The higher the loops, the more the writer seeks to reach into the theoretical domain. For the mental activity to be productive, the height should be in balance with the lower zone and the middle zone.

The upstroke goes away from the self and moves out toward other people before returning to the baseline, bringing what it has learned. If the writer is successful in incorporating the new information into her life, she will make a strong downstroke. A weak downstroke shows avoidance of reality: the writer has trouble integrating what is real (MZ) with what is theoretical (UZ).

Fine Points

Some graphologists call extra-wide lower loops "money bags," because they symbolize an emphasis on money and enjoyment of the good things in life.

Moderate upper zone: Hazel Dixon Cooper, Cosmo's Bedside Astrologer.

Tall Upper Loops

A moderately tall upper zone suggests the writer is searching for greatness—reaching for the stars. If the upper zone is twice as tall as the MZH, the writer is more concerned with the theoretical than the practical. Driven to understand the universe, if she thinks there's more to know about a subject she finds interesting, it makes her crazy until she has ferreted out every last bit of information there is to find.

Tall upper zone: Elvis Presley.

I Love it. Sir I can and will be of any Service that I can to help the country out. I have no concern or motives other than helping the

Too Tall

When the loops reach too far into the upper zone, the writer is dissatisfied with who she is. The movement is away from the self, towards something else, something "out there," so she is looking outside herself to get her needs met. The loops seem to be reaching up, aspiring to please an authority figure, probably the writer's father, whether she is aware of it or not.

An extra-tall and narrow upper zone often signifies someone who had an ultra-religious upbringing with an abundance of rules and regulations to follow. Interestingly, like Charles Lindbergh, many pilots have a disproportionately tall upper zone. Perhaps this reflects their desire to fly up-up-and-away. At least one research project is currently under way to answer this question. It takes longer to make extra tall loops, and the writer often wastes time expounding on theories that have little basis in reality. And the longer she spends on thinking, the less time there is to act.

Tall, narrow upper zone:
aviator Charles Lindbergh.

Any organization thru which such education is distributed is worthy of the fullest support.

Charles A. Lindbergh

Narrow or Retraced Loops

Retraced loops, where the downstroke covers the upstroke, suggest no room for intellectual growth. The writer is narrow-minded and prejudiced against new ideas. Uninterested in broadening her horizons or coming up with something innovative and revolutionary, she continually recycles the ideas and concepts she learned while growing up.

def•i•ni•tion

Retracing refers to laying the final stroke on top of (retracing) the original stroke, and may be found in any zone.

Tall and Wide

Tall, moderately wide loops are a sign of imagination. The writer leaves room to create new thoughts and listen to new ideas. She is able to learn from experience and keep a reasonable perspective on what others have to say. She's not afraid to hear anyone else express an opinion, and finds it easy to visualize unfamiliar concepts.

When the loops are more than twice the MZH, the writer lacks discrimination in what she takes into her mind. An overdeveloped upper zone is a way of compensating for dissatisfaction in one or both of the other zones. The writer prefers to escape into daydreams or intellectual woolgathering, rather than return to the reality of the middle zone. Her ideas are many, but tend to be impractical and unrealistic. They'll probably never get off the drawing board.

Tall, moderately wide upper zone: astrologer Lee Holloway.

Look Ma, No Loops!

Some writers simplify their writing by making straight, unlooped downstrokes. They think in a direct, pragmatic manner, no frills, preferring to cut to the chase rather than spend time in the imagination.

Unlooped upper zone: President George W. Bush.

I understand that you have volunteered for my campaign. I am grateful to have you on my team.

Short Upper Loops

The person who hasn't the energy or interest to rise above the middle zone is rooted in the real world. She finds intellectual discussions boring and will quickly seek an excuse to leave when the conversation turns to abstract ideas. For her, people and things are more interesting topics. She doesn't spend time planning, but prefers to "just do it." Whatever you do, don't give her a book for her birthday, it probably will never be opened. She cares that things happen, not *why* they do.

Short upper zone: Princess Grace of Monaco.

my fear of those instuments increases daily so I find it necessary to turn to other forms of communication —

Variable Upper Loops

As you might guess, the person whose upper loops are short or wide in one word or letter, and tall or narrow the next, is inconsistent in her thinking. She doesn't have a steady opinion or point of view to offer on any subject. The same topic might be viewed from totally opposite directions from one moment to the next.

Down in the Boondocks

The lower zone is the area of activity, sexual and otherwise. It contains our attitudes towards the material and biological areas of life. An emphasis on lower-zone length and/or width shows a strong interest in money, sex, and the material life. Loops that are too short show either a lack of interest in biological urges or little energy to invest in satisfying them.

De-emphasized Lower Loops

It doesn't take much determination or persistence to make short strokes into the lower zone. The writer probably shouldn't take on projects that can't be quickly completed, because she may lose interest or become discouraged over a period of time. If there is strong pressure, she may work hard but has limited endurance and stamina and just doesn't have it in her to keep on going. Because she stays close to the middle zone, she focuses her energy on the necessities of daily life. On the other hand, with other positive elements, some highly productive people may have a short lower zone because they emphasize upper-zone activity, like Jonas Salk, who developed the polio vaccine.

De-emphasized lower zone: Jonas Salk.

Medium Lower Loops

The writer of a moderate lower zone is active and productive, but she also likes to relax and recharge her batteries. If there is moderate width, endurance and persistence increase as the lower-zone loops increase in length.

Slightly wide lower loops suggest a conventional lover who does what is expected and no more. This is not the type you would find searching the Internet for websites featuring kinky sex.

> ### Tales from the Quill
>
> Max Pulver, one of the most quoted early graphologists, said, "The dangers of intellectu- alism are lack of persistence, of perseverance with projects, and of attention to material, physical and sexual matters. Those who write in the opposite way remain to some extent imprisoned in the foundations." If you find Pulver's meaning a little obscure, here's my interpretation: people who live in their heads (too tall upper zone) are often impractical, but those who spend too much time in the lower zone (the foundation) tend to get stuck in material concerns.

Long Lower Loops

The longer the loops, the greater the interest in satisfying physical and material desires. The writer of long lower loops prefers to jump right into activities without a lot of planning (especially when she has short *upper* loops). She reacts on a physical level and enjoys sex. She is motivated by opportunities to acquire money.

When the lower loops are more than twice as long as MZH, the writer can't sit still. She is constantly moving, drumming her fingers on the table, tapping her toes, or pacing around the room. She can't relax and hates routine in anything. She uses sex as a tranquilizer, and may have a long list of partners to call on when she's feeling frisky. Sex relieves her anxiety, but only temporarily.

Narrow Lower Loops

Just as in the upper and middle zones, narrowness in the lower zone signifies inhibi- tion. If the lower zone is long but narrow or retraced, it will take some doing to get the writer to act on her desires. Because she's afraid that she won't be able to perform adequately, she creates a self-fulfilling prophecy.

Moderately Wide Lower Loops

Moderately wide loops balanced with moderate length are made by a self-confident person who is not afraid to act spontaneously in intimate relationships. She has a strong sex drive and is resourceful and willing enough to branch out and go where she hasn't gone before. Long after the honeymoon is over, the writer of wide lower loops (as long as they aren't *too* wide) will be finding new adventures to try with her lover. Imaginative and fun-loving, she's ready for anything.

Long and wide lower zone: Eric Idle of Monty Python's Flying Circus.

Extremely Wide Lower Loops

As the lower loops swell to more than twice the width of the MZH, there is a danger of fantasy overtaking reality. This writer overreacts to everything, exaggerating and distorting the facts until they are unrecognizable. She may brag about her sexual prowess, yet be unable to perform.

Some Last Remarks About Zones

As in all other aspects of handwriting, extremes upset the balance and often are a sign of immaturity. Excessive size or lack of harmony in any zone is a negative indicator and intensifies the possibility of instability.

Never make an analysis based on one sign or one zone, because it is impossible to know a person based on just one aspect of her personality. There are always confirming, verifying factors, and contradictory ones that must be considered in developing an accurate picture of personality.

The Least You Need to Know

- ◆ Writing size tells how much space you feel you deserve.
- ◆ Middle-zone height reveals how much your ego needs; width shows how willing you are to get your ego needs met.

◆ Upper-zone height symbolizes aspirations, principles, and standards; width shows how open-minded you are.

◆ Lower-zone length and width tell how active and productive you are.

Part 3

Let's Dance: Movement

Here's where we'll move even deeper into handwriting. The basic rhythm, speed, pressure, and other vital aspects are explored in detail. These are some very complex concepts, but once you grasp them you'll be able to analyze any writing in any language.

You'll find it's worth the effort to study this section over and over again, until you feel comfortable with the theories presented here. It may be tempting, but don't just skim through it. You'll miss out on a vital part of your graphological education.

9

I've Got Rhythm: Writing Rhythm

In This Chapter

◆ Going out and coming in—the ebb and flow of rhythm

◆ Rhythm versus regimentation

◆ Will you or won't you? Rhythm and willpower

◆ A rhythm all their own

In this chapter, we'll explore *rhythm* in handwriting. You'll learn how to recognize the individual rhythms of space, form, and movement, and understand the writer's unique movement patterns. If you can learn to unravel the complex enigma of rhythm, it will take you far along the road to becoming a good handwriting analyst.

It may seem heavy going at first, but learning how to identify rhythm is an indispensable part of your graphological education. You'll probably want to review this chapter until you are confident you've mastered it.

Rhythm involves movement, and handwriting is movement, as surely as you put one foot in front of the other to walk from here to there. The pen touches down on a sheet of paper and it begins moving from the starting

def•i•ni•tion

Rhythm is movement characterized by regularly recurring elements or activities.

point to your goal, the end of the line. Without movement, all that would result is a dot on the paper.

But more than just the hand is involved in writing movement. Writing is controlled by the central nervous system, and every part of the brain is bound up in the act. Both physiological and psychological factors affect the movement you produce on paper.

Different Strokes for Different Folks

Calm or excitable, stilted or natural, the rhythm of movement expresses the writer's basic life force. There's a world of difference between a mechanical, dull temperament that functions like a robot, and an intense, vivacious one that treats life as a party.

The inherent rhythm in writing movement reveals, perhaps more than any other factor, how the writer adapts and functions in the world. Many different types of rhythm exist along a wide spectrum, from extremely irregular, to weak, to disturbed, to strong, to overcontrolled. We begin our discussion with the smallest element of writing movement, the stroke.

Handwriting is composed of two basic types of stroke: curved and linear. Curved strokes are smooth and continuous. They move in two directions—centrifugal, or counterclockwise (outward and away from the center); and centripetal, or clockwise (inward and toward the center). Linear strokes are straight and sharp. They go in one direction at a time. To change the direction of a straight line, you have to make an abrupt stop and an acute turn. A combination of both types of stroke is needed to produce good rhythm.

As they thrust or slink or dance their way onto the paper, the various combinations of strokes fall into a pattern, a portrait of how the writer experiences the world and how he expresses his experiences. A predominance of straight strokes draws one type of picture; a predominance of curved strokes draws another.

Energy Balancing: Contraction and Expansion

All living organisms have their own natural rhythms. The ebb and flow of energy that comprises rhythm involves two types of movement: one contracts, the other expands. In breathing, for instance, you inhale in an expanding movement; you exhale in a contracting movement. Ebb and flow, in and out, give and take, anticipation and realization, centripetal and centrifugal.

Think of winning the lottery. How would you react? Doesn't it make you want to leap out of your chair just to think of it! You even start breathing a little faster! When you're excited and happy (or excited and angry), you act *expansively*. Now think back to a time when you felt really sad about something. Your body *contracts*, you seem almost to fold up and go inside yourself. It's as if you actually take up less space.

Fine Points

Rhythm is one of the most important and one of the most difficult aspects of handwriting to learn. Think of it as the ebb and flow of energy.

So, as energy expands and contracts it forms a pattern of activity called rhythm or "periodicity." That's a fancy word for doing the same thing over and over, but not in exactly the same way every time. Each breath you take is similar to the others, but not identical. Some breaths are shorter, some are longer; some are ragged, some are smooth, but always, there is an in-and-out motion you can count on.

Handwriting with good rhythm suggests a harmonious personality. The various elements, the physical, emotional, and spiritual, are all working together to pro- duce balance. Writing that is not rhythmic reveals a lack of unity within the personal- ity. Something is out of whack. The writer's day-to-day functioning is impaired in some way.

Chicken Scratch

Beware of mistaking poor rhythm for a "bad" person. Rhythm simply tells you how well integrated the various parts of the writer's life are. Poor rhythm says that something is out of whack.

Will Power or Won't Power?

Rhythm is affected by one's strength of will. As defined for our purposes, will is the quality of mind that sets activity in motion and also controls it. Willpower provides the impetus to get things done and the self-control to call a halt at the appropriate time.

Handwriting that shows good willpower is rhythmic. Rhythmic writing allows impressions from the outside world to impact the writer, which he then assimilates and expresses outwardly in a reasonable manner. There is a periodicity in his behavior and his writing, a sameness within a particular range, but not so much that the writing looks mechanical or machinelike. The will regulates natural impulses and inhibits some of the basic urges that might be harmful.

Strong willpower: Donald Trump.

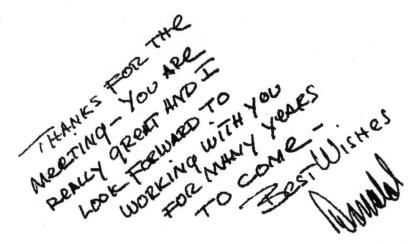

The Regularity Continuum

Socrates wrote, "In all of us, even in good men, there is a lawless wild-beast nature, which peers out in sleep." The person who controls every impulse is inhibited, afraid to allow his emotions free reign, ever. He believes, deep in his psyche, that if he fails to keep every urge in check with the strictest controls at all times, he will become completely wild. This is unacceptable, so he invests enormous amounts of energy denying the very existence of the beast.

The more regular the handwriting, the greater force the will exerts on the personality. The rigid writer's behavior is stiff and formal, emotionally withholding. The energy returns to the self in a centrifugal, contracting movement, which is reflected in his handwriting.

Fine Points

Willpower keeps us from doing things that are harmful to us, such as abusing drugs or alcohol, or engaging in promiscuous sex. A person with weak willpower tends to be self-indulgent and doesn't know when to quit. One who lets the world act upon him instead of being proactive has weak willpower.

The contracted movement pattern of a person who maintains extremely strong self-control tends to be highly regular, such as a clock, or a metronome, or your heartbeat. A high degree of regularity in handwriting is not considered good rhythm. Writing that looks as regular as a ticking clock indicates psychological problems with its rigid, mechanical sameness. The writer is inflexible and unable to adapt to the ups and downs of everyday life.

At the other end of the continuum is the highly released movement pattern. The irregular rhythm is wild and uncontrolled, which is just as problematic as the over-controlled personality. The irregular writer is so impressionable that every input is immediately expressed in action.

> We wonder who he is & who has been given the sedative.
> "Lark Sorenson is dead."

Moderately regular rhythm: Elizabeth George, author of the Inspector Lynley mystery series.

> a chance together — We let it die. And through death ... something new always grows. I agree with what you said 6 or 8 months ago. The next time

Mechanically regular rhythm: murdered ex-wife of O.J. Simpson, Nicole Brown Simpson.

The degree of balance between expansion and contraction is what creates our own particular rhythm. It reveals how receptive we are to outside stimuli, how we assimilate it, and, finally, how we express it outwardly.

Remember, movement comes in and goes out. Someone who only takes in and doesn't give out has no emotional growth. Someone who only gives out, but doesn't renew and refresh the spirit by taking in from the outside, depletes his energy and has nothing left to give.

Irregularity Breeds Contempt

If you've ever seen a seismograph (an instrument that measures earthquakes), you'll have an idea of what the irregular writer's emotional life is like. There are magnificently soaring highs and profoundly plunging lows, with little uniformity or order. Some call this type of personality "high-strung."

The writer is never sure of how he feels, what he wants, even who he is. He is deeply impacted by external events. Every urge, every need, every desire is seen on his face, heard in his tone of voice, acted out in his body language. There is little or no restraint of emotion. Others experience him as superficial or shallow. A woman of this type is often referred to as an "airhead."

Irregular rhythm: Elvis Presley.

I Love it. Sir I can and will be of any Service that I can to help the country out. I have no concern or motives other than helping the

Irregularity in handwriting is seen in variable size, a wavering baseline, and changing slant. Strong rhythm is lacking, which negatively impacts the aesthetic quality of the handwriting and indicates a temperamental, capricious disposition.

Past, Present, or Future? Left and Right Trend

Carl Jung suggested that we can properly meet the demands of the outside world only if we have first developed inner harmony. Writing rhythm reveals how well inner harmony has been achieved.

Jung spoke at length about the importance to personal growth of progression and regression. Psychic energy (life force) flows both backward and forward. When energy is regressive it reduces the impact of what is experienced when it is progressive. For example, someone hits a tennis ball toward you at 70 miles an hour. Moving backward would allow some of the tremendous force to dissipate, so that when the ball strikes, some of its impact will be lost.

Psychologically, too, we have to go backward to go forward. Like backing off from the tennis ball, stepping back to look at past experiences seems to lessen the impact of going full-bore into new experiences unprepared. It allows us to learn from our successes and our mistakes. In handwriting, this back-and-forth movement is seen as contraction and release.

def•i•ni•tion

Left trend is movement toward the left side of the page. **Right trend** is movement toward the right side of the page.

Any movement to the left (the past) in handwriting is called *left trend*. Movement to the right (the future) is *right trend*. Thus, any part of the writing movement—strokes, letters, words, margins, space—that travels in a leftward direction is left trend. Any part of writing movement that travels in a rightward direction is right trend. Both are fundamental to writing. You can't have one without the other, unless all you want is a straight line in the middle of the page.

When the left-trending elements are stronger than the right-trending ones, the writer is seeking refuge in the past. For some reason, he fears the future and does everything he can to avoid going there. It's like a tug of war, with the left side winning.

Writers with excessive right trend appear to be in a hurry to get to the right side of the paper. In that case, they may be running away from something in the past, or enthusiastically pursuing a future goal.

Strokes that travel opposite to the direction they properly should are called counter-strokes because they contradict the original intention. In Western writing, we move from left to right. Elements of the writing that migrate to the left when they should have gone right suggest either a rebellious personality or, perhaps, one that seeks comfort in the familiarity of the past.

Counterstrokes.

Rhythm and Blues

Rhythm in handwriting is an indicator of how well the writer controls his impulses. Good rhythm is a sign of healthy impulses and reasonable impulse control. Disruptions in the rhythmic flow of energy suggest some sort of inner physical or mental imbalance that manifests in the writer's inner and outer life.

Although we judge the overall rhythm of writing, the chief aspects—spatial arrangement (the way the handwriting is arranged on the page), form (the chosen style), and movement (the way the writing progresses across the page)—have their own rhythms and their own functions. To create a harmonious balance, all three must work together.

Movement consists of several elements. These include the basic stroke, pressure, left-right movement, slant, zonal proportions, beginning and ending strokes, and degree of connectedness from one letter to another. If these elements stand out more than any others, the writing has a dominance of movement. Dominance of movement reveals an impulsive person whose emotions and instincts rule. He goes with his gut reactions, is spontaneous and unconventional, and may not have adequate impulse control.

The elements of space include the overall arrangement of the page, margins, alignment, and space between letters, words, and lines. A dominance of space indicates someone who has overdeveloped his intellect at the expense of his social life. He relates to the world through his rational mind and carefully filters every experience through his intellect before acting on it.

Form is the most conscious part of handwriting. It consists of the writing style, which may be school type, simplified, elaborate, or printed. Writing that has a strong dominance of form reveals someone who is more concerned about appearances than substance. Social standing is usually a high priority for this type of writer.

If one part of personality is weak or disturbed, generally, another aspect takes over or compensates for it. Someone who suffers a physical loss, such as loss of eyesight, develops his hearing or another sense to make up for the loss. The same thing happens psychologically.

For instance, the person with poor social skills may compensate by exercising his intellect to make up for what he's missing socially. The compensation will be reflected in his handwriting through a disturbed rhythm of form (relates to the ego). The compensated intellect will have a better developed rhythm of space (relates to the intellect). If the compensation took place through physical activity rather than intellect, it would be evident in a stronger rhythm of movement (relates to the physical).

By zeroing in on the elements that are weak or disturbed, we can determine which parts of personality are affected. When there are problems in all three elements, a serious underlying disturbance that affects the entire personality is at fault. In the following tables, we'll use the categories "strong," "weak," and "disturbed" to examine the rhythms of movement, space, and form in graphic expression.

Tales from the Quill

Surprising results came from a survey I conducted on self-image and handwriting. In most cases, respondents whose handwriting was rhythmic and well balanced stated in their self-assessment that they had a poor self-image, while those whose handwritings were less rhythmic felt they had a good self-image. Just goes to show—no one aspect of hand-writing should be judged by itself. As important as rhythm is, it must be evaluated as part of the whole picture.

Rhythm of Movement Table

Strong	Weak	Disturbed
Rhythmic	Slack	Curved letters changed to angles
Sharp turning points	Sluggish	Straight strokes
Swinging	Listless	Angular
Curved	Dragging	Jerky
Elastic	Hesitant	Brittle
Fluid	Awkward	Stiff
Firm	Lacks pressure	Uncontrolled
Natural	Passive	Lacks harmony
Dynamic	Lethargic	Choppy strokes
Complex movements	Simple movements	Hesitations
Centrifugal movement	Centripetal movement toward center	Uneven tension
Moderate regularity	Emphasis on inner direction	Irregularity
Without constant fluctuations	Monotonous	Fluctuations in size, slant, pressure, form, connectedness

Rhythm of Space Table

Strong	Weak	Disturbed
Good proportions	Conventional	Awkwardly spaced
Well-arranged margins	Extra-wide spaces	Irregular gaps, margins, word spacing
Balanced margins, lines	Poor distribution of space	Overall size too large; writing stands out too much
Words clear and evenly spaced	Drifting margins	Overlapping lines
Good balance of zones	Upper-zone emphasis; lower-zone emphasis; letters too wide	Zones not balanced
Initial strokes missing	Letters too narrow; emphasis on end strokes	
End strokes missing or emphasis on initial strokes	Overall size too small; emphasis on white space rather than the writing	Letter spacing too wide or too small

Rhythm of Form Table

Strong	Weak	Disturbed
Lively	School model	Exaggerations
Spontaneous	Conventional	Unnatural forms
Departs from school model	Monotonous	Distortions
Legible shortcuts	Narrow or retraced loops and ovals	Overembellished
Original	Awkward	Inharmonious
Harmonious	Undeveloped	Highly angular
Some embellishments		Ungraceful
Creative forms		Poorly developed

Do You Wanna Dance?

Various types of rhythms make dance and music fun. The graceful 1-2-3 waltz rhythm is unlike the steady 1-2-3-4 of a military march. The brisk 1-2-1-2-3 of a cha-cha bears little resemblance to the laid-back beat of reggae, or the mercurial sound of acid rock. The following handwritings illustrate some different types of rhythms.

Lively, jumpy rhythm: Michael Connelly, author of the Detective Harry Bosch series.

Strong march rhythm: actress Julie Newmar, the original Catwoman.

Released waltz rhythm: spiritual author and lecturer Marianne Williams.

Extreme, Dude!

Extremes in handwriting hint at some form of compensation for a lack in one area or another. The writer prefers to deny what is really going on inside, so he tries to cover it up by distracting you with the exaggerations. Until you get the underlying picture of personality in mind, try to ignore the exaggerations, as they may draw you away from the truth.

Extremes in handwriting detract from good rhythm. Some handwritings have extremes that seem to jump off the page and hit you in the eye:

- Lower loops so long and wide they look like big, sad teardrops on the page

- Upper loops slanting so far to the right that the writing looks like it could fall over in a breeze

- Pressure so heavy it tears through the paper

- Ornaments that wouldn't even look good on a Christmas tree

Extremes in writing.

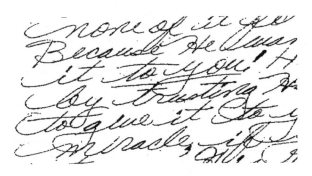

"Perfect" balance can never be attained because humans experience continual input that requires adjustments and growth. "Good enough" balance, however, is absolutely attainable.

The Least You Need to Know

- Writing is movement.

- Movement expands and contracts. As always, look for the degree of balance in how much the writing expands and contracts.

- Movement to the right is natural. Strong movement to the left is contrived.

- There are many different types of rhythms, which symbolize different types of temperaments.

- Extremes or exaggerations are never given a positive interpretation because they impede good rhythm and balance.

Chapter

10

Contents Under Pressure: Pressure

In This Chapter

- ◆ Energy gets things done
- ◆ Choose your instrument carefully
- ◆ How intense are you?
- ◆ Keeping up with the flow

Whether a task is physical or mental, it takes energy. The energy needed for physical tasks comes from the food we eat. Psychic energy, which is used to accomplish the work of the personality, comes from emotional experiences. Since the human body is a closed system, what happens on a physical level affects thoughts and feelings, and what happens on an emotional level affects thought. When the flow of energy is smooth and the human system is working harmoniously, things get accomplished. When the flow is disrupted, the entire organism is impacted.

Writing pressure is the characteristic that most closely expresses the energy of the personality. Like blood pressure, which strongly influences physical energy, writing pressure regulates the flow of ink as it is expelled from the pen. In this chapter, we'll cover which factors affect the stability and quality of the ink flow, and a few other items that it probably never occurred to you to ask about.

Ready for Action—Tensing and Flexing

Energy produces movement and, for any part of the body to move, it requires muscular tension. Without tension, we'd be as limp as the characters on cartoonist Gary Larson's boneless chicken ranch. Tension keeps the body in a constant state of readiness to act. We've already learned that the degree of tension and release creates a pattern of activity.

Too much tension means the body is always on the alert, which eventually results in physical and mental fatigue. Too much release results in flabbiness and an inability to react quickly when a response is called for. By now, you know what I'm going to say next. Say it along with me: a reasonable balance between the two extremes gets the most positive interpretation.

The physical movement of the hand when writing involves two sets of muscles that allow it to tense and flex. Downstrokes use the tensing muscles and upstrokes use the flexor. The motion of the downstroke—the tensing, contracting movement—brings the pen back to the self. At that moment the emphasis is on conserving energy and self-preservation. Therefore, if a handwriting demonstrates extra heavy emphasis on downstrokes, the writer is excessively concerned with the most basic of instincts, personal survival, more than other aspects of life.

The motion of the upstroke is the flexing, stretching movement, which takes the pen away from the self, toward others. During that movement the energy is expended on moving outward toward the ideals, and in releasing stress. If the writing emphasis is more on the flexing movement, the writer's focus is on outer concerns, such as altruistic or idealistic efforts or developing her spiritual side, more than her basic instinctual needs.

Tension is created by a need. Release comes from satisfying the need. Bottom line: the strength of the writer's needs and desires, whatever they are, is expressed in her output of energy. They will affect her writing pressure and the tension/release pattern.

External Influences

Several factors influence writing pressure. They include the type of writing instrument, pen hold, choice of paper, and writing surface.

Writing Instrument

Choice of writing instrument can make a tremendous difference to the writing trail it produces, yet some handwriting analysts insist on analyzing only samples written with ballpoint pen—I'm not sure why. If forced to use an instrument she doesn't like, the writer with a strong preference for a particular type of pen may not produce her normal style, and that could skew the analysis. Let the client use the pen she likes best.

Pen Hold

The way you hold the pen influences the width of the stroke it creates. Here's an experiment: hold your pen near the tip (called a *short hold*). You'll find the pen wants to stand almost upright, and the ink line it produces is thin and sharp with a very precise stroke. Now, grasp the pen further back on the barrel (a *long hold*), about 1½ inches from the tip. When you write, the ink flows more readily and spreads out in a thicker line. The type of line that results from either hold is called the *ductus*.

def•i•ni•tion

Ductus is the quality of the pen stroke produced by the flow of ink. A **short hold** means the pen is held near its tip. A **long hold** means the pen is held further back on the barrel.

Choice of Paper

If the writing paper is thick and porous, the ink soaks into it like blotting paper and the ductus looks fuzzy or blurred under magnification. Very smooth or glossy paper leaves the ink sitting on its surface and may not give a true impression of pressure (forgive the pun). Twenty-pound bond seems to be the easiest type of paper for accurately estimating pen pressure.

Writing Surface

Where you choose to write is another factor that affects handwriting. Here's another experiment: place your paper on a hard wooden surface to write and check the pressure. Then put a soft pad underneath the paper and see what a difference it makes. A hard writing surface doesn't allow as much play on the paper, so the pressure doesn't leave as much of an impression

Chicken Scratch

A handwriting sample that looks very shaky may have been written on a rough surface. When you see something out of the ordinary, don't analyze it until you have obtained further information.

on the paper. A softer surface allows too much play and makes the pressure appear heavier than it really is.

A Gripping Tale

There are three types of pressure in handwriting. The first is grip pressure and refers to how tightly you hold the pen. That's part of our earlier discussion about tension and release. Do you cling to your pen like a limpet, leaving a dent in your finger? If you often get writer's cramp, your grip pressure is probably too strong.

The second type is called primary pressure. That's how heavy-handed you are as you press the pen into the paper. Primary pressure shows how much you assert yourself in the world.

The third type is secondary pressure, which shows the rhythm of tension and release. Rhythmical secondary pressure creates a pattern of light/dark strokes. Remember: upstrokes should be lighter than downstrokes because the upstrokes release the tension. Sometimes it's easier to detect the secondary pressure pattern on a photocopy.

Types of pressure.

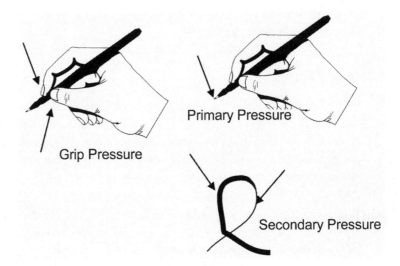

Internal Influences

In addition to all the external influences on pressure, health and mood can have an effect. When you're feeling ill, the pressure may get lighter because you don't have the energy to invest in the writing movement. The same is true of someone who is depressed. She just doesn't feel like making the effort. On the other hand, the angry person tends to write heavier, digging into the paper.

Pussycat or Storm Trooper?

Graphologists view pressure as the third dimension of handwriting. The writing zones carry movement across, as well as up and down on the paper. That's the first and second dimension. Pressure moves *into* the paper and has been labeled the depth component. It reflects, in a very literal way, the impression the writer makes on the world.

The timid, shy person tiptoes onto the paper in her house slippers without making a dent. The medium pressure writer has healthy self-confidence and isn't afraid to make her presence known. The angry, frustrated girl who rages at life storms onto the page in combat boots, leaving deep gouges in her wake, perhaps even ripping holes through the paper.

Fine Points

Dimensions of Handwriting:

♦ Movement across the paper from left to right

♦ Movement up and down across the page

♦ Movement into the paper

What Does It Weigh?

Pressure is not an indication of physical strength. A 98-pound grandma may have much stronger writing pressure than a 300-pound fullback. The degree that the writer presses into the paper depends on the amount of psychic energy she expends.

Don't worry about measuring pressure exactly. Light, medium, or heavy is close enough. How can you tell how heavy the pressure is? Easy! Turn the paper over and feel the back. Can you feel the words pressing into the paper? Or is the back totally smooth, the pen having made no impression at all? If you can't feel anything, the pressure is light. If you can barely feel it through the paper, the pressure is medium. If the paper is heavily scored, and you can feel the writing almost as if it were Braille, the pressure is heavy.

A photocopy or facsimile doesn't allow you to detect absolute pressure (depth), which is an important component of handwriting. This doesn't mean you can't analyze faxed or copied handwritings, but not until you have some experience under your belt and know how to gauge the writing depth.

The truth is, sometimes a photocopy offers a better idea of the pressure pattern than the original. Set the copier on a "lighter" mode and often, the light/dark pattern will stand out.

Breaking the Surface: Medium Pressure

Medium is the most common pressure, so we'll start there. Medium-pressured writing will be moderately dark, and you may feel a slight indentation on the reverse of the paper. In terms of need for physical contact, the writer is moderate and conventional.

As pressure is an expression of one's vitality, a good pressure pattern suggests someone with adequate willpower, stamina, and a moderate sex drive. If other characteristics support it, the writer is reliable and dependable, with sufficient backbone to help her get through difficulties.

Running on Empty: Light Pressure

The pen dragging on the paper produces friction, which the moderately light-pressure writer prefers to avoid. It may be that she's had to face a lot of conflict in the past, and can't stand the thought of dealing with any more. Consequently, she avoids obstacles whenever possible and takes the path of least resistance every chance she gets. She would rather fight than switch.

More spiritually than physically oriented, the light-pressure writer's sexual energies are sublimated into the mental realm. She probably doesn't expend a lot of energy on sex or other activities requiring a lot of vitality and stamina. It's not that she doesn't work hard. In fact, she may work very hard, but in bursts of energy which leave her absolutely exhausted.

The light pressure writer is usually very sensitive, sometimes (if the writing is also irregular) to the point of being temperamental. She can't afford to let things touch her too deeply, so her emotions tend to stay on the surface. An emotional event may flatten her momentarily, but then she'll let it go and move on.

Blowing in the Wind: Extremely Light Pressure

Extremely light pressure has a ghostly quality. Lacking in substance, the writing barely glides over the page, leaving almost no mark. Depression is often a factor, as the writer feels overwhelmed by life's stresses. For her, friction of any kind is like rubbing a towel over a sunburn—unbearable! It may help the analysis to find out why her will to make an impact is so weak.

The extremely light writer is highly suggestible and doesn't have the inner strength to stand against someone with strong willpower. Because she has little interest or drive for experiencing life in all its fullness, she compensates by living in her mind.

Anything that suggests power and vitality disturbs her sense of equilibrium, so she may choose a quiet environment with light colors and unseasoned foods.

Pressure Fades Away

Downstrokes that start strong but fade away before the releasing upstroke suggest someone whose energy peters out before the effort is complete. If the pressure returns just before the end of the upstroke, a short rest may be all she needs to revitalize and complete what she started. If your lover has this habit, give her a little break at strategic moments. You may enjoy the results!

Mount St. Helens: Slightly Heavy Pressure

Moderately heavy pressure can be easily felt on the reverse side of the paper. The writer sees the writing surface as a force to be overcome, and she believes she has the will to overcome anything. The heavy-pressure writer is a hard worker who, with a good contraction/release pattern, gets things done. When other people get tired and quit, she keeps on going.

Her stamina takes her through a long day, and she's still got the energy to party at night. She's a sensual, hearty lover with a strong sex drive. Activities that call for bodily contact and physical strength attract her. She enjoys pitting herself against difficulty and, especially with strong downstrokes, is determined to beat the odds. She's not afraid to demand what she wants.

The moderately heavy pressure writer is the type who enjoys spicy foods, fine wine, bright colors, and rough textures.

Tales from the Quill

Jennifer, a 26-year-old "California girl," works 9 hours a day in a busy county office as a secretary while she attends medical school 3 nights a week. On weekends and free evenings, she's haunting the nightclub scene with her friends or spending time with her boyfriend. Her two cats have almost forgotten what she looks like! Jennifer's stamina is evident in the moderately heavy pressure of her handwriting.

Playing the Heavy: Extremely Heavy Pressure

Extremely heavy pressure is a primary sign of frustration and anger. The increased tension on the pen results in deep scoring of the paper. If pressure is the degree to which the writer wants either to embrace or pummel the world at large, extremely heavy pressure suggests hostility and aggression. The writer is stubborn and inflexible with a nasty temper (especially when the pressure is combined with a strong right slant, slashing *i*-dots, and heavy *t*-crosses).

There is likely to be a ferocious drive for sensual gratification, but she has no finesse and may be brutish in satisfying her needs. For her, everything is brought down to its basest level. When she wants something, she shouts. If you disagree with her, she shouts. If she is unhappy, she shouts. "Bull in a china shop" comes to mind.

If there is a positive side to the extremely heavy pressure, it is that she isn't afraid of doing the dirty work. When something unpleasant needs handling, this person will do it.

Sudden Bursts of Pressure

When you see a sudden burst of pressure, check the word in which it appears, as it may be emotionally charged. Otherwise, the sudden pressure signifies a flare-up of suppressed emotion that has been smoldering for some time. If the pressure subsides right away, it simply symbolizes a quick burst of irritation that passes.

When the sudden burst is on the horizontal axis, especially on an end stroke, the writer is forcing her will on the world. She must have the last word. If the horizontal stroke is in the lower zone, she probably is not even aware of this tendency to be domineering. Certainly, she won't admit to it!

Sudden bursts of pressure: musician David Byrne of the Talking Heads.

..THIS GUY HAS HUGE HANDS AND

EE SOME FILMS OF AFRICAN DANCE

OTO A REHEARSAL OF THE DANCER

Life's Hard Enough–Displaced Pressure

To stay balanced, it is just as important to take time out to play as it is to work. Without regular times to relax and let go of the tension that builds up from day-to-day events, the body eventually rebels. Tension without release can lead to stroke, heart attack, and other unpleasant health problems.

Some people find it extremely difficult to relax and do nothing. They keep on pushing and don't know when to quit. Sometimes the tension is displaced, or channeled into an area where it doesn't belong. In handwriting, this results in a phenomenon called *displaced pressure*.

def•i•ni•tion

Displaced pressure occurs when, instead of the upstrokes being lighter than the downstrokes, the pattern is either reversed or emphasized on the left-right movement.

Pressure Displaced on the Horizontal

Pressure which is displaced onto the horizontal, as in *t*-crosses, rather than the vertical (up/down) axis of handwriting is a sign of excessive domination and force of will. Instead of directing the energy where it properly belongs, into the unconscious instincts of the lower zone, it gets hijacked. Extra strong, long *t*-crosses are symbolic of aggressive willpower. The person whose pressure goes horizontal rules others with an iron fist. Oh, it may be camouflaged in a pretty velvet glove, but there is no doubt about who has the say-so.

When the horizontal pressure appears in underlining, it is a matter of emphasis. The writer is trying to exert her authority like an instructor who thinks you don't understand her. If the horizontal stroke is a long final stroke at the baseline and not done for the purpose of underlining, it suggests holding off and distrusting others.

Pressure Displaced onto Upstrokes

Very little is written about displaced pressure. It is usually not considered in a positive light, but can be a sign of successful adaptation. Psychologist Dr. Klara Roman often found it in the handwritings of successful women who, for whatever reason, had sublimated their sex drive into their work.

The reversal of pressure means that when the writer should be releasing energy (light upstrokes), she is actually contracting (pressure on the upstrokes). She is, in effect, swimming against the tide of libidinal energy, making things much harder than need be. By forcing her will against the environment, she doesn't allow things to flow naturally.

On the surface she may appear quite calm, but the lack of inner balance causes frustration. The pressure moves away from the middle zone (ego activities) where it belongs, and toward the upper zone, displacing energy into an area where it doesn't belong at that time. In other words, the writer is thinking when she should be feeling and feeling when she should be thinking.

When pressure is displaced in the lower zone (light downstrokes, heavy upstrokes), sexual energy is displaced into the middle zone area of daily life. This doesn't mean the writer isn't interested in sex. Quite the opposite might be true, but there is no appropriate outlet for the sexual energy. The expenditure of energy into the middle zone is a compensation for it. According to Roman, if the displacement is carried out without loss of force or rhythm, the compensation is successful.

Manipulative behavior is a natural by-product of reversed pressure. The writer is determined to get done what she wants, by hook or by crook. If she can't get it by being nice, she'll force the issue. Insecurity generally is at the root. The writer's instinctual needs aren't being directly satisfied, so she exerts her will in some other area to make up for it.

Displaced pressure: Margaret Mitchell, author of Gone with the Wind.

A Word About Directional Pressure

When graphologist Felix Klein was imprisoned in the concentration camps at Buchenwald and Dachau during WWII, he discovered a surprising phenomenon in the handwritings of some prisoners. Those who survived had something in common: the strokes on the right sides of letters that were supposed to be straight were bent, or caved in. This seemed to indicate stress coming from the direction of the future. They never knew if they would be alive from one moment to the next. Those whose handwritings were more rigid were killed more often, as they didn't have the same capacity to adapt or bend to life in the camps. Directional pressure doesn't refer to the depth component, but it is pressure nonetheless.

> **Fine Points**
>
> Directional pressure can come from any direction. If the "caving in" is on tops of strokes, there is stress from authority figures; from the left it is pressure from the past; from below it comes from the instincts; and from the right, the pressure is from the future.

Directional pressure: Princess Grace Kelly (the downstroke bends inward, showing anxiety about the future).

Your Erogenous Zones

There is a difference between sensuousness and sensuality. Sensuousness has to do with gratifying the five physical senses: sight, sound, touch, taste, smell. Sensuality, on the other hand, is what results when indulgence in sensuous pleasures goes to its extreme. At least, that's the definition we'll use here.

Pastosity and Clam Sauce

Pastosity. What kind of word is that? A made-up one, actually, and its creation is credited to that prodigious early modern graphologist, Klara Roman. Dr. Roman used the word *pastosity* to describe the broad flow of ink that today we see from felt tip pens. It comes from the word "pasta," and intends to represent a soft, doughy quality.

The stroke is wide, both on upstrokes and downstrokes, but there is no real pressure. The stroke looks as if it were painted on with a brush. The lack of release that comes from heavy pressure on both up- and downstrokes is not present in this case because the pastose stroke is a released movement in itself. Lots of ink is discharged onto the paper.

Pastose writing is produced by those who are physically oriented and very much in tune with their senses. What they can touch, taste, smell, see, and hear are the things that turn them on. The scent of a rose might drive a pastose writer wild, or the sound of the birds singing early in the morning. Warm and earthy, she enjoys sex for its tactile sensations.

The important thing is, for the pastose writer, the sensuous experience must be natural. Don't try to palm some knock-off perfume or fast food on this type of writer. She wants the real thing.

Because the pastose stroke is produced without heavy pressure (it's made by a long hold on the pen), it suggests that the writer wants to enjoy her creature comforts without expending a lot of energy to get them. If the "good things" come to her easily, fine. If not, that's okay, too. But she'd much rather sit in the lap of luxury than on the cold dirt floor.

Unlike sharp writers, pastose writers are not judgmental. There are many shades of gray between black and white, and the pastose writer usually is somewhere in between. On the negative side, this individual lives mostly by her senses, expending far less of her energy developing the philosophical or spiritual side of life.

Pastose writing: composer
Ludwig Von Beethoven.

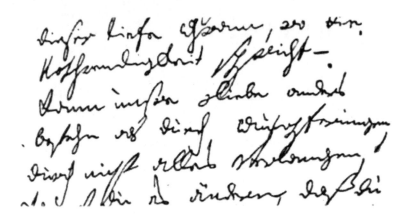

Mud Wrestling

Muddy handwriting, related to blocked pressure, is at the extreme end of pastosity. Writing is muddy when the writing looks smeared and smudged, the oval letters are flooded with ink, pressure suddenly billows, and/or there are numerous heavy cross-outs.

Muddiness comes from eroticism gone wild. That's different from a healthy sexual appetite. Muddiness is found in handwritings of some people whose sexuality may be linked to all sorts of unconventional practices frowned on by society. It suggests unbridled excesses and unbalanced discharge of energy. The flood of ink depicts a flood of impulses which the writer makes little or no effort to curb. Guilt and anxiety are often a big part of the picture.

Muddy writing: James Earl
Ray, convicted assassin of Dr.
Martin Luther King Jr.

Blocked Pressure

When the pressure is unrelieved, the upstrokes and downstrokes are both dark. This is not the same quality as pastosity, which is created without noticeable pressure.

Blocked pressure is heavy and looks unhealthy. In fact, it may be time for the writer to go for a physical checkup. Possibly, circulatory problems, alcoholism, menopause, or heart disease may be a contributing factor.

If the cause is not strictly physical, we can deduce that the writer feels stuck in a rut. What happens if you drive your car into a sandbank? You can't go forward and you can't go backward. You just sit there, spinning your wheels. And that's what life feels like for the writer of blocked pressure.

Signs of blocked pressure are muddiness, combined with …

- ◆ Slow speed.

- ◆ Lack of dynamic movement.

- ◆ Inhibition.

Shading and Sharpness

Looking like the sculpted bas-relief of an ancient temple, writing in relief, otherwise known as shading, results from a fountain pen or calligraphy-type pen, sometimes with a chisel tip. It produces an artistic script, though not a particularly spontaneous one. Aesthetics are of paramount importance to the writer of shaded writing. She is cultured and refined, socially polished, someone who demands excellence in her presentation.

Shaded writing: author Elmore Leonard.

Sharpness in handwriting can best be identified under magnification. A sharp stroke is thin and has clean, clear edges. The aesthetic person enjoys the crispness of this type of stroke, and usually has a critical nature. The sharp writer enjoys an argument, but don't expect her to bend even a millimeter. Her aggressive, dogmatic way of dealing with people may push others away.

For the sharp writer everything is either black or white with no gray area in between. When combined with angles, there is a certain coldness of personality and absolute refusal to adapt. She likes others to see her as moral and righteous. However, the kindness and compassion that go with morality and righteousness appear to be lacking.

Sharp writing: "Catwoman"
Julie Newmar.

I am noticing

emotion alters my

I am feeling both

Energy has been compared to many things: electricity, a horse and its rider, a body of water. Water is probably the metaphor that makes most sense. Look at the ductus under magnification. The ink flow, like water, may be sluggish and slow moving, or a rapidly flowing river that is swollen to overflowing; a smooth, glassy lake; a swift stream; or a stagnant pond where nothing moves. Understanding this component of handwriting will help you know the writer on a very basic level.

The Least You Need to Know

- Pressure reflects psychic energy, not physical strength.
- Pressure in handwriting symbolizes the energy available for the work of the personality.
- Extremely heavy pressure is a sign of frustration.
- Extremely light pressure is a sign of depression.
- Moderate pressure suggests physical health.

Chapter 11

Faster Than a Speeding Bullet: Speed

In This Chapter

- ◆ What the heck is graphic maturity?
- ◆ Putting on the brakes
- ◆ Signs of speed and slowness
- ◆ Speed and personality
- ◆ Speed and legibility

It's easy to gauge speed when driving your car. The flashing red lights behind you on the highway tell you that you were doing more than 65 mph. Drive too slowly and the honking horns will let you know. But measuring speed on paper is more of a challenge, especially when you weren't present to watch the writer's pen as it progressed across the page.

Speed is a very important, though oft-neglected, factor to consider when analyzing handwriting. It relates to intelligence, spontaneity of thought, and dynamic action. Handwriting moves in two directions: forward and backward. In the forward movement we see how the writer approaches the world: enthusiastically, spontaneously, or hastily rushing forward, never quite having enough time to get everything done. When forward movement is inhibited, or there is too much movement to the left (backward), it signifies either caution and forethought or lack of ability and know-how. In this chapter, we'll learn what impact speed has on handwriting and what it says about the writer's temperament.

The Age of Innocence

Many factors, both internal and external, influence writing speed. The most powerful of those is graphic maturity, which is an internal factor. *Graphic maturity* is a term coined in the early 1920s by Robert Saudek, who helped lay the scientific foundation for handwriting analysis.

def•i•ni•tion

Graphic maturity is the ability to write fluidly without having to consciously think about the act of writing.

Saudek published *Experiments with Handwriting* (George Allen & Unwin, 1922, reprinted by Books for Professionals, 1978), which details his research on speed and is still considered the most important work on the subject. It's a tough book to get through, so unless you have a very strong interest in the physiological aspects of handwriting or are a masochist and want to wade through it yourself, I'll summarize some of the basic tenets.

Before learning how to write words, you first must learn how to form single letters. Graphic maturity is the point at which you can write fluently without having to stop and think how to form the letters and the words. There are several checkpoints that must be reached before we can say that a writer has reached graphic maturity:

♦ The writer has learned how to control the writing instrument and feels comfortable with it.

♦ There is no physical impairment that would affect the writer's ability to write.

♦ The writer has become familiar enough with how to form an individual letter that when he hears the name of the letter, a mental picture of it appears in his head.

Before an entire sentence can be written automatically (that is, without thinking about each word before writing it), one more condition must be met: the writer focuses on what he wants to write about to the degree that he isn't paying attention to the details related to the act of writing itself. He ignores or overlooks problems that may be directly related to the writing, such as …

- Poor legibility (sometimes caused by a faulty writing instrument).

- Concern about how attractive the writing looks.

- Uncertainty about the spacing or other parts of the writing pattern that make the writer pay closer attention to the act of writing than the content. (Hesitancy of any kind impacts the flow of writing.)

The next checkpoint in the development of graphic maturity is familiarity with the language. The writer is considered familiar with the language if ...

- He is comfortable with the language.

- There is a change of language midtext and it doesn't disrupt the continuity.

- He is as comfortable with the written word as the spoken word.

Parlez-Vous Handwriting?

Even after a writer reaches graphic maturity, some circumstances impact his ability to write without hesitating. Something in the text itself—a word or a thought that arouses painful memories—can cause the writer to falter or pause momentarily. Or, he may reach a word he is unsure of and is forced to stop and sound it out in his mind.

People write differently depending on the purpose of the writing. Content makes a difference, too. If you're writing a check to the IRS you might go slower because you don't want to do it. Or if you're writing an enthusiastic account of your vacation in Hawaii in a letter to your friend, the writing may be faster than your normal pace. Mood also has an effect on speed. Angry or excited writing is faster than sad or tired writing.

Chicken Scratch

If a handwriting sample shows many stops and starts, ask the writer questions about the writing instrument. Your analysis may be dead wrong if you assume personality traits that are actually the result of a sticky pen or some other external factor.

Speed Bumps

A smooth, fluid writing movement shows that the writer is comfortable with the act of writing, that it comes naturally. What contributes to fluidity, and what detracts from it? Speed in handwriting depends on many details and circumstances. Let's consider them one at a time:

◆ *Direction of movement.* Fast writing moves to the right. Any interruption to the writing movement is like stepping on the brakes when you're driving your car.

◆ *Shapes of letters.* Rounded movement is faster than angular movement. Angles require abrupt stops.

◆ *Size of letters.* Medium-sized writing is faster than small or large writing. Any exaggerations take longer and slow down the writing.

◆ *Extra strokes.* Strokes that are unnecessarily retained or added take longer to make and slow down the writing.

◆ *Pressure.* Heavy pressure takes longer than medium or light pressure because it creates friction on the paper.

◆ *Quality of pen and paper.* A pen that has ink clogging the tip impacts speed. Writing on poor-quality paper also creates pen drag.

◆ *Physical disability.* A disability may influence writing speed. Someone suffering from Parkinson's disease, multiple sclerosis, or another illness that affects muscular control may write slowly out of necessity.

◆ *Mental illness.* A problem such as chronic depression may slow down the writing. Other types of mental illness, such as the manic phase of bipolar disorder, speed it up.

◆ *Drugs.* Prescribed, over-the-counter, or "recreational" drugs and medications may alter writing speed for obvious reasons.

◆ *Unfamiliarity with the language.* If the person is trying to write in an unfamiliar language, speed will be affected.

◆ *Self-consciousness about the appearance of writing.* When the writer is more concerned about form than content, his need to write "beautifully" slows him down.

◆ *Dislike of writing.* Someone who hates to write may have poorly developed script, which will slow it down. Or he may be in a hurry to get the act of writing over with, which will speed it up.

Setting the Pace

The *pace* or speed at which we write is affected by how we respond emotionally. The well-balanced person who expresses their emotions appropriately writes at a steady tempo. Someone who is tense and anxious makes many starts and stops.

Factors Affecting Tempo

Each individual has his own natural tempo. Some people are slow in everything they do, from getting up in the morning to getting around to making breakfast. The day moves at a tortoise pace. They're even slow about going to bed. Others have energy to burn and never sit still. The day flies by in a whirlwind of activity without a second to spare between tasks.

Environmental factors, such as the telephone ringing or someone walking into the room while the writer is in the act of putting his thoughts on paper, temporarily affect speed. If you have to stop to answer the phone or speak to the person who pokes his head around the door, the disruption will appear as a hesitation in the writing speed. Physical illness or emotional crises may precipitate permanent changes in writing speed.

Speed and Speech

Speed in handwriting mimics the writer's personal pace in his day-to-day activities, and even reflects the way he speaks. Those who speak fast tend to write fast as well. When you're in conversation with someone who zooms along so fast you can hardly understand him, ask for some handwriting. Chances are you won't be able to read it because he thinks faster than he speaks or writes, which results in poor legibility.

The slower speaker is more deliberate in his writing as he is in his speech. Unsure of himself and nervous in communicating, he tends to speak and write hesitantly, starting and stopping numerous times before being able to express what is on his mind. Those who speak in short, staccato bursts write that way, too, like machine-gun fire.

Reading the Handwriting Speedometer

Saudek's experiments reduced writing to milliseconds in order to measure the time it took to write. The following table summarizes some of the indicators representing speed and slowness in handwriting.

Rarely will a handwriting sample be composed of either all fast or all slow elements. Some signs of slowness almost always appear in a faster script and some signs of speed almost always appear in a slower script. It is helpful to check the areas where the speed was arrested to find out what caused the slowness and vice versa.

Indicators for Fast and Slow Writing

Speed	Slowness
t crossed to right of the stem	*t* crossed to left of the stem
Long *t* bars	Short *t* bars
Loops balloon slightly to the right	Loops pull to the left
Increased right slant	Left-slanted loops
Left margin gets wider	Upright loops
Right margin gets narrower	Left margin gets narrower
No sudden stops or changes of direction	Right margin gets wider
Moderately connected	Very even margins
Light-medium pressure	Frequent change of direction
Clear ovals	Many breaks within words
Sharp strokes	Heavy pressure
Few covering strokes	Ink-filled ovals
Accents and *i*-dots look like dashes	Retouching or soldering
Fluent, smooth writing	Many covering strokes
Medium size	Accents and *i*-dots round, careful
Garlands, thread, mixed forms	Strong consistency
Illegibility	Large or small size
Words taper off	Angular forms
Simplifications	Slow arcade forms
Neglect of detail	Supported forms
Expansion	School-type writing
Short or missing initial strokes	Elaboration
End strokes to the right	Attention to detail
Slightly rising baseline	Narrowness
Loops moderate in width and length	Long end strokes
Final strokes decrease in size	Blunt, rolled-in, or leftward end strokes

Saudek's rule was that a sample containing at least two more indicators for speed than for slowness is primarily fast but has been slowed down. Conversely, if a sample has at least two more indicators for slowness than for speed, it is primarily slow but has been sped up. The question is, what caused the writer to alter his normal tempo? We may not know the answer. Maybe the writer had a cold and stopped to blow his nose, or he saw something on the news that got him excited. Sometimes it has to be enough just to take note of the difference.

As Slow As Molasses

Just how slow *is* molasses, anyway? Picture a stream of sticky syrup meandering down the side of the jar, taking its time and enjoying the scenery along the way. That's the way the slow writer approaches life.

Assuming no mental or physical causes, slowness in writing indicates a reduction of emotional spontaneity. The moderately slow writer generally uses school-model forms, which are more conventional and less natural than a rapid, spontaneous script.

Fine Points

A slow writer may be quiet and profound, or lazy and timid; it takes a complete analysis to discover which. Remember: not speed, nor any other element of writing, can provide a full picture of the writer's personality on its own.

Moderately Slow Writing

Moderately slow writing is a sign of inhibition and self-control, as well as circumspection. The writer is most comfortable when he has the time to thoroughly prepare and rehearse ahead of time and follow a familiar routine that lets him know what's coming up next.

Passive and thoughtful, the moderately slow writer cannot be hurried along, nor will he make quick changes of direction. He'll only go slower to prove that you don't control him. In fact, when he's under time pressure, his stress level rises significantly. On the other hand, when you need help with a project that requires patience or involves a lot of mundane details, the slow writer is the one to call on.

Chicken Scratch

An interesting paradox of slow writing is that, although the writer takes extra time to ensure correctness, he is more likely to scratch out words or make corrections to the writing than the fast writer who cares less about making mistakes.

P.s. lleed your friends lip wore than ever.

Moderately slow writing: former Secretary of State Madeleine Albright.

The Tortoise: Very Slow Writing Speed

There is a difference between the careful deliberation of the moderately slow writer and the sluggish, plodding movement of one who is mentally impaired. In the case of very slow writing, lack of graphic maturity or mental impairment is generally the cause.

How do you separate moderately slow from very slow? The extreme slowness of the unskilled hand will be obvious, as distinguished from the writing of someone who has reached graphic maturity but has a careful, contemplative nature. Analyzing extremely slow, unskilled writing is beyond the skills of the new graphologist.

Very slow writing due to mental impairment: Donna Yost, a woman with an IQ of 87, convicted of second-degree murder in her child's death (overdose of bedwetting pills).

Tales from the Quill

In a study of children who were performing lower than their grade level, it was found that their writing speeds were significantly slower than those of their higher-performing peers. This was not necessarily an indicator of lower intelligence. Stress may have been a factor, such as problems at home.

Sometimes a writer will *intentionally* slow down the writing pace. He is probably trying to hide something that could be detrimental to him. Fear of betraying what he wants to keep hidden makes him very careful about how and what he writes. Underlying the deliberate slowing down of the writing act may be pathological anxiety or, possibly, criminal acts.

*was just thinking about
I thought I would sit c
and write you a letter. I
enjoyed the interview w
and anytime you want
another with me just be
to let me know and*

Deliberate, slow-speed writing: serial killer Christine Falling.

Steady As She Goes: Medium Writing Speed

Medium speed signifies a conventional approach and reasonable impulse control. The writer's personal tempo is moderate and restrained. He can handle delays without getting too upset (assuming other factors in the writing bear this out), and doesn't mind waiting for someone slower to catch up with him. He likes to process new ideas and thoughts, but isn't fanatical about making sure he has all the latest facts and data to support them. For him, good enough is good enough.

"To Sherlock Holmes, she was always the woman." — my favorite line in the Canon!

Leslie S. Kling

Medium-speed writing: Leslie Klinger, editor of The New Annotated Sherlock Holmes.

The Hare: Moderately Fast Writing Speed

Moderately *fast* writing takes a reasonably good measure of self-assurance. Because the writer is not self-conscious about the way he writes, the focus is more on the message than the style. He reacts quickly and wants to see things happen quickly. Like the guy at a 1-hour photo store, he doesn't like waiting for things to develop. The fast writer is efficient and dislikes waste. He uses his time and resources wisely, and takes the initiative when something needs to be done.

def•i•ni•tion

Fast writing speed is made by a normally rapid writer who is unimpaired physically, intellectually, and mechanically; or by a slower writer who is in a hurry.

His ability to quickly comprehend the essence of a matter says he's a fast learner who can put new knowledge to use almost as soon as he assimilates it. It ticks him off when he has to wait for a slower thinker to catch up. He'd like to put the words in his mouth for him! The moderately fast writer is smooth in his interactions with others. He'll come up with a ready retort and is never short of a quick answer.

Moderately fast writing: actor Ralph Fiennes.

Let's Play Jeopardy!

Legibility is an important factor to consider when judging fast writing. Since we write for the purpose of communicating, it should be legible enough for the reader to understand what the sender wanted to get across. When writing is so fast that it becomes illegible, the words lose their meaning and the basic purpose of writing—communication—fails.

Is it true that all doctors' handwritings are illegible? Busy doctors are often accused of writing illegibly, due to the speed at which they write. When prescriptions are misread by those whose job it is to administer care, their patients' lives can actually be put in jeopardy. This is one case where deliberate slowing of the writing can be beneficial—when the message is one that affects other people's well-being. But like any other writer, a doctor's handwriting reflects his personal style and temperament, and many doctors do make an effort to write legibly.

Moving at the Speed of Light

There's fast, and then there's *hurried*. One has the ability to get things done quickly and efficiently. The other is rash and impetuous, always in a hurry, regardless of the time available.

The difference between the fast writer and the hurried writer is a sense of agitation in the latter. Borne along by the winds of necessity, he turns his attention to whatever is most urgent at the moment. He feels the hot breath of Father Time on his neck and fears he won't be able to accomplish all that he wants to do. But it really doesn't matter how much time is available, as the pressure to hurry up is internal and unrelenting.

Impatient and impulsive, the very rapid writer's thoughts travel almost faster than

Very fast writing: actor Sir Anthony Hopkins.

his synapses can fire. Even when his body is at rest, his mind is never still. Moving at such a pace affects his ability to be thorough and careful, so the knowledge he picks up is usually directly related to what he needs to know right now. In his haste, he may leave out letters, diacritics (*i*-dots and *t*-crosses, for example), and punctuation, all of which contribute to illegibility. When he remembers to dot the *i*'s and cross the *t*'s, the dots and crossbars usually are made in a sharp, jabbing motion, symbolizing his irritability and a tendency to overreact.

If you want to start World War III, put a very fast and a very slow writer in a small room and lock the door. How long do you think it would take them to drive each other to distraction? All bets are off!

The Least You Need to Know

- ◆ Speed of writing depends on the graphic maturity and skill of the writer.

- ◆ Speed and spontaneity are closely related.

- ◆ Speed depends on the direction of the movement, shape of the letters, size, and pressure.

- ◆ Fast thinkers write fast. Deliberate thinkers write more slowly.

- ◆ Slow writing is an important contributing factor for determining a writer's premeditated dishonesty.

Chapter **12**

Reach Out and Touch Someone: Connections

In This Chapter

- The writing impulse pattern
- Writing in the air
- Connecting the dots
- Breaking the bridges
- You can analyze printing

Can you imagine a conversation where there were no pauses between the words?

Itwouldbereallyfrustratingtryingtofigureoutwhatthemessageis.

See what I mean? Pauses in conversation give both the speaker and the listener a chance to catch their breath and contemplate for a moment what was just said. Without pauses, information floods in, obscuring the meaning of the message. On the other hand, pauses that are too long impair continuity. Ideas become discrete bits of information without any means of linking them together.

h o w   c a n   y o u   r e m e m b e r   t h e   l a s t   t h o u g h t
w h e n s o   m u c h   t i m e   h a s   e l a p s e d ?

In this chapter, we look at the connections between words and the different writing impulse patterns they reflect.

Impulse Patterns

Handwriting consists of a series of impulses echoed on paper. The spaces between them are like pauses in conversation. Some pauses are short, some are long; some are smooth, some are choppy. The smallest writing impulse is found in a single stroke, which proceeds to the next impulse, the letter, then the word, and finally, the sentence impulse. A writing impulse begins when the pen starts moving on the paper and ends when it is lifted.

Writing impulses mimic speech. Some people speak rapidly, rushing to get their thoughts out, while others are more deliberate and careful in delivering their message. Someone who speaks with many starts and stops creates a considerably different impulse pattern on paper than another person who speaks smoothly and expresses herself well.

Early in the 20th century, Klara Roman discovered that poor writing impulses had a relationship to problems in speech. She found that those who spoke fluently and articulately wrote with smooth, continuous writing impulses. The handwritings of those who stuttered or stammered, or who had other difficulties in communicating coherently, also matched the way they spoke. Using handwriting movement as therapy, Dr. Roman was able to help many speech-impaired people improve their ability to speak. As a result of her research, clinics in Europe began using handwriting analysis to help diagnose and treat speech-impaired patients.

Fine Points

Collect handwriting samples from people whose speaking styles differ radically. Chart the impulse patterns of slow, smooth speakers and compare them to samples from rapid, uneven speakers.

Unquestionably, different impulse patterns reflect behavioral styles unique to each individual. These patterns tell us about the writer's ability to function in the world intellectually, socially, and emotionally. The degree and type of linkage from one letter to the next is symbolic of how well the writer …

- ◆ Connects thoughts.

- ◆ Functions in social relationships.

- ◆ Coordinates activities.

Some People Say I'm Psychic: Airstrokes

Handwriting exists in several dimensions. One of those dimensions is "above" the paper. Yes, writing actually starts in the air. Like an airplane on final approach to the runway, the hand hovers briefly above the paper as the writer decides where to bring the pen in for a landing. In between writing impulses, too, the pen rises off the paper momentarily before moving into the next writing impulse.

Ideally, while the pen is raised, the hand proceeds in the same direction through the air as it was moving on the writing surface. When the pen touches down again, the flow of ink resumes as if there had been no interruption. Movements above the paper are called *airstrokes*. Smooth airstrokes are created when the writing continues moving in the same direction. Blunt ones are created when the writing movement stops abruptly or makes infinitesimal changes of direction.

The hesitant writer who is unsure of her next move stops suddenly to reconsider or adjust her path. The confident writer creates a continuous, smooth airstroke that advances along the *graphic path* in the same direction. Use a stylus (or work on a photocopy) to trace the movement along the graphic path from the end of one writing impulse to the next. If you can't trace the movement in a smooth line from one stroke to the next, the airstrokes are abrupt.

def•i•ni•tion

The **graphic path** is the trail of ink made by the writing movement as it proceeds from left to right. An **airstroke** is the movement of the hand in the air, which continues in the same direction as the writing on the paper.

You'll need to whip out your trusty magnifying glass and examine the starting and ending strokes to find out whether an airstroke is smooth or not. Under magnification, the point at which the movement tapers off as the pen was raised will show a lightening in the trail of ink. Stopping to change direction creates an abrupt airstroke where the ink does not taper off.

Disruption of the writing movement affects the rhythm. In handwriting, frequent stopping and starting is like walking along a dark street at night, breaking stride every few yards to look back and see if anyone is following. It suggests a lack of self-assuredness, unlike someone who has a strong commanding presence and moves forward with a sense of purpose and self-confidence.

Abrupt (above) and smooth (below) airstrokes. Above: Green Beret Dr. Jeffrey MacDonald, convicted of murdering his family. Below: actor Christopher Lee's airstrokes don't always leave the ground!

A handwriting with smooth airstrokes is produced by a mind that makes leaps of logic faster than a speeding bullet and grasps whole concepts in a single bound. The writer spends a lot of time "in the air," which, in graphology, symbolizes the mind. She seeks efficient solutions to problems, avoiding the friction caused by contact with the paper.

Ties That Bind

Connectedness refers to the degree to which a group of writing impulses joins together to form words. The correct term for the connecting strokes is ligature. (Yes, that's the same word referred to in crime stories where the victim was tied up or strangled.) It means something that ties or binds. The more friendly meaning in handwriting is to unite two or more letters into a single unit.

A handwriting is considered connected if shorter words, about six or eight letters long, are joined together. If there are breaks, they should be after syllables or in other expected places, such as breaks to dot the *i*'s or cross the *t*'s. When the connections are broken in unexpected places, or the connections in a short word are mostly or all broken, the writing is considered disconnected.

Connectedness is one of the indicators that shows how well the writer strings her thoughts together, and how comfortable she is dealing with the outside world and adapting to her present circumstances.

Connections between letters are made by joining upstrokes and downstrokes. Downstrokes are the spine or backbone of writing. Without them there is nothing to support the body. Legibility may be impaired somewhat, but you can still decipher the message. When the downstrokes are removed and you are left with only upstrokes, it is impossible to read what the writer is trying to get across.

Writing without downstrokes (above) and writing without upstrokes (below).

Let's Stay in Touch: Connected Writing

"Connected" doesn't mean that every single element in every single word is linked together. Pausing after syllables for *diacritics* doesn't count as breaking the impulse. *Where* the breaks occur is important. If they come at the beginnings of words, it signifies something different than if they are made at the ends. If they occur in the middle zone, it affects a different area of behavior than in the upper or lower zone.

def•i•ni•tion

Diacritics, also called diacritical marks, are *t*-crosses and *i*-dots and other marks added to words to help with pronunciation, such as accents.

Moderately Connected Writing

Moderately connected writing, which is connected (except for letters after syllables and diacritics), is made by the moderately adaptable person. Provided the airstrokes are smooth, she is able to use either logic or intuition, whichever is appropriate to the situation. Her thoughts flow smoothly using deductive thinking, and she is able to string together a series of ideas into a whole concept. She needs to be able to relate the small details to the bigger picture for it to make sense.

Socially, the moderately connected writer wants to relate to others in some way. The writer is attracted to group activities and (with supporting evidence, such as a well-developed lower zone) welcomes other people into her life. Feeling connected to a circle of friends she can count on makes her feel emotionally supported and comfortable.

Moderately connected writing (above) and over-connected writing (below). Above: actor Burt Lancaster. Below: convicted serial killer Robert Long.

Highly Connected

The highly connected writer links most of her letters. She may pause occasionally after capitals but, for the most part, she connects everything else.

She has a good memory for facts, although she may not be as quick to associate them with the events they represent. For instance, she might remember that November 9 is an important day for some reason, but not that it's my birthday (well, it's important to me!). She enjoys handling details, putting things where they belong, and dealing with the practical necessities of life. Once she has started a project, don't bother to interrupt her; she needs to keep going until she's finished it, the same way she finishes writing a word before taking a break.

Linking letters is a progression from left to right, from me to you. The highly connected writer feels a strong need for involvement with others. Her behavior and attitudes are consistent from one day to the next, and she can be counted on to respond similarly in like situations.

Overconnected

The overconnected writer makes no breaks at all, even after capital letters. If the writing is also narrow or crowded, what was consistency in the moderate to highly connected writer has burgeoned into obsession. The unrelieved effort reflected in overconnected handwriting is the hallmark of a refusal or inability to let up, even for a moment. The persistent connections at the baseline are made by someone who needs to feel her feet firmly in contact with the ground. She expends much of her energy taking care of the practical, material aspects of her life. She doesn't trust her intuition, but needs to gather as much logical data and as many facts as she can before making a decision.

The overconnected writer can be overwhelming. Her need for contact, if combined with close word spacing, suggests someone who doesn't have good social boundaries. She discharges an avalanche of thoughts and ideas without giving you a chance to assimilate them. Just as she can't seem to relinquish the writing impulse, she goes on and on, whether you want to hear her or not. She may give lip service to allowing others to have their say, but doesn't really hear them. She's too focused on her own thoughts.

In extreme cases, the emotional excitation implied in overconnected writing is sometimes a sign of a psychological disturbance. The writer's refusal to give anyone else any space suggests some sort of paranoia. She doesn't trust anyone else, so she feels compelled to control as much of her environment as possible.

Chicken Scratch

In discussing the overconnected writer, Klara Roman said, "Overconnected configurations are produced by rhetoricians, verbose persons, time wasters, individuals who make much ado about nothing."

I Need My Space: Moderately Disconnected Writing

Writing that has many smooth breaks, when simplified and original (that is, when it's made simpler than copybook), is the sign of a quick, facile mind. The writer is able to leap nimbly from one thought to the next without waiting to have all the data before her. Especially if there are smooth connections and airstrokes in the upper zone, it shows an ability to proliferate a series of ideas and combine them into a workable system.

With her propensity for sailing off the page with many airstrokes, the moderately disconnected writer tends to be more mentally than socially oriented. She is generally more comfortable in the theoretical world than in the company of others. Although she may have plenty of friendships, it isn't quite as easy for her to connect with others as it is for the connected writer.

If the airstrokes are choppy, the writer's emotions are less controlled and a bit more erratic. Her behavior is not so consistent, and she may surprise you by suddenly changing her attitude. You may think you're having a very pleasant conversation, when all of a sudden she abruptly gets up and walks off. She abruptly disconnects her written words in the same manner.

Mixed connectedness (above) and disconnected (below). Above: Steve Hodel, author of Black Dahlia Avenger. *Below: chess genius Bobby Fischer.*

Looking for Breaks in All the Wrong Places

Extreme disconnectedness is different from printed writing. Here, we're talking about cursive writing that has been chopped up into very small writing impulses. It's unusual to find many smooth airstrokes in totally disconnected writing. Constant, restless movement in many directions and nervous activity are the order of the day for the extremely disconnected writer.

The extremely disconnected writer is often highly creative. But can she put her creativity to work productively? The ideas gush out, spattering in all directions like paint from an aerosol can. Some of them may be pure genius, but others are just flights of fancy. She isn't always able to clearly define which is which. Often moody and inconsistent, you never know how she is going to react from one minute to the next. Establishing close relationships is much more difficult for this individual. The breaks between letters suggest a breaking of the bonds between herself and the outside world. She finds it easier to stand alone than to bother cooperating with others.

Making a Break for It

Some handwritings are generally connected, but the writing impulse breaks consistently in one particular spot, perhaps always after the first letter, or always after the last letter. What does that mean?

Let's say you start to write a word, but after the first letter you pause and reconsider. Is that what I really wanted to say? Yes, it is. And, having broken the connection, you go on to finish the word. Art is imitating life. When the writer pauses after the first letter of a word, it mirrors a tendency to reconsider after having made a decision. The writer feels she needs to step back and take a deep breath, or to wind herself up before carrying on.

> **Fine Points** _____
>
> When the disconnected final letter is _g_, the writer is often someone who has trouble making emotional commitments in intimate relationships. Such a writer may live with a lover for years, and even get married, but it's as if she feels compelled to withhold that last little bit of herself.

Let's Break It Off

Do you know someone who has trouble making and keeping commitments? Chances are, the last letter of some words will be separated from the rest. This often happens when the writer rushes headlong into a new relationship or makes a major decision. As the time draws closer for her to put her money where her mouth is, she gets cold feet and pulls back. After reconsidering, she may move forward and fulfill the commitment, but first she's likely to do this push-pull cha-cha several times.

Disconnected final and initial letters: President George W. Bush.

Bring Me My Soldering Iron

Sometimes a writer will realize that breaks have crept in where she didn't intend, or doesn't want them. So, she goes back and tries to connect them after the fact. Strokes that are made in an attempt to fix a break are called mending, retouching (going back over the strokes), or soldering.

A soldering iron, such as you'd find in a machine shop, is used to melt and apply solder to two pieces of metal in order to join them together. In effect, that's what happens when the writer wants to connect a "hole" in her writing, only the soldering material in this case is ink.

The significance of mending and soldering is that the writer is anxious to make things look better than they really are. She doesn't want to be seen as wrong, so she makes an effort to correct and improve herself. Some writers use this method to hide something they don't want seen, so it may be a form of dishonesty. As usual, it all depends on the whole configuration of the writing. Often, the retouching (in the form of mending or soldering) just makes matters worse, as the following example illustrates.

Retouching.

Viva Variety! Printscript

Some people combine printing and writing. Graphologists call this writing style printscript. Depending upon whether the overall graphic picture is harmonious or not, the writer may be wonderfully creative, or merely impulsive and erratic.

Creative Printscript: actress Emma Thompson.

> The best day of my life. Nine hours synching & 1 LOVED EVERY MINUTE OF IT!

Reading the Fine Print: Printed Writing

There are several types of printed writing, block printing and manuscript printing being the most common. Block printing is done in all capital letters, while manuscript printing uses upper and lower case letters. Manuscript printing is taught as a lead-in to learning cursive writing.

Using the principles of gestalt graphology it's almost as easy to analyze printing as cursive writing. As graphic movement, printing utilizes space, form, and movement just like any other style of writing.

Some people (most notably police officers, architects, and engineers) print because it's a requirement of their type of work. If they print only at work, but write cursive at home, we would analyze the cursive. However, if they print in social settings, too, such as writing personal letters, the printing will reflect the true personality.

Interestingly, many printers, while breaking the connections between their letters, place the letters close enough to touch. This suggests that while their conscious desire is to keep their distance, their inner need is for closeness.

Some types of printing, like cursive, allow the writer to go into all three zones (upper, middle, lower), but block printing isn't one of them. Block printing is viewed in the same manner as writing with an emphasis on the middle zone. The writer's energies are concentrated in the day-to-day area of routine and social interaction. Like other middle-zone writers, the block printer's ego is central to all aspects of her life. She doesn't mind sharing her opinions, and expects you to agree with her. But if you don't, it won't change her mind.

Printed writing.

The Complete Idiot's Guide to Handwriting Analysis will make an excellent addition to an already spectacular series.

The Bare Bones: Skeletal and Disintegrated Writing

Skeletal, fragmented, or disintegrated writing is stripped down to its absolute bare minimum, but still retains legibility. That is, the downstrokes are still present, but not the upstrokes. The writer is ascetic and stingy in attitude and manner. There is no flesh on the bones of her writing—no loops or flourishes to enrich it. Her emotional detachment hints at little or no connection between herself and the world. If she is not just plain eccentric, mental illness (impending or present) is a possibility.

In cases of severe mental illness or distress where the mind begins to break down, it is manifested on paper. As the mind deteriorates, the writing regresses through the various stages, all the way back to the basic stroke impulse. At that point, regression to an infantile stage is complete. The writing of a Down's syndrome adult is a stunning example of her ability to organize the page, while being entirely unable to go beyond the basic stroke in communicating with others.

Writing of an adult with Down's syndrome.

Tales from the Quill
The handwriting of American poet Emily Dickinson, in her later years, disintegrated almost to the point of illegibility. As she became more reclusive, the letter forms became more difficult to read. You can see from the next sample that the letters bear absolutely no resemblance to any copybook. Emily created her own original forms, but the positive interpretation that normally comes from originality is lost due to their eccentric, even hieroglyphic appearance.

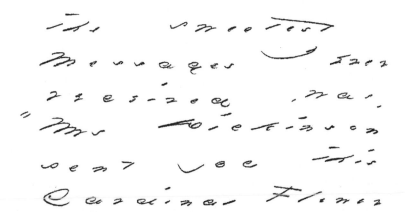

Emily Dickinson's disintegrated writing.

I Don't Know How I Know It, but I Do

Everyone has it, but not everyone uses it. Some people develop it to an astounding degree, while others prefer to shun it altogether. What is it? *Intuition.* What can handwriting uncover about this special means of perceiving?

For our purposes, intuition is an instinctive, unconscious process that begins in the lower zone, the area of the unconscious. It is quite unlike the deliberate theorizing, measuring, and computing of a series of ideas you would do in conscious thought. But neither is it stuff just popping into your head out of the blue.

Intuition seems to have some relationship to previous knowledge. When the unconscious (lower zone) recognizes a truth about something within the realm of your experience, the perception quietly germinates, unfettered by logical thought processes. When insight is ready to manifest, it erupts into the conscious mind above the baseline and blossoms in that "aha!" sensation. If the perception happens to come midword, a smooth break or an airstroke results.

But what if the airstrokes are not smooth; isn't that also intuition? Well, sort of. As we've said earlier, abrupt breaks signify a torrent of ideas popping into consciousness, but more on the order of sudden hunches that are not connected to anything in particular.

It is extremely difficult to force a change in the degree of connectedness in an individual's handwriting. Try to print for an extended period if you normally write cursive; or try writing cursive if you only print. It feels yucky (that's the technical term). Once a writer has reached graphic maturity, her tendency to connect or disconnect comes naturally.

The Least You Need to Know

◆ The disconnections (airstrokes) between letters are just as important as the connections.

◆ Connected writing shows an ability to connect thoughts.

◆ Overconnected writing is a sign of argumentativeness.

◆ Disconnected writing shows a break in the flow of thought.

◆ Printed writing is not the same as disconnected cursive writing.

Chapter 13

From Me to You: Connective Forms

In This Chapter

- ◆ Adapting, inside and out
- ◆ Rounded, angular, or thready forms
- ◆ The secondary connective forms
- ◆ A shark's tooth in handwriting can bite

How well do you adapt to different environments? Are you flexible and quick to adjust to new situations and people? Or do you stubbornly stick with what you know and insist that others defer to your habits? The answer is found in your basic temperament.

Temperament is most clearly seen in the shapes of letters and the connections between them. These provide the next piece of the personality puzzle—*how* we relate to others—and are called connective forms. In this chapter, we'll see what the connections between letters have to do with the way the writer relates in social situations.

The Four Forms

There are four major connective forms: two rounded (arcade and garland), one angular, and one thready (or indefinite), which combines the two rounded ones. Of the rounded forms, the arcade is open at the bottom and the garland is open at the top. Angular forms are closed at both the top and the bottom. Thread is open on all sides.

Fine Points _____

If the *m* or *n* is rounded on top, the primary form is arcade. If they look more like a *w* or *u*, the primary form is garland. A wavy top is thready; a pointed top is angular.

The easiest way to find the connective form is to check the tops of the lowercase letters *m* and *n*, and the connections from one letter to another at the baseline.

The school model teaches a combination of the garland, arcade, and angle forms, and most adults adopt one of these three types as a primary way of forming letters and linking them together. Generally, all the forms will also be used to some degree. We add to the school model the thread type, which is a combination of the garland and arcade, but is flattened out.

A mixture of all the connective forms suggests an innate ability to relate to many different types of people on their own level. Someone who uses one type of connective form exclusively tends to be a one-dimensional personality. His behavior is regimented and premeditated; he lacks the capacity to act spontaneously.

Swiss graphologist Max Pulver describes the connective form as defining the way the writer adapts, both to his inner and his outer world. For instance, the choice of mostly rounded forms is made by the more passive individual (the more rounded the form, the more passive the person), mostly angular forms are chosen by resistant people (the more angular, the more resistance), and mostly thready forms are adopted by those who refuse to make any choice at all.

Changing the form that is natural to you is extremely difficult. Here's an exercise for you: the following figure shows the four major connective forms. Pick one that is unlike your own writing and copy it for several lines. How did that feel? Probably pretty uncomfortable, since you were imitating a form that reflects something other than the way you naturally function.

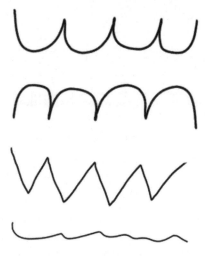

The four major connective forms: garland (top), arcade (second), angle (third), thread (bottom).

Why Can't We All Just Get Along? Garlands

The first of the major connective forms is called the garland. There are several variations of the garland, but the basic form has firm pressure and a natural, free flow of left-right movement.

Although both sexes use all the connective forms, the garland is viewed as having more feminine qualities. Rounded on the bottom and open at the top, the garland is like a bowl, ready to receive whatever you are prepared to give.

Remembering that the writing movement is from me to you, you'll recognize the garland as a spontaneous movement outward, opening itself up, extending itself toward others. Sociability is implied in this movement, and a willingness to please.

Because the bowl is open from the top, it is influenced by outside forces. The garland writer is trusting and open, the type of person who reaches out to others with a smile and expects you to smile back. The rounded form symbolizes emotions, so you can expect warm responses from this writer.

Kind and compassionate, a little on the sentimental side, the writer's basic needs frequently are tied to home and hearth. Very rounded writing is often done by those who are more comfortable with kids and animals than with other adults. This writer won't argue or fight about anything else, but when it comes to defending his home and family he can be a tiger.

Wilting Garlands

When the garland lacks firm pressure and a strong right trend, much of the positive interpretation is lost. Instead of being merely receptive, *flat, shallow,* or *weak garlands* indicate extreme susceptibility and dependency. Certainly, the shallow or weak garland implies weakness of character. In some cases, it might be plain old laziness.

def•i•ni•tion

In the **flat garland,** the connecting strokes hug the baseline. In the **shallow garland,** the connecting strokes droop. Strokes of the **weak garland** are made without pressure.

Made by those who talk much but say little, the writer is easily influenced and may go overboard in indulging himself. He lacks the energy to resist outside pressure and allows others to push him in a direction he might not be eager to go. He's gullible and naïve, ready to believe anything he hears, so if he happens to fall in with the wrong crowd, he's likely to find himself in hot water, right along with them.

The shallow garland is sometimes a sign of depression. The writer simply doesn't have the heart to withstand the onslaught of a stronger-willed aggressor. He goes with the flow to avoid having to fight for what he wants.

Faking It—Sham Garlands

The sham garland (sometimes called "clothesline garland") is made without the free flow of movement of the genuine garland. The letter connections are rounded on the bottom but the movement is restricted, slow, and careful. Upstrokes are partially concealed by downstrokes, which implies a need to hide something. Since connecting strokes generally occur at or near the baseline, the concealing is taking place in the middle zone, the zone of relationships, emotions, and day-to-day life.

The sham garland writer wants to *appear* affable and adaptable, but something in his environment has him worried or afraid to act naturally. Consequently, he covers his fear with a veneer of congeniality. The friendliness of the normal garland has become a mask.

Occasionally you'll find looped garlands. Since the loop is made by a slight turn to the left, it is a regressive or counterstroke. In other words, it's going the wrong direction. Dr. Klara Roman says the looped garland is a case of balancing tension and release by momentarily going inward. Trait-oriented graphologists call it the "worry stroke," and say it is made by those who carry the woes of the world on their shoulders.

For Raul,
All the best,

Elmore Leonard

Garland forms: thriller writer Elmore Leonard has surprising garlands in his text, but an angular signature.

Best of Luck
Lionel
Hampton

Musician Lionel Hampton's garlands, nicely balanced with other connective forms.

Enjoy "singing"
the Blues

Roelle Krich

Rochelle Krich, author of the Molly Blume mystery series, makes a perfect garland form in the n *of enjoy.*

Cover Me, I'm Going In: Arcades

The second type of rounded major connective form is the arcade, named for its arch-like shape.

The arch is a superstrong structure that may be used as a bridge to travel over; an aqueduct to carry life-sustaining water under; or a means of protection under which to hide from a variety of hazardous conditions. It becomes an impenetrable bulwark against the outside world. Consider Marble Arch in London, or the Arc d' Triomphe in Paris—some very impressive architecture that have stood for eons and weathered all sorts of assaults, including WWI and WWII.

> **Chicken Scratch** _____
>
> In graphological literature, the arcade has traditionally been given a bad rap. It usually is listed as a major sign of dishonesty, as well as other nasty stuff. While that may be true in slow handwriting, it isn't always the case. Speed is the modifying factor.

The arcade form turns the bowl of the garland upside down, making it rounded on the top instead of the bottom. While the garland is open to influences from the outside, the arcade closes off at the baseline, making it inaccessible from any direction except within. If you put an apple on the kitchen counter and place a bowl over it, how accessible is the apple? And that's the effect of the arcade form in handwriting. There's a sense of impenetrability.

Like the garland writer, the arcade writer is basically an emotional person. The difference is he doesn't like to show it, preferring to hide his emotional responses under the arches. The need for the arcade writer to be strong and conceal his emotions sometimes gives others the impression that he is cold or unfeeling. Nothing could be further from the truth. However, he would rather let them believe that than have to explain himself.

An arcade in fast writing is interpreted differently from an arcade in slow writing—they even *look* different.

Fast Arcades

The fast arcade begins with a releasing movement toward the upper zone, which shows the writer's interest in achieving great things. Driven toward success and accomplishment, he pushes himself to ever greater heights. The arcade ends with a downstroke, coming back toward the self and the lower zone, and indicates strong determination. The writer keeps his eyes on the goal, not allowing obstacles to deter him. Because the arcade is closed at the top, the writer is able to shut away outside distractions and single-mindedly pursue his objectives.

The negative side of the fast arcade writer's one-track mind is that others may see him as pushy and overbearing. Especially when the pressure is displaced onto the upstroke, the energy is sublimated from other areas and permits the writer to keep on driving himself until he has achieved his goal.

Many times, fast arcades are seen in the handwritings of highly creative people. Those who work in the arts, as well as architects ("arch"-i-tects—get it?) tend to use the arcade form because the structural appearance appeals to them. Similarly, structure and form are important to the fast arcade writer. In fact, he may be quite attracted to architecture on one level or another.

Fine Points

When the arch is tall and comes at the beginning of a word, the writer wants to make an impact. He wants to be seen as impressive and imposing, without having to say a word.

The fast arcade writer tends to be very interested in the past. Remember, the arcade is open at the bottom, toward the past and the subconscious. He wants to know where he came from, what his roots and genealogy are (especially when combined with a long lower zone). A traditionalist, he would like to maintain life the way it was, and it takes some time and effort on his part to accept progress.

Concern with appearances indicates a more formal approach than the garland writer, which puts the brakes on spontaneity. Some fast arcade writers are reserved, even a bit shy. Others are simply snobbish and class conscious. Look at the whole picture.

Slow Arcades

In a handwriting with many slow arcades, the statuesque arch is now more like a baseball cap, pulled down low over the forehead to conceal the wearer's identity. Or a turtle who has retreated inside his shell. The maker of the slow arcade is self-oriented and defensive. He doesn't wait to be attacked, but barricades himself behind the walls of the arch, just in case. The slow arcade is a controlled form, unlike the free and easy movement of the garland.

Tales from the Quill

When the last stroke of a word returns leftward in an arcade, it is a sign of deliberate secretiveness and withholding of information. Pulver, who was big into symbolism, likened the final arcade to the writer biting his lip to keep from saying something that he doesn't want you to know. The return to self also suggests selfishly keeping things to himself for his own ends.

Especially when the arcade is narrow, it signifies secretiveness and inhibition. Some graphologists see it as the sign of a hypocrite, or a wolf in sheep's clothing. An arcade at the end of a word is a deliberate, inhibiting movement. The writer withdraws the outgoing gesture and returns it to himself. This may indicate defensiveness, embarrassment, or insincerity.

Arcade forms: actor Omar Sharif (Doctor Zhivago) makes beautiful fast arcades.

Actress Kate Beckinsale combines her fast arcades with natural garlands.

Convicted murderer Lyle Menendez: slow arcade forms.

No More Mr. Nice Guy: Angles

Okay, I've got my boxing gloves on. Now we can move on to discuss the angular writer. Why the gloves? Because the angular writer always seems to be looking for a fight or argument. Friction is part of his daily diet. Inasmuch as the garland writer seeks peace and harmony, when things are going too smoothly, the angle writer gets unsettled and feels compelled to make waves.

In order to form an angle, the hand is required to make an abrupt stop and change of direction. There is little room for flexibility in the writing movement or in the angle writer's nature. He refuses to adapt to the needs or desires of others, but expects, even insists, that others should accommodate him. He sees every situation as a new opportunity to exert his will.

The angle writer is driven to make decisions and act, especially when acting gives him a chance to provoke a power struggle. He's unlikely to sit around waiting for something to happen. With the addition of heavy pressure, the writer may treat people with a ruthless heavy hand. The handwriting of Heinrich Himmler, head of the dreaded Nazi SS in World War II, is an extreme case in point.

One of the angular writer's positive characteristics is that when he uses his power for good, he can be extremely effective. When he needs to stand firm, there is no shaking him. He doesn't give up, no matter how high the odds are stacked against him. Some call it stubbornness, but he sees it as persistence.

Your Guardian Angle Is Watching

When the angle is slightly rounded rather than making a completely sharp point, it's called a soft angle. The softness mitigates some of the more difficult aspects of the angular form and gives the angular writer moderation. His obstinacy becomes a gentler persistence, and inflexibility becomes just plain firmness.

All in all, the soft-angle writer is much easier to get along with than the sharp-angle writer. He has developed some tolerance and adaptability; but while he may still have strong opinions, they will not be expressed so directly and severely. The better nature of the angle is allowed to shine through.

Biting with the Shark's Tooth

So named because it looks like one, the *shark's tooth* form is an angle with a bend in it, which you can see in the following figure. The stroke bends inward, as if something from the right side were pushing it. That makes it a counterstroke (going in the opposite direction to the way it should go).

The shark's tooth is a smooth-looking stroke that hides cunning, crafty behavior under a courteous exterior. The writer smiles at you while calmly stabbing you in the back. If this form is seen only once or twice in an otherwise positive script, the inference is that the writer can be pretty nasty when pushed, but that the trait pops out only under duress.

Angular forms: Heinrich Himmler's writing is filled with angry angles. Himmler was the founder of the Nazi concentration camps.

Margaret Mitchell, author of Gone with the Wind, *used a combination of forms with many angles.*

Don't Pin Me Down: Thread

The thread form isn't taught in any schools. It combines the arcade and garland, but breaks them down so it isn't easy to identify which is which. The result is a rather flat and wavy form that is at once ambiguous, indefinite, and equivocal.

Like the arcade, the thread form is often treated negatively in graphology texts. It is assumed that all thread forms should be treated equal, which is not so. There are two distinct types of thready formations—primary and secondary.

It is impossible to make either type of thread form slowly. Thus, the mind that makes it thinks fast. In primary thread, legibility remains unimpaired and the form helps the writing movement progress to the right because it accelerates the speed. Secondary thread produces illegibility because the writing thins out, in many instances, to a mere wavy line.

Chicken Scratch

The thready writer is generally unassertive, avoiding, and evasive. He dodges conflict even more than the garland writer does. The thready writer is like an eel, twisting away from unpleasantness.

Primary Thread

Primary thread is made with moderate pressure and is seen mostly at the ends of words. The last letter breaks down and to some extent thins out. Or some letters (most notably the *m*'s and *n*'s) lose their definition and become slightly wavy-looking. Overall though, the letters retain their basic shape.

The primary thread writer thinks and acts fast. He's not so interested in plumbing the depths of information, but rather, tends to skim the surface. Although he's at his best when handling complex matters, he tends to get impatient when someone tries to feed him too many details.

If connective forms symbolize the writer's ability to adapt, then the thready writer is the King of Adaptability. Adaptability is his very essence. We could call him the chameleon, because wherever he is, he fits in. He takes on the shape of his environment.

The thready writer lives by his instincts and goes with his gut reactions. He quickly jumps to conclusions—often too quickly—without the benefit of logic. So, his basic assumption may be correct but the final judgment can sometimes be flawed due to lack of supporting information.

By equivocating, he hopes to avoid having to take a stand and promote a particular viewpoint. He won't expend the energy to fight and would rather avoid friction or conflict at all cost. Interestingly, though, when forced into a corner with no other way out, he'll come out swinging.

Once again, connective forms are found in the middle zone, which has to do with day-to-day functioning, ego needs, and social activities. When word endings thin out in a thready form, it suggests diplomacy and tact. Why? Because the thready form is able to penetrate the defenses of others and get under their facade. When this talent is not used for good, the writer can become manipulative and exploitative, as is the case with secondary thread.

Secondary Thread

Secondary thread is made either without pressure or with very light pressure, resulting in a formless scrawl in the middle of words. It is a sign of inner hysteria. The writer feels crushed by life's burdens and feels as if he can handle no more. The secondary thread writer is like a rubber band that has been stretched so many times it has lost its resilience. His motivation is self-preservation, which means hiding out. The only strength he has left is for flight. He always leaves a back door open so he can wriggle out in case of trouble.

When the writing is illegible (and assuming no mental or vision problems), there is a total lack of concern for others. If he doesn't care whether they can read his message, what does that say about his level of compassion and fellow-feeling? His only concern is to stay afloat.

Secondary thread is the connective form of choice by the con artist, the person who refuses to make a commitment of any kind, and one who feels unable to take a stand. Actually, it's no use for these people to make a choice, because once they make one, they're just as likely to abandon it for something more attractive. Their favorite road is the path of least resistance.

The Double Bow

The double bow is a fairly uncommon form. Like the thread, it combines the arcade and the garland, but retains more of their form. The writer wants to appear conventional and sincere, but doesn't want to have to make a choice. The writer is always working at maintaining equilibrium, hopping from one foot to the other, changing sides. He has no opinion of his own and won't give you his point of view because it depends on who he is with at the moment.

The double-bow writer could be called an opportunist who does what he believes is expected in order to avoid conflict. If he finds himself in a position where he could be taken to task for his actions, he simply slides over to the other side. His main objective is to avoid the complications and responsibility that comes with having an opinion.

Thready forms: co-author of the Nikki Hill mystery series, attorney Christopher Darden uses a combination of forms that emphasize primary thread.

Former President Richard M. Nixon used secondary thread forms.

Combining Forms

Some combinations of forms are particularly desirable, such as the garland/angle combination. The softness of the garland derives strength and support from the angle, so the writer is not a complete pushover, driven by his emotions. The angle is made softer by the garland, showing a greater willingness to adapt.

Some garlands in arcade writing temper the arcade writer's reserve and allow for greater spontaneity. Likewise, some fast arcades in a generally garland writing bring a little more reserve and caution to the more gullible garland writer.

The angle/thread combination is a primary sign of the exploiter who capitalizes on the weaknesses of others. He is sneaky and undependable. The worst of both connective forms is found in this duo. Don't trust him with your kitchen trash!

The Least You Need to Know

◆ The shape of connections between letters and within letters reveals the writer's style of relating to other people.

◆ Rounded forms are made by passive, accepting types.

◆ Angular forms are made by active, self-assertive types.

◆ Thready forms are made by avoidant types.

◆ A combination of forms are used by the healthiest personality types.

◆ The least desirable combination of forms is the thread and angle.

Chapter 14

In the Mood: Slant

In This Chapter

- ◆ Handwriting is like body language
- ◆ How to measure a loop
- ◆ Right, left, or indifferent, which way do you slant?
- ◆ All over the place—variable slant
- ◆ What about lefties?

Writing slant tracks the moment-to-moment flow of feelings and responses. Upslant demonstrates surface reactions but not the deeper emotional expression found in some other areas of handwriting, such as pressure. Downslant shows how well the writer controls those immediate gut reactions.

Because it is the easiest characteristic to change deliberately, slant is considered one of the superficial signs in handwriting analysis.

Slant is a lot like body language. When you are interested in what someone is saying, the tendency is to bend forward to hear better and pay closer attention. If you don't like the message, you may lean backward as a show of resistance. With a so-so attitude your posture might be upright—you don't care, either way.

All About Slant

As we've discovered, in handwriting symbolism the left represents self (the personal "me"), and the right represents other people (the global "you"). The degree to which handwriting slants to the right or left reveals how much the writer wants to be involved with "you."

Graphology pioneer Alfred Mendel wrote that slant indicates the writer's position between the mother (left) and father (right) or, according to Klara Roman, between male and female leadership. The more left-slanted, the more inclined the writer is toward females. The greater the right slant, the more the writer is influenced by males.

> **Fine Points**
>
> If the slants could speak, they might say: "I think, therefore, I am" (vertical slant); "I'd do anything for you" (right slant); "Nothing exists except me" (left slant); and "Oh dear, what should I do?" (variable slant).

The person who uses a right slant is the type who leans forward to listen in a conversation and openly shows her interest in the speaker. One whose writing reclines to the left wears a more skeptical expression. The vertical writer assumes a neutral posture until she decides whether or not she approves of the subject matter.

Slant shows how spontaneous one's emotional reactions are and how receptive the writer is, both to internal and external events. It also reveals how well she controls her responses after filtering them through her rational mind. Slant reflects how quickly the writer responds and reacts. The *consistency* of the slant reveals how stable the writer's emotional equilibrium is.

Culturally Speaking

Nationality has some influence on slant. The United Kingdom school model teaches an upright writing position. British people have the reputation for being generally more cool-headed, which is one characteristic of the neutral slant. In the United States, the learned slant is moderately rightward, but there is a wider range of variability in the handwritings of Americans, which, in itself, is an indicator of cultural independence, a well-known American trait.

At some periods in history, writing was far more right-slanted than it is now; at other times, it was more upright. In his book, *The Psychology of Handwriting* (George Allen & Unwin, 1926; reprinted, Books for Professionals, 1978), Robert Saudek describes some of the changes in handwriting slant in various European countries over time.

That's another reason why it's important to check the school model if you are analyzing writing done by someone from another country. Deviating from school model is as significant as if school-model style is retained.

Gauging Slant

Two types of slants exist in handwriting, and both are found in all three zones. They are the upslant, which is made by a stroke moving upward, away from the self; and the downslant, which is made by strokes moving downward, back toward the self.

In the upper zone, slant is measured by drawing a line from where the upstrokes and the downstrokes of an upper loop cross at the baseline, to the top of the loop (see the next illustration). The angle is now determined between the line we've drawn and the baseline. This clues us in on how responsive the writer is intellectually to outside influences. The letters *l*, *b*, and *h* are the easiest to use in measuring upslant.

The downstrokes of middle-zone letters are also measured, using the last stroke of the letters *m*, *n*, and *h*. Because the middle zone is where we live from day to day, we can learn how quickly the writer reacts outwardly on her inner responses, her gut reactions.

A 90° angle is vertical, or upright. Slants between 90° and 45° in either direction are considered moderate. Any slant leaning further than 45° to the baseline is extreme. Some writers can't seem to make up their minds and adopt a variable slant. As you might guess, variable slant has a meaning all its own.

Chicken Scratch

Some graphology schools require students to measure 100 slants on a page! Exact measurements are less important than developing your judgment.

The most profound effect on slant is produced by the angle at which the paper is placed on the writing surface. Pen hold and the position the arm is held in relation to the writer's body also affect the slant.

An inexpensive plastic protractor will do for measuring slant. The flat side of the protractor should line up with the baseline of the writing you want to measure. Slide the gauge along the upper loops until one of the slanted lines passes directly through the middle of the loop (or close to it), from the apex (top) to where the downstroke crosses the upstroke at the baseline. This allows you to find the angle between the upslant and the baseline.

Measuring upslant (above) and downslant (below) angles.

Slant gauge.

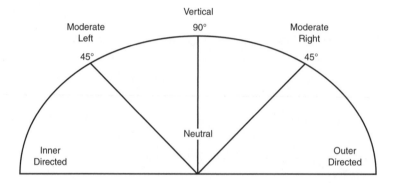

To measure the downstrokes in the middle zone, simply find the slanted line that most closely approximates the final downstroke on the *m*'s, *n*'s, and *h*'s. This allows you to find the angle between the downstroke and the baseline.

If you don't have a protractor to measure slant, you can photocopy the slant gauge shown in this chapter and print it out on a transparent sheet. Lay it over the handwriting to see where the slant falls.

Feeling It in the Heart: The Right Slants

The degree of right slant tells how much the writer is willing to spontaneously show her feelings. If your spouse brought home a new friend to meet you and you wanted that person to feel welcome, how would you act? You might reach out, maybe even with both hands, to grasp her hands in a warm clasp and tell her how glad you are to meet her. The act of reaching forward and extending yourself is reflected in right-slanted handwriting.

Moderate Right Slant

The writer with a *moderate right slant* is sociable and affectionate. A stronger right slant, however, suggests someone who might impulsively throw herself on you and give you a big hug and kiss. She is expressive and enthusiastic, a bit sentimental, and easily able to love others and show it.

Slanted writing suggests some degree of subjectivity. The writer doesn't care so much about logic and reason, she just knows how she feels. With a moderate slant she uses some restraint and doesn't get totally carried away with her feelings. She may share her opinions and viewpoints with others, but is not afraid to allow someone else to influence her when the situation calls for it. Emotions are involved, though, so the writer's decisions may be colored by her feelings about the subject matter.

The kind of warmth and sincerity found in a moderate right slant are desirable characteristics. As the slant moves further to the right, emotional controls begin to weaken.

def•i•ni•tion

A **moderate right slant** is where the upslant in the upper zone measures between 120° and 130°, and in the middle zone, between 110° and 130°. These numbers are approximate, not absolute.

Moderate right slant: singer/ songwriter Judy Collins.

P.S. Call me & will talk about you know what —

Strong-Extreme Right Slant

The stronger the slant, the more subjective the writer. When the slant becomes extreme, the writer is responding on a purely gut level, seeing things only from her own point of view. Her attitude says "How will this affect me?" She is too impatient to put the brakes on and examine the facts before acting, so it doesn't take long for her to make a decision. She just reacts, regardless of the consequences.

The very strong right-slanted writer is quick to jump to conclusions and overreact. She makes assumptions and proceeds accordingly. There are times when her rash, reckless responses might put others at risk, but it never occurs to her that she might be at fault when things go wrong. Taking time to check things out before hurtling into them headlong would probably save everyone a lot of grief.

With supporting evidence, such as narrow word and line spacing, the extreme right-slant reveals a writer who responds hysterically at the drop of a hat. Especially when letters and words become progressively more slanted to the right, real emotional problems are a strong possibility. Whatever she experiences is expressed in an instant. Expect her to broadcast her feelings openly and extravagantly. When she is angry, she is explosively angry. When she is loving, she is passionately loving.

Strong right slant: Vice President Dick Cheney.

Upright, Uptight?

A vertical or upright slant is midway between left and right slant. Self-control and self-discipline are needed to maintain such a neutral posture. Try standing up straight for an hour and see what a strain it can be! If handwriting is like body language, the vertical writer is standing very straight and projecting a rather austere manner.

His unsentimental, levelheaded demeanor may make him look as cool and detached as James Bond, but the apparent lack of emotion is not because he isn't emotional; he would simply prefer to deny that he is. Being very concerned with controlling his behavior, he weighs his words before speaking and thinks before acting. The closer the slant is to upright, the more the writer curbs his initial impulses.

He won't blindly go where fools rush in; he listens to his inner voice, which speaks the language of logic, not emotion. Being fair is very important to the vertical writer, so he takes great pains to stay impartial and carefully weigh the facts before making a decision. He thoughtfully considers the various sides of a matter, balancing all the pros and cons.

Upright handwriting: actor Michael York.

You'll Never Know How Much I Really Love You: The Left Slants

When you have a real aversion to someone and unexpectedly run into her on the street, what do you do? You might turn away, giving her the cold shoulder. In effect, that's what left-slanted handwriting does. The left slant is a formal rejection of the world at large; a literal turning away; a slap in the face to anyone who wants to approach the writer with social overtures.

Even a moderate slant to the left shows an oppositional attitude toward the world in general. When the writer needs encouragement and emotional feeding, to whom does she turn? Herself. The writer is leaning away from "you." She doesn't feel comfortable asking anyone else for anything important. It would be too much of a risk.

Risk of what? Rejection, perhaps. She's felt it before and prefers not to repeat the experience. It doesn't have to be childhood experiences that prompt the left slant. In one case an individual said she switched her slant after her parents divorced; another, when his wife left him for another man. And another after he discovered his lover had an abortion without discussing it with him.

The left-slanted writer is just as impressionable and emotional as the right-slanter, but she keeps her responses to herself. The greater the degree of left slant, the more emotional and the more self-contained she is likely to be. In fact, if you mentally flip the angle of left slant to the same angle of right slant, the emotions indicated are doubly strong, yet doubly inhibited.

> ### Tales from the Quill
>
> Graphologist Marcel Matley says of women who choose a left slant, "She says in her heart, if not out loud, to the father figure who threatens her, 'I'll show you, you bastard, I will become a better man than you are.' So she tends to become the kind of male he is, outdrinks him if he drinks, out-sexes him if he is a sex addict, outperforms him in business if he is a businessman, etc."

Such a writer may be very friendly and outgoing, yet, even after a long period of acquaintance, reveal little of herself beyond what you see on the surface. You are left to guess at what left-slanters are thinking and feeling.

Left-slanted writers are almost always pleasant to work with and they make an effort to do a good job. When things start going wrong, however, they may take refuge in an "everyone for themselves" attitude. They'll watch their own backs before covering for someone else.

Teenagers who are feeling rebellious about knuckling under to their parents' and teachers' influence often use left-slanted writing. Since the right symbolizes authority, one who deliberately turns to the left is defying authority and convention. Think of it as "thumbing their nose" at the rest of the world, saying, "I'll do what I want, regardless of how you feel about it."

Left slant is never taught in school models, so when someone adopts one, she's made a conscious choice to reject the norm. It takes sustained effort to preserve a left slant over a long period of time. Thus, while a moderate right slant is considered spontaneous, a left one is always viewed as unnatural.

Moderate Left Slant

Chances are, the person with a *moderate left slant* was the victim of some really nasty experiences. As a result, she feels compelled to protect herself at all costs. In a man, the left slant often stems from early conflicts with his father, stepfather, an older brother, or some other influential male. He may never have been acknowledged by his male role model, or worse, he may have been abused.

def•i•ni•tion

A **moderate left slant** is where the upslant in the upper zone measures between 80° and 90°, and the downslant in the middle zone measures between 80° and 90°. These numbers are approximate, not absolute.

A boy's response to the disappointing relationship may be to repudiate any behavior or attitude that approximates anything close to that person. Sometimes he'll compensate by growing into an especially sensitive or refined young man. More aggressive boys may even accuse him of being a "mama's boy."

To the moderate left-slanted writer, being in control is all-important. Consequently, she takes the time to screen her emotional reactions through the fine mesh of logic. She believes she can think her way through life (or perhaps uses a chemical substance) as a substitute for experiencing her feelings.

please thank all the help at W.H who stay up till dawn at these parties + never

Moderate left slant: Jacqueline Kennedy before she became Mrs. Onassis.

Extreme Left Slant

Alfred Mendel conducted a study of famous authors who wrote with a strong left slant. It turns out that they shared a common background: a very unhappy childhood and parents who were out of harmony with each other. Mendel concluded that left slant is an indicator of unresolved difficulties very early in life, resulting in a generally negative attitude.

Even when she wants to respond emotionally, the extreme left-slanter feels paralyzed by her inability to trust. Surely, she thinks, if someone is "acting nice" to her, he must have an ulterior motive. She desperately wants to avoid being susceptible to any more emotional damage than she already has experienced. Her self-protective attitude makes her like a turtle refusing to come out of her shell.

The extreme left-slanter is preoccupied with the past, where mothering and nurturing were supposed to be. She is looking for something to hang on to, some stability. Someone who didn't get what she needed in the past returns there again and again, hoping to find some way to make up for what was lacking—in this case, by slanting her letters to the left.

Staying aloof takes a lot of energy. The extreme left-slanted writer is exhausted by the conscious need to repress her reactions, and her lack of energy may lead others to wrongly conclude that she is passive and lazy. If she is able to find some way to successfully compensate for the disappointments she experienced in the past, there will be signs of strength in the handwriting, such as good pressure and vitality, and a well-formed middle zone.

Chicken Scratch

Convicted Oklahoma City bomber Timothy McVeigh's handwriting reveals a strong left slant in combination with a tiny middle zone (lack of reality); wide letter and word spacing and printing (isolation); and heavy pressure (frustration). It looks like a slingshot, pulled taut, ready for launching.

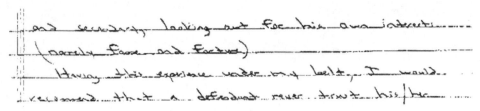

Strong left slant: Oklahoma City bomber Timothy McVeigh.

Every Which Way but Loops: Variable Slant

If slant were an electrical current, it would be important for the current to flow smoothly. What happens to a computer when it isn't protected by a line conditioner or a surge protector and there are spikes of electrical current? The motherboard is fried. No more computer. When electricity doesn't flow smoothly it leaves a lot of damage in its wake. The person whose loops slant in every direction is like someone who is being zapped with electrical current every five seconds or so. Yeow!

Decisions, decisions. The variable slant writer turns indecisiveness into an art form. She is consumed with ambivalence. Making up her mind about anything and sticking with it is close to impossible. She can't even decide which way to write, for heaven's sake! Oh, she tries to control her responses, but the constant excitement and restlessness subject her to the capricious waves of emotional input which fling her in every direction.

She can't decide which way to go, what to do, whom to believe. An inner battle rages, and, what's worse, it's not a war she has a chance of winning because the enemy is within. And just when she finally makes up her mind, someone comes along with a better argument and she switches over to the other side. Of course, she may just as quickly switch back, and for those who were counting on a firm decision, this can be extremely frustrating. Of course, if you want her on your side, you're in luck, as she willingly explores all sides and is on all sides.

Variable slant: fifteen-year-old Charles Bishop, who deliberately flew a small plane into a bank building after 9/11.

Lefties Are in Their Write Minds

The left-handed person has many more challenges in the graphic field than the right-hander. As the mother of a left-handed son and daughter, I remember how much harder it was for them to learn to write than it was for my right-handed son. According to Klara Roman and other graphological trailblazers, the natural mode of the left-hander is to write upside down or backwards (mirror writing), which goes against the grain in the right-handed world we live in (supposedly, only about 15 percent of people are left-handed).

We've already established that left-slanters are rebellious, but Roman further claims that when a left-handed person adopts a left slant, she is protesting the pattern that is imposed on her by the outside world. For a lefty to be able to write with a right slant, she is forced to turn her paper in a counter-clockwise direction. When the paper is absolutely straight to the edge of the writing surface it is nearly impossible for her to write correctly because she would be dragging her hand across what she had just written. Try it. You won't like it.

The lefty who manages to successfully compensate for writing in a right-handed world should get extra credit. So, when a left-hander adopts a right slant, pat her on the back for having made the adaptation. The same goes for when she makes rounded forms, which are more difficult for her to make than angular ones.

> **Fine Points**
>
> The late Pauline Clapp and I compared 120 writers, 60 left-handed and 60 right-handed. Each group had 30 males and 30 females. Of the entire sample, only two wrote with a left slant. Both were right-handed.

Slant and the Sexes

Women who use a left slant seem to find it especially difficult to relate to men and, even more so, male authority figures. Sometimes they are highly competitive with men, either directly or indirectly challenging their leadership. The pull to the left suggests that any close relationships they develop are likely to be with mother substitutes. Especially when the writing is also rounded, these women tend to be more possessive than some other types and have trouble letting go of a relationship once it's over.

Women whose lower zone slants right, while the rest of the writing slants left, are also rebelling against male authority. With a left-slanted upper zone in addition to the right-tending lower zone, they probably won't rebel openly, but find more passive ways to express their defiance. Additionally, the right-slanted lower zone in either men or women pulls away from the left, the mother influence. Therefore, there is probably conflict in the relationship with the mother or some other close female role model, such as a sister, aunt, or other mother substitute.

A left-slanted upper zone in men's writing is fairly uncommon. It suggests a strong attachment to ideas about women, particularly the mother. The writer prefers to steer clear of situations where other men can dominate him. Such men are often eager to please and work hard to make relationships succeed. However, when the left slant is in the lower zone, it implies disappointment in his intimate relationships and he may have doubts about his ability to satisfy a lover.

Other Stuff About Slant That Doesn't Fit Anywhere Else

An unvarying slant, like any other mechanical-looking handwriting, is a sign of over-control. The writer is predictable and consistent, but also emotionally inhibited and passive. She is afraid to let go and respond to her feelings.

Sometimes one letter in a word will unexpectedly tip over toward the baseline. Some handwriting analysts call these "maniac" letters because they're a mini-volcano of emotion. This is not a particularly uncommon characteristic, and certainly not always the sign of a maniac (I even make them myself, once in awhile).

Maniac d: *the so-called Zodiac Killer, who was never caught.*

The personal pronoun "I" that slants to the left in a normally right-slanted writing suggests feelings of guilt. The writer is pulling away from others, and since the single letter *I* represents the self, she wants to hide something from the world.

When the upper zone slants in a different direction from the lower zone, it indicates conflict between the way the writer thinks and acts. If the upper zone slant conflicts with the middle zone slant, the disagreement is between thoughts and feelings.

The Least You Need to Know

- Slant is a gauge of emotional responsiveness.
- Upstroke slant shows your gut reactions.
- Downstroke slant shows how quickly you respond to your gut reactions.
- Left-slanted writing is never natural.
- Slant is one of the easiest elements of handwriting to deliberately change.

4

Just My Style: Form

Flamboyant Fanny? Ostentatious Oliver? Simple Susan? Elegant Elfred? Plain Jane and no nonsense? You'll find out what the style of writing says about the way a writer presents himself or herself to the world.

You'll also discover what part form plays in the big picture.

Keep It Simple, Sweetheart

In This Chapter

- ◆ Copying the copybook
- ◆ Simplifying matters by cutting away the extras
- ◆ Going to extremes—embellishments galore
- ◆ Adding something beautiful with stylized writing

Handwriting is not like walking or breathing, which comes naturally—it's a learned behavior, more like speech. The penmanship teacher spends many hours instructing her students in how to create the strokes and forms that make up the letters of the alphabet. But regardless of whether the copybook is Zaner-Bloser, D'Nealian, or any another, students all start out learning to write alike.

We've already discussed graphic maturity—the point at which a young writer no longer needs to consciously think about the letter forms as he writes them, and letters and words begin to flow naturally. Then, at some point, and the timing depends upon the child, something else happens. The margin may begin to move away from the left side of the page. Or the writing size begins to shrink or grow beyond copybook size. The slant, baseline, and letter forms may look entirely different from what the school model dictates. What's going on here?

The letter forms and their placement on the page have begun to deviate from what the young writer learned in school. A more personalized writing style is taking shape that mirrors the youngster's personality development. As he grows and matures, cultivating his own style and tastes along the way, his handwriting will gradually reflect the internal changes he experiences.

Let's say he loves sports and has energy to burn. His lower zone will probably expand and the pressure will increase. If he is shy about meeting new friends and venturing forth into the world, his right margin may grow and the writing size contract. If he is running for class president and has a flamboyant style, he may enlarge and decorate the capital letters. He didn't learn to make those flourishes and ornaments from his penmanship teacher—they just appeared naturally. The aspect of handwriting that exhibits personal style is called "form," and it's the focus of this chapter.

To Conform or Not to Conform, That Is the Question!

Form is the most conscious aspect of handwriting and represents a deliberate choice of writing style. It is how the writer wants others to see him. He may choose copybook, simplified, printed, or embellished styles to project his unique self-image.

Follower or Leader?

Those who stick close to the school model tend to be followers more often than leaders. They are most comfortable when the rules are clearly stated and they have a good idea of their parameters. Rather than the maverick who is prone to go off on his own, adult copybook writers prefer to follow instructions and guidelines given to them by someone else. They like to do things the way they have always done them, feeling threatened by major changes. Their motto is, "If it ain't broke, don't fix it."

Lest you jump to the conclusion that continuing to write copybook style is a "bad" thing, consider this: many who adhere to copybook style perform some extremely important functions in our society. Grade-school teachers, secretaries, and administrators often choose copybook style, and where would we be without them? But while teachers might be happy if their students all maintained copybook writing style, the healthiest relationships, groups, and organizations embrace a variety of styles of being.

Chicken Scratch

Some people believe that it's good to write just the way they learned in school. The truth is, many convicted felons write exactly the way they first learned. It's a matter of conforming, and some people conform to the wrong crowd. Of course, most copybook writers are not felons!

Please use them with our sincere continued support.

Pleasant copybook style writing: actress Marlo Thomas.

working them out. Please enroll me as a member.
please print) King Martin Luther
s., Mrs., Rev., Prof.)   LAST   FIRST   MIDDLE
ss. 309 So. Jackson St.
Montgomery   STATE   Ala.
            (zone)
tion Clergyman — Religious Affiliation Baptist
    (if student, please mention school)
n in the 18-26 age group. Please enroll me in the Youth Section.

The copybook writing of Dr. Martin Luther King Jr.

Straying from the Straight and Narrow

Almost everything we do says something about us. We project our style in our body language, facial expressions, tone of voice, and handwriting. Some people feel more comfortable blending in as part of a crowd. Others are more original, individualistic, doing things their own way. They don't much care what people think of them. And, within that group of "original" people, there is a wide range of styles.

The form the writing takes on—the way it *looks*—demonstrates the writer's own personal style. Using copybook as a starting point, the degree to which the handwriting departs from the school model is the degree to which the writer feels compelled to express his own unique way of being.

There are numerous ways to depart from the school model. The shapes of the letters may be different, or the size, slant, beginning and ending strokes, and margins. Or, the writer might strip away some of the nonessential strokes, change the basic form, or add ornamentation.

Tales from the Quill

Teachers have a strong influence on the young mind. One woman reports remembering when her third-grade teacher very seriously informed the class, "You need to join up all your letters and write cursive—not printed—capitals, or else when you grow up, they won't let you vote, they won't let you have a job, they won't let you drive a car." Children tend to believe what adults tell them. A seemingly innocent remark such as this may have a long-range effect on an impressionable young mind.

Originality in handwriting can be expressed either by simplifying the school model or elaborating on it. A tremendous number of possibilities falls between one end of the spectrum and the other. Let's start with copybook as the midpoint and work our way backward toward simplification.

The simplification to elaboration spectrum.

The accompanying figure demonstrates just six ways the letter *s* might be made along the spectrum from highly simplified to extremely elaborate. Apply this illustration to all of handwriting to get the idea of what it means to simplify or elaborate.

Just the Facts, Ma'am

Writing is done for the purpose of communicating, so it needs to be clear and easily readable. It doesn't have to be fancy or ornate. To qualify as "simplified," a handwriting will have less ornamentation and less superfluous elements than copybook. To some degree, the unnecessary parts will be stripped away.

def•i•ni•tion

The **beginning stroke** leads into a letter but is not an essential part of the letter. The **ending stroke** follows the end of a letter or word but is not an essential part of the letter.

For example, *beginning strokes* are dispensable. You don't need them to make a word understandable. The same is true of *ending strokes*. Upper loops are also optional. It's quite possible to make a downstroke that steers directly into the next letter without first moving into an upstroke. The following handwriting sample is simplified down to the bare bones.

The bare bones: actress Natasha Richardson.

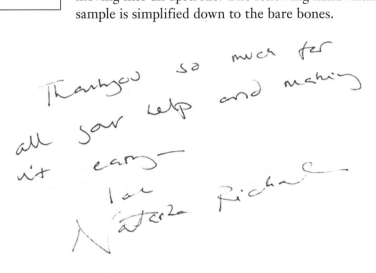

Simplified Handwriting

Simplifying handwriting is a way to take shortcuts and get the message across quicker. Writing that is simplified overall is made by one who wants to be efficient and expeditious. He gets impatient if you bombard him with a lot of extraneous details, as he wants to get down to basics. Don't waste his time with long explanations—he isn't listening anyway.

The simplified writer's home, like his handwriting, may be sparse in decorations, with a few high-quality knickknacks gracing the bookshelves. In combination with an overall wide spatial arrangement (which is common in simplified writing), the writer feels uncomfortable in a crowd. The simplified writer takes his time getting to know you before he will allow any type of intimacy. Whenever possible, he elects to spend his free time with a few carefully chosen friends.

Simplified writing that is low on loops signifies a direct personality that "tells it like it is." The writer can't stand verboseness and doesn't indulge in the kind of flowery speech that is liberally sprinkled with flattery. What you'll get is the bare facts with little embellishment. The emphasis is on the intellect more than the emotions, and the writer is generally objective and realistic. It takes a fast thinker to cut through all the irrelevant matter and get to the bottom line.

> I feel quite nervous to inscribe this book for you— it will say so much more to you than to anyone else! Thank you so much for

Simplified writing: naturalist Jane Goodall.

Ingenious Solutions

Because one of the aims of simplified writing is efficiency, writers who like to cut out the details often create very interesting shortcuts. The next figure illustrates some nifty ways to get from one letter to the next, which the writer certainly never learned in penmanship class!

Ingenious shortcuts: actress Miranda Richardson finds unique solutions to the problem of how to get from one letter to the next.

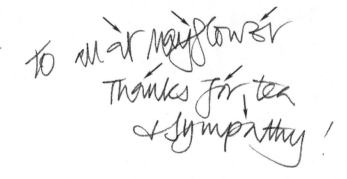

The ability to find efficient means to get from one place in writing to the next suggests that the writer is proficient at constructing solutions to problems without relying on the standard, tried-and-true methods. He is resourceful and innovative, finding fresh, sometimes even revolutionary ways of doing the same old thing.

There is, however, the danger of (as my grandmother used to say) "throwing the baby out with the bath water." In his need for efficiency and innovation, the simplified writer may reject what worked well in the past simply because it isn't new.

Tales from the Quill

Sometimes simplifying takes time. Writing a concise letter, for example, isn't always as easy as it sounds. Benjamin Franklin once wrote to an acquaintance, "I would have written you a shorter letter but I didn't have the time." It's easy to write at great length about a subject, but making the writing clear and concise takes much more effort.

I Go to Pieces

It is possible to achieve simplification without damaging the basic structures of the letters. To deserve a positive interpretation, the handwriting must be spontaneous, natural, and easy to read.

Keeping the bare essentials: actress Susan Sarandon.

When too many details are eliminated the writing may look emaciated, like someone who has been fasting too long. There is little meat on the bones. We say the form is neglected. Yet, if the downstrokes are present, the bare essentials are still there and the writer generally manages to function in the world.

The overly simplified writer is ascetic. He has little interest in form. Creature comforts and the extraneous trappings of life mean nothing to him. He views the world through objective eyes, sustained by purely intellectual interests. He doesn't consider other people's needs; in fact, he is probably barely aware of their existence. Reason and intellect are developed at the expense of his emotional life.

> **Chicken Scratch**
>
> The *extremely* simplified writer often is not considerate of other people. He lives at a high level of stress and is too impatient to put a little meat on the bones of his writing. His behavior in the world is just as impatient and irritable as his writing.

Overly simplified writing: poet Emily Dickinson, who withdrew, even from her family, and stayed in her room for years.

Skeletons in the Closet

As in many other aspects of handwriting, "simplification" is a matter of degree. When the handwriting is so overly simplified that it has deteriorated to the most basic strokes and legibility is totally abandoned, it is called fragmented or skeletal writing. Whereas the writer of simplified writing wants to be clear and efficient, the skeletal writer achieves the opposite result—the writing becomes hard to read because it lacks some of the essential structure, the "backbone."

Extreme simplification is a sign of emotional self-denial and an impoverished spirit. The writer may feel so profoundly stressed and unable to deal with the pressures of his daily existence that he is forced to divest himself of every emotion or experience that might add to the fullness of life.

Neglect of form in handwriting can also be a sign of narcissism or egocentric behavior. The person who is so consumed by his problems tends to become wrapped up in himself—to the point that he ignores the people and events around him. Emotional reactions are withheld and responses kept to the barest minimum. His emotional life is decaying, falling apart, and so is his handwriting. Communications with the outside world are impaired at best, nonexistent at worst.

Dressing Up Is Fun

At the other end of the spectrum from simplification is the enrichment/elaboration continuum. While simplification is fast, spontaneous, and unconscious, any type of ornamentation added to handwriting is done consciously. Again, we have to ask ourselves: is the writing legible and is it spontaneous and natural? If answers to both questions are yes, then the interpretation can be positive. If, on the other hand, the elaboration detracts from the message or legibility in any way, a negative meaning results.

Think of handwriting as a sponge cake. Simplified writing is the plain, unadorned cake. Add a little frosting and you've got copybook writing. From there, your imagination can run wild. Do you like birthday cake with flowers made of purple frosting? That might be embellished writing. How about wedding cake with bride and groom, sugar bells, and silver sprinkles? Now, that's elaborate!

Elaborated writing can run the gamut, from richly enhanced to gaudy and overly dramatic. Someone who decorates his writing with many extra strokes, wide loops, and other embellishments is a visual person for whom form is often more significant than content. This is not a value judgment. It's a fact: the writer spends more time making the writing beautiful (remembering that beauty is in the eye of the beholder) than on what he writes.

The elaborate writer is likely to have a home filled with objets d'art—pictures and sculptures—with an emphasis on design. He is attracted to flamboyant, eye-catching, showy things. His manner is dramatic, sometimes to the point of theatricality. You can bet he'll make an entrance when he arrives at a meeting or party. When he describes an event, it's not a dry recitation of the facts, it's a full-blown story. In his life, everything is BIG and EXCITING.

Ornamented handwriting: true-crime writer Ann Rule's glamorous signature.

Artistic Additions

To be considered artistic, the ornamentation must add to the form picture, not detract from it. In other words, if the form stands out too much, it may reduce the positive meaning. Usually, positive ornamentation includes some type of flourish and original or unique letter forms.

Ornaments that are superfluous and overly complex become mere gaudy junk that serves no useful purpose. Always keep in mind that legibility is the first consideration.

Artistic printed writing: actress Reese Witherspoon.

Distinctive Details

Writing that is full and round without being overly elaborated suggests fullness of emotion and imagination. In a harmonious writing where the forms are balanced in a well-organized space, the interpretation could be an exuberant spirit with a zest for life.

Elaboration in disorganized, inharmonious writing, on the other hand, could signify one who overexaggerates or overestimates himself. Both types of writers have an abundance of ideas, but express them differently. Think of it as the difference between having a gift wrapped by a professional or by someone who is all thumbs. Either way, the gift is wrapped, but which would you rather give?

Elaborate writing of William Peter Blatty, author of The Exorcist.

WILLIAM PETER BLATTY

> **Chicken Scratch**
>
> Writers of highly embellished handwriting devote many hours attending to details that will make their environment look impressive without leaving time to handle the mundane obligations that pay the bills.

There's a big difference between enriching writing and overembellishing it. The difference is an aesthetic one. When the adornments are in good taste and not overdone, the analysis will be more positive than one where the handwriting is bedecked with a myriad of curlicues, inflated loops, and extra strokes. Both types of writers are attempting to beautify their scripts, but for different reasons. The enriched writer wants to enhance his writing and improve it. The embellished writer wants to impress others for his own self-aggrandizement.

The *overly* embellished writer is likely to be vain and ostentatious in his presentation, drawing attention to himself. His need to be in the limelight is an overcompensation for a poor self-image. He believes that the only way he can get the recognition he so desperately craves is to demand it. Unfortunately, his overornamentation trivializes his efforts, and the attention he gets is likely to be of the negative variety.

The more extravagant the flourishes and ornaments, the more inflated the capital letters, the less the writer is in touch with reality. He may be conceited and narcissistic, boasting of his supposed accomplishments, which probably exist only in his mind. Such people are often social climbers who are impressed with other people's money.

The Icing on the Cake

Everyone has different faces or masks that they use in different situations. Carl Jung called them our *persona.* We wear our masks to cover up the less desirable parts of ourselves (Jung's shadow side) so others won't see them. The masks we wear change according to circumstances. We don't wear the same face when dealing with the boss as the one we wear in bed with our lover (at least, one would hope not!). The mask we wear when a policeman pulls us over in traffic is probably not the one we wear at a party, and so on.

Some people are more concerned than others about controlling their shadow side, and consequently develop a stronger persona to keep it under wraps. Those who are most afraid of their shadow peeking out and giving them away develop a strong persona, which means lots of self-control.

def•i•ni•tion

Persona is the outer self that masks the shadow side of personality. An overly strong persona is seen in carefully constructed handwriting called persona writing.

Strong self-control requires a lot of maintenance and energy, and is developed at the expense of spontaneity. It shows up as a pictorial-style handwriting, like Elizabeth Dole's handwriting. The writing looks more as if it were drawn, rather than written naturally and spontaneously. It is more of a work of art than communication.

The writing is elaborate and ornamented, but with little spontaneity. Mrs. Dole has a reputation for having extremely strong self-control that rarely, if ever, slips. Her mask is kept firmly in place, and the public sees only what she wants us to see.

Persona handwriting of U.S. Senator Elizabeth Dole.

Persona writers are often successful in the world of culture or design. They may be performers, artists, or orators who keep their private selves completely separate from the one they show to others. The persona writer is generally polite and formal, sophisticated and charming, but onlookers may get the sense that the smile is painted on and unchangeable, regardless of what is happening inside.

The important question is: what is the purpose of the mask? Is it an attempt to deliberately disguise and hide something, or is it adopted out of a need to appear more beautiful, more sophisticated, more charming than the writer feels?

Persona handwriting is somewhat more difficult to analyze than natural handwriting, but the careful graphologist will be able to peek behind the mask and see what's there. Certainly, the person who maintains his individuality, who is courageous, independent, and strong-willed in his drive to break away from the norm, stands out from the rest. Those who insist on "doing it their way" feel less need to adapt to the world than the copybook writer does.

The Least You Need to Know

- Copybook style is the point of departure in analyzing handwriting.
- Communication's the thing—whatever the style, the handwriting needs to be legible and clear.
- Simplification means cutting away unnecessary elements.
- Too much simplification breaks down the ability to communicate clearly.
- Overelaboration is a sign of perfectionism called persona writing.

Chapter 16

A Rose by Any Other Name

In This Chapter

- ◆ Who are you?
- ◆ Signing on the dotted line
- ◆ Ideal self versus real self
- ◆ Who am I?

We've just completed a discussion of the most conscious aspect of hand-writing, its overall form. In this chapter, we'll delve into some very specific form choices—capital letters, the signature, and that extra-special letter, the personal pronoun I.

When someone discovers that I'm a handwriting analyst, very often they'll thrust their signature at me, expecting an instant opinion. It's doubtful that the same person would go to the doctor's office and expect to get a diagnosis based on a quick peek down her throat; yet she thinks a hand-writing analyst should be able to draw a full personality portrait from just a signature—the equivalent of a cursory glance at her tonsils. The doctor can see that her tonsils are enlarged, but must order tests to find out the all-important *why*.

Clearly, the signature is a very meaningful part of the whole handwriting picture. It explains some things about the way the writer functions that the other text might not. Some graphologists are willing to make an analysis based on the signature alone, but the old masters always cautioned against it. The signature represents the personality on its best behavior, but it doesn't tell what goes on behind closed doors.

Tales from the Quill

A woman who suffered through a long, difficult marriage finally got a divorce, whereupon she completely changed her signature. One day she got a call from her bank. They wanted to know if she had written a particular check, since the signature was so different from the one they had on file. Her public image had changed and the change was reflected in her signature.

How Do I Look?

In the days before handwriting, people used pictographic drawings to transmit information. These symbols represented the message they wanted to get across. When you sign your name to a document, whether it's a legal contract or a personal letter, you are leaving a symbolic representation of who you are, not so unlike those early pictographs.

One's signature is crafted to project what we want others to know about who we are. It identifies us as us. Once we've chosen a signature that we like, it usually remains constant. Only after undergoing major life changes is a signature likely to alter in any significant way. We have compelling examples in Napoleon Bonaparte, Adolph Hitler, and Richard Nixon, whose signatures all suffered dramatic changes as their power declined.

Changes in the signatures of world leaders.

According to Klara Roman, sometimes the signature may be symbolic of a wish, rather than the reality. When one's self-image is tied strongly to their profession, or there is some other significant life event, a symbol may appear in the signature.

The symbol of a ship is clear in a cruise-ship captain's signature. Liberace drew a little piano beside his name. George Foreman's signature has a boxing glove, and news anchor Peter Jennings, who died of lung cancer, seems to have made a lung in his signature. Then there's the knife in the signature of John Bobbitt, famous for having suffered the unkindest cut of all at the hands of his wife. It's probably safe to assume that the knife was added to his signature after the event.

Apparent symbols in signatures: 1. Liberace. 2. Peter Jennings. 3. John Wayne Bobbitt. 4. George Foreman.

Developing one's signature is a highly individual and personal matter. It's rather like choosing a suit of clothes. Someone who believes her body is covered with horrible blemishes might select a heavy overcoat to cover herself. Or perhaps she feels the need of a suit of armor as protection from a world that seems threatening. On the other hand, maybe the writer is a nudist who doesn't mind if others see her, er, well, you know.

Your signature is your public image; it's how you want to be seen. A signature that is congruent with the rest of the writing is a primary sign of a genuine, up-front person who has nothing to hide. Her personality is consistent and dependable. Text that looks entirely different from the signature suggests duality. Either the writer has something to hide, or else is hiding from something. The body of writing uncovers the true story.

Do You Read Me?

The readability of a signature speaks volumes about the writer's willingness to be known. Following are some of the ways people commonly present themselves in their choice of signature:

◆ *Clear and legible.* What you see is what you get, warts and all.

◆ *Illegible signature.* Makeup, dentures, hair dye, high-heeled shoes—the methods we use to change our outer appearance are many and varied. There's nothing wrong with wanting to improve on the basic model, unless it's for the purpose of deliberate deception. An illegible signature may result from someone who is in a hurry and has had to sign many documents. Or, the writer doesn't want others to know the truth about her. Desire for privacy, or something more ominous? Examining the body of writing will tell.

◆ *Both.* Some people, especially those in public life, have two entirely different signatures. The public one is more like the gift wrap on a package. What's inside may not look exactly like what the wrapping implies. The one chosen for private correspondence is more revealing of the real person. Grammy winner Paula Cole has a very private side that is seen in her illegible signature. The legible signature is much more like her handwriting.

Singer Paula Cole's hand-writing and her two different signatures.

This is ballpoint pen.
I actually have 2 signatures: because
my official signature is so illegible,
I sometimes sign like This.

Paula Cole

◆ *Middle name or initial included.* Including the middle name or initial is a sign of pride. It's a formal, official way of presenting oneself. Like William H. Macy, for example.

All in the Family

The family name represents one's ability to interact on a social level. The given name symbolizes one's personal ego. If the person behind the signature is balanced and harmonious in both roles, the first and last names will be compatible and congruent. Sometimes they're not, as we'll see next:

> **Fine Points** _____
>
> The height that the capitals reach indicates to what degree the writer is driven to achieve. Extra large initials are frequently employed as compensation for low self-esteem.

- *Surname larger.* Pulver spoke of one's surname as being her history or trademark. In the case of a man, it reveals his regard for his family (or, for a woman who takes her husband's name, her husband's family). If the initial letter of the surname or the whole name is made larger than the given name, it denotes great respect for tradition and pride in the family name.

Signature of Nicole Brown Simpson with its larger surname capital.

- *Given name larger.* The person who writes her given name larger than the family name may not be too enamored of her family. She may have suffered some disappointment at the hands of her father or other family member and devalues their name by making it smaller. A woman who hates her husband may symbolize her animosity by shriveling up his name. A larger first name suggests that the writer would rather be known as "Bill" than "Mr. Clinton," for example.

Signature of former President Bill Clinton.

- *Slant.* If the given name and the surname slant in different directions, it's a good bet that there is an inner conflict being waged between the writer's ego and her social life. Check the body of writing to discover the cause of the conflict.

- *Surname illegible.* If the given name is written clearly but the family name is illegible, the writer has issues (that's a nice way of saying "problems") with her father. An illegible given name with a clear surname points to an insecure ego.

All the Trimmings

When my kids were little I used to spend a lot of time in fabric stores. They hated it, because naturally they would rather be playing outside. But one thing they did enjoy was helping me choose which trimmings I would sew onto the clothes I was planning to make for them.

Some people enjoy ornamenting their signatures, much like sewing fancy buttons and beads onto a garment. It makes them feel important, or it's just fun to dress things up. The question for the graphologist is, is the writer choosing to do it for fun or because she feels compelled to do it? The answer will be seen in how natural and genuine the embellishments are. A free and easy movement that adds attractive swirls is interpreted differently than carefully drawn ornamentation.

The autographs of (1) actor Brad Pitt and (2) rapper Eminem look more like logos than signatures.

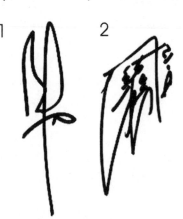

The Wrapping on the Package

Anything that goes beyond the plain and simple writing of one's name is considered an embellishment. From ornate capitals to flourishes and swirls, there are countless ways to elaborate a signature. When placed underneath the signature, these decorations are called *paraphs*. Commonly used in bygone days, the paraph is rare in the United States today. It is still used in some Middle Eastern and South American countries.

def•i•ni•tion

A **paraph** is a flourish appended to the signature. It may take the shape of an underscore, wavy line, scroll, or other decorative form. In "olden days," it was used as a means of preventing forgery.

What is the significance of underlining and other additions to the signature? That's our next area of discussion.

◆ *Signature embellished.* Embellishments represent a need to draw attention to oneself in some way. The writer feels her accomplishments deserve recognition.

Flamboyant signature of actor and California Governor Arnold Schwarzenegger.

◆ *Signature underlined.* Underlining the signature is a way to emphasize it. The writer is proud of the poise and confidence she projects. It may be either a bold statement or a defiant, compensatory gesture.

◆ *Signature crossed through.* When the final stroke of the signature goes back to the left and lines through it (or an intended underline slashes through it), it represents a gesture of canceling oneself out. A wife who detests her husband might unconsciously cross right through her married name, or a man who hates his father might cross through his own name.

◆ *Signature with a covering stroke.* This extra encircling stroke is used to cover over or protect the ego and *cover up* some part of the writer's life.

◆ *Signature with period or dot at the end.* Is a sign of caution, of backing off, inhibition, and mistrust.

Ups and Downs

The position of the signature and its size are also significant.

◆ *Signature smaller than text.* Either the writer underestimates herself or wishes to appear more modest than she really is. The text will tell the truth.

◆ *Signature larger than text.* This is a show of bravado. The writer wants to appear supremely poised and self-confident, even though she really feels quite small inside. She needs to impress others with her competence and stature.

◆ *Ascending signature.* The writer whose signature soars is ambitious, hopeful, and goal-oriented, especially if she also makes tall capitals with strong rhythm.

◆ *Descending signature.* This indicates extreme discouragement, fatigue, or illness. The writer may have lost all hope and is simply giving in to depression.

Memories of Bygone Days

Leftward tending strokes suggest a return to past memories. When the leftward stroke is in the upper zone, the emphasis is on cultural or philosophical recollections. A final stroke that gets larger in a rightward direction, on the other hand, is an emphasis on the self and outer life. The writer is pleased with herself and wants others to know it.

Right-tending strokes in the signature of Senator John Kerry.

John F. Kerry

> **Chicken Scratch**
>
> A signature written at the far left side of the page is a danger sign! Especially when the writing is also small and narrow, the writer may be contemplating suicide.

The placement of the signature on the page has its own story to tell. Normally, we expect to see the signature toward the right-hand side. The writer who exceeds that expectation and goes all the way to the right drives herself mercilessly. The nearer the signature is to the center of the page, the stronger the inhibiting movement. Since the right side represents the future, the more the signature hangs back, the greater the writer's fear of the future.

The Man Behind the Curtain

In the *Wizard of Oz*, when Dorothy and her companions finally made it to Emerald City, they stood quaking in their boots in front of a frightful image with a booming voice. That is, until Toto the dog revealed the little man behind the curtain. Capital letters are the big scary voice the writer projects, and the small letters are the reality behind the curtain: the ideal self and the real self.

School models call for capital letters of two to three times the height of the middle zone. Some writers exaggerate their capital letters to extremes. Others shrink them to barely copybook height. Capitals may also be more elaborate or more simple than copybook. The next list covers what various styles mean:

- *Capitals copybook.* Conventional and conservative, the writer has little interest in breaking away from what she was taught and going out on a limb.

- *Capitals plain and simple.* The writer has no illusions about who she is. Her manner is direct and up front.

- *Capitals ornate.* The writer may be overly impressed with herself, and thinks others should be, too. Attracted by status, wealth, and social prominence, some degree of narcissism is evident in this showy display.

- *Capitals very small.* Modesty and constraint are indicated here. The writer wants to shrink into the woodwork, rather than be swept into the limelight. She may be submissive and pliable, or just plain spineless.

- *Capitals large.* The person whose capitals are large but not extreme has self-confidence, pride, and ambition. She believes in her ability to accomplish what she sets out to do.

- *Capitals extremely large.* This is the self-aggrandizing person who comes on strong. She makes herself the center of attention and exaggerates her accomplishments to anyone who will listen. Whether what she says is based on reality or is mostly in her mind is another story.

> **Tales from the Quill**
>
> A graphologist was shown the handwriting of a young radio announcer who wrote with extremely tall capital letters. "You're looking for bigger and better things," she told the announcer. The announcer laughed and shared that she had just accepted a more prestigious job at a much larger station.

- *Capitals well formed.* With a sense of pride and dignity, the writer presents herself well.

- *Capitals poorly formed.* The self-concept is not well developed. If this is the writer's "ideal self," she may need some help in improving her image.

Let's Get Personal

English is the only language besides Russian Cyrillic in which a single letter represents the personal pronoun. In French it is *je*, in German *ich*, but in English, I stands on its own as the personal symbol. That makes I a highly significant letter.

Entire books have been written on the subject of the personal pronoun I, which will be referred to as PPI from here on. Jane Nugent Green's *You & Your Private I* (Llewelyn, 1975) goes into great detail to describe the various aspects of the self in relation to the PPI. My personal favorite on this subject, *The Freudian I* (Reprinted, Graphex, 1998) by Terry Henley, uses Freudian concepts to explain the complexities of this single letter.

The school model calls for a PPI of about twice the height of the middle zone. Anything higher than that is considered tall; anything shorter is short. Besides the height, the width, or scope of the letter is important. So is the pressure, placement, and most telling of all, the shape of the I. Of course, these aspects of the PPI must always be considered within the gestalt of the handwriting you are analyzing.

Copybook PPI.

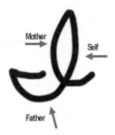

According to Henley, the downstroke or the backbone of the PPI represents the self. The straighter the downstroke, the more independent the writer. Conversely, the more curvature there is in the downstroke, the more the writer depends on others for emotional support.

As in all parts of handwriting, the initial writing impulse represents mother, and the final stroke represents father. According to copybook, the first stroke starts at the baseline and moves into an upstroke, which turns at the apex, returns to the baseline, moves left into a curve, and finally ends to the right. Thus, when made this way, the upper loop (the sail) represents mother and other females, and the bottom loop (the boat) represents father and other males.

Fine Points

One way to tell if a PPI is written in reverse is to find another word in the text that begins with a capital *I*, such as Indiana. If the capital connects to the word, you'll be able to trace the writing movement and see whether the writer began at the top or the bottom of the PPI.

In some schools, children are taught to write the PPI in the reverse of what was described earlier. Also, some writers who were not taught to reverse it, do. "In reverse" means that the bottom part of the I is made first, then the top. It's not always possible to tell which way the I was made unless you check the pressure pattern under a magnifying glass. The heavier pressure will usually be on the downstroke.

The following list describes some of the common types of PPI.

- *Copybook PPI.* The writer has conventional attitudes. She probably had a "normal" family life in a two-parent home. Whatever issues she had with her parents as she grew up did not do any long-term damage to her ego.

- *Reversed PPI.* Henley says the reversed PPI (when not taught) is a sign of rebellion. Others define it as the writer seeing herself differently from how others see her.

- *Printed PPI.* The PPI made in one single stroke (called a *stick figure I*) or with a crossbar at the top and bottom (called a *Roman I*) is a sign of independence, making yourself number one.

def•i•ni•tion

A **stick figure I** is a PPI made in one single downstroke. A **Roman I** is a PPI with a crossbar at the top and bottom added to the downstroke, like a Roman numeral I.

- *PPI with upper loop only.* The writer was strongly influenced by her mother (or other female figure). The father may have been missing, physically or emotionally or both.

- *PPI with lower loop only.* The writer's mother image is missing from her life. She may not have been present for her, either physically or emotionally. The male image was a stronger influence.

- *Very small PPI.* The writer is modest and unassuming. She doesn't like to draw attention to herself. She may have been devalued at home, and hasn't developed a strong self-image.

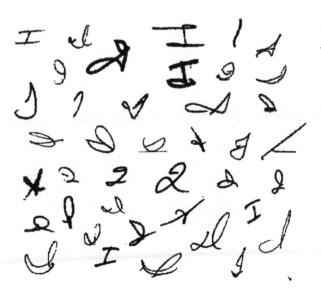

A small sampling of various forms of the PPI.

- *Lowercase PPI.* This may be an affectation, as in the writing of e. e. cummings, who wrote almost everything in lowercase. Or, if other signs in the writing bear it out, the writer's self-concept may be poor. She feels she doesn't deserve to give herself the reward of a capital I.

- *Large and wide PPI.* The writer takes up a lot of personal space. When the upper loop is wide it suggests that the writer has an expansive, open view of women in her life. The same would be true in reverse if the lower loop were wide—men are given a lot of latitude.

- *Lower loop turns left.* When the final stroke of the PPI ends toward the left, it is a gesture of rejection. The writer's father has disappointed or hurt her and she can't deal with it.

- *Angular PPI.* Angles are not prescribed by the school model PPI; therefore, there are significant ramifications when they are added. The angle is a sign of inflexibility. In the upper loop of the PPI it signifies anger and resentment toward the mother/females. Angles in the lower loop show aggression directed toward the father.

- *Retraced PPI.* Sometimes you'll find a retraced upper loop in the PPI, which suggests that the writer squeezes her feelings about her mother into tight little packages that she doesn't want to look at. In some cases, the writer who blames her mother for a separation from her father retraces the PPI's upper loop.

- *Very round PPI.* The soft, bloated PPI looks like a fetus, and the behavior of the writer may be babyish. She needs a lot of mothering and may have come from a home where she was pampered and overindulged. As a result, she has a hard time standing up for herself. This type of PPI is often found in women and some gay men.

- *PPI with a figure eight.* A figure eight lying on the baseline is a counterstroke and indicates unresolved issues or conflicts with the father/males.

- *PPI looks like a number 2.* The writer sees herself as a second-class citizen in her own life. She puts everyone else first, herself second, third, or last.

- *Top and bottom loops are separated.* The upper and lower loops are made separately. Frequently, if you question the writer, you'll find that her parents were separated, either physically or philosophically, maybe both.

- *PPI is isolated.* When the PPI stands away from the other words with an island of space around it, the writer either feels alone or needs to be alone.

- *PPI leans left*. In handwriting that otherwise is right-slanted, this is an indicator of guilt feelings. The guilt usually has something to do with sex or religion.

- *PPI lays on the baseline*. If you see a PPI that looks like it's fallen over on its side, chances are the writer is disappointed in her father but has decided to accept him for who and what he is.

These are just a few of the many possibilities. I encourage you to do your own research, questioning as many people as you can about their history and try to see how it fits in with the PPI they choose to represent themselves.

The Least You Need to Know

- Your signature is your public image. It's what you want the world to know about you.

- Capital letters represent your ideal self, while lower case letters represent your real self.

- The personal pronoun I (PPI) tells about your self-concept and your attitudes toward your parents.

- The PPI should be examined for size, shape, and placement relative to the words that come before and after.

Part 5

Sweating the Small Stuff

Now that you've got all the hard stuff out of the way, it's time to coast for a while. Learning about the character traits that have been assigned to various letters is something like learning how to play chords in music after you've learned the theory. It fills out the melody.

This is where we'll also cover important information about some of the more unpleasant aspects of handwriting—the danger signs.

Chapter 17

The Finer Details

In This Chapter

◆ How it all begins … and ends

◆ Tying things up

◆ Digging in with hooks

◆ Too much punctuation is negative!!!

Finally, we've come to a discussion of beginning and ending strokes. If it seems odd to wait so long, it's a case of going from the general to the specific. You had to learn about the vagaries of space, form, and movement before we could get to the fine points. But now, here we are.

As in all the other areas of handwriting, depending on where they start and finish, beginning and ending strokes can be interpreted on several levels: the physical (lower zone), social/emotional (middle zone), and intellectual (upper zone). And, always, the movement from left to right symbolizes going from me to you.

Beginning strokes show how the writer moves from within himself out into the world. On a physical level, the type of beginning stroke provides clues about how eager he is to get going on a new project or activity; on a social/emotional level, his sense of independence; on an intellectual level, how much preparation he needs before starting out, and how well he understands the basics.

def•i•ni•tion

In copybook writing, all letters have a **beginning stroke** that leads into the letter. It's also sometimes called an "initial" or "lead-in stroke." All letters also have an **ending stroke** that leads into the next letter. It is sometimes called a "final stroke."

Ending strokes tell us how the writer relates to the outside world. On a physical level, they indicate his eagerness to move forward; on a social/emotional level, his attitude toward his fellow man; on an intellectual level, his ability to think progressively.

The variety of beginning and ending strokes is astonishing and diverse. They come in all shapes and sizes, and, as small an element as they are in the overall writing sample, they can fill in some very important details about the writer's personality.

In the Beginning

Remember when you got your first bicycle? Your dad attached training wheels so you wouldn't fall over and hurt yourself. You needed that extra support to help keep your balance until you learned how to stay on the seat and ride in a straight line by yourself. Before long, though, you wanted Dad to get rid of the training wheels because you felt all grown up and could now ride without help.

Initial strokes are the training wheels of handwriting. In the beginning, when you're first learning to form the letters, initial strokes provide the beginner with the support he needs to steady his hand as he proceeds into each word. Once graphic maturity is reached, however, most initial strokes become superfluous and can be discarded without losing legibility.

There is a second aspect to retaining or rejecting those lead-in strokes. As part of the original handwriting training, keeping them might signify one's willingness or desire to follow the rules. Once one understands the reasons behind the rules, he can choose his own path and follow them, or not. No one will be harmed should the writer choose to discard this particular rule, and he can prove his spirit of independence by omitting the expendable initial stroke.

When the initial strokes are jettisoned, it reveals a self-confident, independent writer who relies on himself. He has the capacity to act quickly, without spending a lot of time on preliminaries. He no longer wants or needs training wheels to guide him along his chosen path. He understands what is important and what is not.

Can't Let Go

The writer who retains the initial stroke is either unable or unwilling to remove the training wheels. He believes he needs a crutch, and has difficulty letting go and "riding" on his own. He has difficulty getting started, either with a new project or activity, or making a social connection. The shape of the initial stroke will tell us whether the inability of the writer to let go of the past and move from me to you is because the past was a comfortable place where he'd like to stay, or because he's afraid to leave it and go forward.

Any type of long initial stroke indicates that the writer feels compelled to think about it for a while before starting anything new. He isn't comfortable going into unfamiliar territory unprepared.

Fine Points

Few men make long, curved initial strokes. Adult women who do are usually very attached to home and family. They may have been babied long past babyhood, which has impacted their ability to act independently. The longer and the more curved the stroke, the more the writer has been sheltered from the big bad world.

The very long, straight initial stroke that starts well below the baseline is known as the "springboard stroke," and hints at difficulty in the past. However, the stroke is made with great energy going into the middle zone, and that suggests a strong desire to take past difficulties and turn them into achievements. The longer the stroke, the greater the obstacles the writer has had to overcome in order to feel successful.

An example of a long, straight initial stroke in author Mary Higgins Clark's handwriting.

The shorter, straight stroke has been called, by the trait-stroke school, the "resentment stroke." Whether the writer is actually resentful or not, theory tells us that this type of stroke forms an angle with the following stroke, and is a sign of tension and aggression. The aggressive acts take place in the middle zone, and the writer's behavior is quarrelsome and contentious. He is on the defensive, always on guard against criticism, seeing himself as a victim, rather than as someone who is powerful in his own right.

A long, curved initial stroke has a friendlier implication, but is still a sign of immaturity. Chances are, the writer was babied at home, which can be a very seductive memory when things aren't going well. So he returns to old friends and/or family for support and encouragement, rather than standing on his own and trying to sort things out for himself.

Curved initial strokes that start high in the upper zone look like a smiley, and the writer has the demeanor to match. You'll find that people who begin with a curved or wavy initial stroke smile a lot and are generally cheery folk. They have a good sense of humor and prefer to look on the bright side.

Curved initial and final strokes in novelist Nora Roberts's handwriting.

Tales from the Quill

Graphological icon Felix Klein used to say that the person who retained the long initial stroke needed a second cup of coffee before he could get going in the morning. He would have to wind himself up before he could face the day. The long extra stroke symbolizes the need of the writer to put a little distance between himself and the new activity. He has to think about it for a while before getting going.

The small, cramped loop on an initial stroke has been called the "jealousy loop." I'm not sure of the reason for that one, but the definition offered by the trait-stroke schools is "jealousy focused on one person."

A special case is the large initial letter. When the first letter of a word (not a capital letter) is larger than the rest, it shows a need for recognition and superiority. The writer comes on strong at first, to make his presence known. After the initial burst of energy he backs off.

The End

The last stroke of a word signals the end of an effort. The project is done and it's time to rest. What does the writer do? Does he want to reach out and socialize? Or does he put up a wall between himself and others?

Where there is no final stroke and the last letter is abruptly cut off, the writer is likewise often abrupt or even rude in his social transactions. He is very impatient and hates "wasting time" on the polite amenities. You may be speaking with him, when suddenly he turns on his heel and walks off without a word.

Chicken Scratch

A final stroke left suspended in midair is called "trait suspendu." It is like ending a conversation in the middle of a sentence. There is more to be said, but the person has thought better of saying it. He would rather keep the information to himself.

The long garland final stroke is like a hand reaching out generously, in friendship. The writer wants to move forward and take others along with him. He is kindly and empathetic, willing to share his resources and time. In the same gesture, he is holding his hands out to be filled, showing readiness to receive, as well as to give.

When the long final stroke is not garlanded, but is straight, the meaning is entirely different. It is a holding-off gesture, as if the writer were putting out a stiff arm to keep others away. He doesn't trust people and doesn't want them getting close enough to hurt him, as seen in the next sample.

Former California Governor Gray Davis's long, straight final strokes.

In some writing, the long final stroke is made only at the end of lines, filling up the space between the last word and the edge of the paper. In this case, it signifies a superstitious sort of "touching the wall" for safety, as we did as children.

A final stroke that returns to the left, arching back over the word like an umbrella, is a self-protective gesture. Think of someone crossing his arms over his head to ward off a blow. This type of ending stroke also effectively builds a wall between the writer and others who might like to become friends with him.

When the final stroke returns to the left *under* the word, below the baseline, it is a way for the writer to emphasize himself. He wants to draw attention to his achievements and have others applaud him for his contributions.

Covering return strokes: novelist and poet Margaret Atwood.

S for your letter. I'm taking advantage
unts of spare time on this book tour to
- I get home, I'll have too much to do!!!
nourn the loss of the art of handwriting

Final strokes that rise into the upper zone are said to denote someone with a tendency to worship. It is also a seeking for higher truths. The writer who goes into the upper zone when he doesn't need to is interested in philosophy and exercises his intellect every chance he gets. He may also be ambitious and optimistic, especially if the baseline also rises.

A final stroke that ends abruptly with pressure on the downstroke is self-assertive; the writer can be dogmatic in defending his point of view. Add to that an increase in the pressure and you get belligerence.

Final strokes that tend to turn down show a pragmatic, matter-of-fact way of dealing with the world. There is a certain ponderousness in this seeking of the baseline or below. If other signs support it, pessimism is possible.

Heavy-pressured final strokes suggest that the writer experiences unbearable surges of emotion. If the final stroke is in the middle zone, the writer will have unexpected outbursts of temper and aggressiveness. If it is in the lower zone, he may turn the aggression inward in depression and self-sabotage.

Heavy down-tending finals of muralist Diego Rivera.

A final letter that grows suddenly larger than the rest of the word is made by one who blurts out whatever is on his mind. He has a childish, immature way of demanding what he wants, using no finesse or tact.

Most handwriting samples will have more than one type of initial and final stroke, with one standing out more than another. Look for a preponderance.

I Love You, Period: Punctuation

Not much is said in the classical texts about punctuation, and we're not going to say much about it here. However, there are a few things to be aware of when considering those seemingly insignificant exclamation points and question marks!?

Some writers use excessive punctuation, adding heavy underlining, quotation marks, and exclamation points. Some add little asterisks or smiley faces here, there, and everywhere. The effect on the page is often confusing and disturbing. The person who turns punctuation into ornamentation doesn't really understand where things belong. He overdoes everything. He is theatrical and melodramatic, and simply doesn't know when to quit.

Overdone punctuation is done by someone who feels obliged to draw attention to himself in some way. He craves excitement and adventure. He can't sit still and is always on the move, looking for action. When making a period or a comma, he goes over and over the same spot, grinding the pen into the paper. Dot grinding is a form of compulsion, often seen in the handwritings of both abusers and victims of abuse.

Round, careful commas and periods suggest a careful, meticulous mind. The writer is a methodical thinker who wants to take the time to do things properly. More often than not, this type of punctuation is found in copybook writing and is a sign of the conventional personality.

Periods that look like commas, with the final stroke fading into a tail thanks to a fast pen, denote impatience. The writer may have a quick temper and an irritable nature. He can't stand to wait, and wants to get on with it. His rather careless attitude implies that it's okay with him if some of the details fall through the cracks. He has more important things to do than hang around, trying to get it right. Thready connective forms usually will also be found in the sample.

Tales from the Quill

People suffering from some types of mental illness often use excessive punctuation. Particularly those diagnosed with paranoid disorders write with extremely heavy punctuation of all types: periods, commas, quotation marks, exclamation points, and question marks. They also tend to underline more than normal, and, in some cases, write all around the edges of the page. They feel compelled to control all space on the paper.

Yoo-Hoo! Here I Am!

Inappropriate or lavish underlining is done for emphasis and signals someone who wants to feel important. He draws attention to his own words, as if to say, "Here I am! Listen to me!" Very heavy underscores that almost (or actually) tear through the paper are a sign of a strong emotion, usually anger or frustration. If the writer makes a habit of using this form of punctuation, he probably has an explosive temper.

Heavy crossing out demonstrates a need to be right. The writer doesn't want you to see that he's made a mistake, so he completely blacks it out. He simply can't bear to be told he's wrong or take criticism from anyone. He demands his own way, no matter what. As long as things go according to his wishes, everything is fine. But push him or expose his weaknesses, and you can expect an unpleasant eruption of anger and hostility.

Heavy cross-outs in O. J. Simpson's handwriting.

Don't Let Go! Hooks and Ties

You may use a plastic or metal hook to hang your robe on the back of the bathroom door. You use hooks if you go fishing. Grappling hooks are used by those who like to climb mountains. Hooks are made for many different situations, but they all have the same basic purpose: holding onto something.

In handwriting, too, hooks symbolize holding on. Some hooks are large and round, such as the garland initial or final strokes we discussed earlier. Others are tiny, seen only under magnification. Each type has its own significance. Where they appear, along with their shape and size, add yet another piece to the personality puzzle.

In this section, we'll talk about hooks and ties (another form of holding on). Hooks are generally found in angular writings more often than they're found in garland writings, but depending on the type of hook, they may be present in fast or slow writing. Ties are often seen in rounded handwritings, and may serve the purpose of lending some strength to the normally flexible writer.

Chicken Scratch

Beware of the sneaky little hook at the ends of words. The writer may appear generous in extending himself on your behalf. At the last minute, though, he throws out a hook to keep hold of what he had offered and selfishly pulls it back.

Hooked on Handwriting

Hooks have two basic meanings: tenacity and acquisitiveness. They can be made on initial or final strokes, or both. In the upper zone, a hook means grabbing onto an idea and holding it. In the middle zone, it could represent a refusal to let go of a social attachment. In the lower zone, it usually has to do with sexual attitudes.

Hooks at the beginning of a letter or word suggest holding on to what is past, while hooks at the ends of letters or words imply reaching out and actively attempting to acquire something new. Because hooks are superfluous appendages, they are not usually considered a positive sign.

Fine Points

Hooks can appear in any part of handwriting. They may be large, such as the kind of hook that you hang your bicycle on; or they may be tiny tics that are barely seen.

Small initial hooks are made with speed and express impatience and irritability.

Large initial hooks represent holding on to past experiences. Large final hooks may be a sign of greed and a desire to acquire as many possessions as possible.

Writing with many hooks is done by someone who can't let go—of the past, of relationships, of anything. It's even hard to take the trash out on pickup day. If the writing is also narrow and cramped, you can bet the writer's a packrat whose home is filled with all sorts of miscellaneous stuff.

The easiest place to spot a hook is on *t*-bars, as well as initial and final letters. Use your magnifying glass.

Lots of hooks in the hand-writing of actor Christopher Walken.

The Old School Tie

Like the hook, a knot or a tie holds something together. In handwriting, knots are a sign of persistence. It's not enough that this writer forms the stroke or letter, he has to tie it up with a neat bow, too.

Ties in the handwriting of actress Kirstie Alley.

The knot is made by someone who, once he gets hold of an idea, will not let it go. He stubbornly persists in his beliefs. There is a tendency for him to get caught up in the small details, so he may miss the importance of the big picture. By wasting energy on trivia, he has less time for important considerations.

Another, slightly more sinister interpretation for knots and ties is secretiveness. When the tie is in the form of a double looped oval in the middle zone, the writer is locking his lips and hiding the key. We know he's got something to hide, but we don't know what it is.

Chapter 18 is designed especially for those who need something tangible to hold on to. We'll be diving even deeper into the particulars, to find the meanings that have been assigned to some of the individual letters.

The Least You Need to Know

♦ Initial strokes reveal how comfortable the writer is in leaving the past behind, as well as how he deals with essentials.

♦ Final strokes tell about social attitudes and whether the writer is interested in extending himself on behalf of others.

♦ Punctuation plays an important part in handwriting analysis.

♦ Some hooks may be seen only under a magnifying glass, but their significance should not be underplayed.

Chapter 18

Making It in the Minors

In This Chapter

- ◆ *t* time
- ◆ Looking them in the *i*
- ◆ *x* marks the spot
- ◆ *p*, *r*, and a bunch of other small letters
- ◆ It's all Greek to me
- ◆ The oral *o*'s and *a*'s

If you have been a teensy bit frustrated by the seemingly nonspecific aspects of the gestalt method, this chapter is for you.

Here, you'll find some of the "this-means-that" minor indicators that appeal to the left-brained graphologist. Of course, everything you see in handwriting should always be analyzed in context, but there are some specific letter forms that we can pick out, just for fun. It's sort of like learning how to play chords on the piano rather than studying the theory behind the music. You might not be able to play the really complicated pieces, but you can make it sound pretty darn good.

def•i•ni•tion

The **trait-stroke school** of handwriting analysis assigns personality-trait names to individual writing forms. This method builds a picture of personality as if using bricks, laying one atop the other, and seeing what results at the end.

The interpretations that follow are taught by the atomistic or *trait-stroke school* of handwriting analysis. These are the bits you can use to "amuse your friends and amaze your neighbors." They are literally minor points and are not for the serious analyst unless taken as secondary information to fill out the analysis. I can't always give you the theory behind them, because no one seems to know it! But the interpretations do seem to "work." The discussion that follows applies to lowercase letters, which may be printed or cursive.

Don't *t*'s Me

The letter *t* has two parts, a stem and a crossbar. The crossbar requires a dynamic left-right action (or right-left in some left-handers). Traditionally, the *t*-cross represents one's ability to set goals and meet them. According to the book *Tattletale t's*, by Geri Stuparich (American Handwriting Analysis Foundation), there are more than 400 ways to make the letter *t*. We'll cover a handful of the more common forms.

The Stem

The height of the *t* stem is a clue to how strong the writer's self-image is in regard to her work life. If the stem is moderately tall, about twice the height of the middle zone, she feels good about herself and is independent enough to assert herself when the situation calls for it.

- Very tall (more than 2.5 times higher than the middle-zone height): pride that has grown to the extreme of vanity. We often find that the writer of a very tall *t* stem had a strict, demanding father who was never satisfied with the writer's accomplishments. Consequently, whether she realizes it or not, she continually tries to impress her father. Yet, she feels she never quite measures up.

- Short: the independent person who follows a different drummer. Her own self-approval is more important to her than what anyone else thinks. She doesn't need the approbation of others to feel good about her successes.

- Copybook: more comfortable following than leading. She's conservative, conventional, and happy to go along with the crowd, so don't expect her to branch out on her own.

♦ Looped: sensitive to criticism about her work. Of course, *any* wide loop is a sign of emotionalism and sensitivity because loops are containers for emotions.

Height on the Stem

The height at which the *t* is crossed tells us how high the writer sets goals. Copybook height is around two-thirds up the stem. It's important for most of the *t*-bars to actually cross the stem because that keeps the writer in touch with reality—the baseline, where the *t* sits.

The person whose *t*'s cross at copybook height sets her goals at practical levels that she knows she can accomplish. She doesn't reach out for attainment greater than she feels she can reasonably meet.

There are two possibilities for a *t* crossed very low on the stem. It may denote depression and a lack of energy for creating new goals. The writer sets her sights on easily attainable aims to ensure that she won't fail. It is also possible that the writer has recently achieved a goal and is resting on her laurels for a while.

A *t* crossed higher than what copybook demands indicates someone with high goals. The writer seizes opportunities to advance herself and is willing to work long and hard to get what she wants out of life.

Some *t*-bars fly high above the stem into the graphological stratosphere. If it's just a few of them, it is the sign of the visionary who looks ahead and sees the possibilities of tomorrow. Otherwise, the writer is out of touch with reality. It is important to balance those "visionary *t*'s" with others that stay in touch with the stem.

Former President John F. Kennedy's "visionary t's."

t-Bar Length

The *t*-bar length reveals how much willpower the writer puts into attaining goals. Copybook has a short bar, which shows a conventional, conservative attitude. The writer pursues goals with a practical outlook and, with other supporting signs, can be counted on to finish what she starts.

♦ Very short *t*-bar: insecure person whose willpower is only so-so. Sticks to what she knows and does her best not to annoy anyone by pursuing her goals too heartily.

♦ Long *t*-bar: dynamic will. The left-right thrust distinguishes the writer as someone who knows what she wants and is not afraid to push herself forward to get it. Forceful and with an ability to direct other people, her enthusiasm and excitement help get things moving.

♦ An extremely long *t*-bar that crosses entire words: an extremely controlling and forceful person who tends to bully others into doing things her way.

t-Bar Pressure

The pressure exerted on the bar as it moves from left to right is an important indicator of stamina. It tells whether the writer has the sustained energy to meet her objectives.

Strong pressure throughout the *t*-bar indicates that the writer has the stamina and vitality to withstand pressure in the pursuit of her goals. A weak-pressured *t*-bar is made by one who runs out of steam and gives up too easily.

Pressure that starts out strong and fades away before the end of the effort symbolizes the same behavior in reality. The writer starts out strong, but her energy peters out before she completes the job.

Various *t*-Bars

The form of the cross bar has to do with ideas, attitudes, and theories, since it is in the upper zone. *t*-bars come in an amazing variety. Here are just a few:

♦ *Slants downward* (especially with heavy pressure): the "domineering *t*." Can be quite the tyrant who wants to boss others around.

♦ *Points upward:* optimism, ambition, hopefulness. Looking forward with excitement to moving ahead and succeeding.

◆ *Concave* (bows downward, as if someone were pressing down on it): is easily
persuaded to change course and often
allows others to take advantage of her.

◆ *Convex* t-*bar* (an arcade): self-protection.
The writer stands alone and rejects
help. She isn't about to open herself up
and make herself vulnerable by accepting a helping hand.

◆ t-*bar connects to the next letter, or is connected to its own stem:* quick intellect.
Makes easy mental connections and is
resourceful when dealing with problems.

> **Chicken Scratch**
>
> The most bizarre and
> strange forms of *t* crossings
> are found in the handwritings of
> prison inmates. These idiosyncratic
> thinkers see the world differently
> from the way others see it. They
> make their own rules and disre-
> gard the standard, normal ways
> of behaving in favor of their own
> selfish aims.

Unusual forms of t-bars.

◆ *Lassolike* t-*bars* that swing to the left before returning to the right: suffers guilt
feelings and mentally returns to the past, trying to figure out why she didn't
handle things better. Often found where a violent death (murder or suicide)
occurred close to the writer.

◆ *Uncrossed* t's or crossed to the left: procrastination. The writer has a hard time
crossing through the *t*, so you can imagine what it's like for her to make a decision and follow through on it!

- t *crossed to the right:* enthusiasm and excitement. The writer is so anxious to get going on a new project that she can hardly wait.

- t *made in one stroke at the end of a word*, with the bar coming up from the baseline in an arcade movement called an "initiative *t*": doesn't wait to be told what to do. She jumps right in and gets started without a blueprint or instructions.

- *Pointed t-bars:* The sharp point on the end of the bar is used like a dagger to cut others down to size. Ridicules others with sarcasm and make others feel "less than." Her cruel and cutting remarks are a defense against her own insecurity.

- t *crossed twice:* compulsive behavior. Insecure and anxious; the type who goes back into the house several times to make sure she turned off the gas. May take on a sinister cast when combined with other negative indicators, such as heavy pressure.

Although a moderate variety is normal and acceptable, when one handwriting contains a wide spectrum of *t* forms, it suggests that the writer is uncertain about where she wants to go and what she wants to do. Look for balance.

Original thinker

Flexible

Self-protective

Sarcastic

Enthusiasm

Quick thinker

Controlling

Death consciousness

Procrastinator

Ambitious

Hypersensitive

Authoritarian

Initiative

Various types of t-*bars.*

Seeing *i* to *i*

The only difference between an *i*-dot and an idiot is *i*. The small letter *i* may look insignificant, but it has its place in handwriting analysis. The style and placement of the *i*-dot add some valuable information about the writer.

The careful, precise, round dot placed close to the stem is said to mean that the writer is loyal. Okay, I guess that makes sense— the dot loyally sticks by the stem. A dot flying high and to the right is made by an impatient, adventurous person who is interested in the future. Missing *i*-dots are an indication of a poor memory and/or a tendency to procrastinate. In some cases it is an act of rebellion—"I'm not going to do what I'm supposed to do!"

Fine Points

The trait-stroke method uses the *i*-dot to determine the writer's attention to details. The closer to the stem and the rounder the dot, the greater attention the writer pays to details.

A circular dot is generally made by one who has not yet reached maturity, usually a teenager. The writer of the circle *i*-dot is usually gullible and naïve. She presents a paradox: on the one hand she wants to stand out from the crowd, but on the other hand needs their acceptance. A notable exception is Walt Disney, whose signature was created for him by the art department.

When the *i*-dot takes the form of a heavy slash, brutality is often the cause. It may be that writer has a mean mouth, or worse.

If *i*-dots are formed like a dash or a comma, it signifies an ironic sense of humor. When there's also a little hook, it's a sign of irritability.

The circular i-*dot of Walt Disney.*

Let's Get Organized

The letter *f* is the only tri-zonal letter: it passes through all three zones. The top and bottom of the *f* are, theoretically, supposed to be the same length and width. Thus, the *f* can be used as a gauge for the writer's sense of organization. If the top and bottom loops are the same height and width, she is said to be well organized. An emphasis on the upper loop suggests someone who plans better than she executes. Conversely, with an emphasis on the lower loop, she is more interested in doing than planning.

A fluid *f* is made in one smooth stroke, and signifies efficiency and effortless movement. Louise Rice (the newspaperwoman who originally brought graphology to the United States) believed it typified altruism, possibly because of its graceful rightward movement.

The *f* with a large knot around the stem means pride in one's family—perhaps because *f* stands for family? Well, it stands for lots of other things, too, like food. Some graphologists believe that an inflated lower loop on the *f* is an indicator of a particular love for food.

The letter *f* also stands for father. Shirl Solomon, who wrote a wonderful book called *Knowing Your Children Through Their Handwriting and Drawings* (Crown Publishers, 1978), believes that the lower loop of the letter *f* represents father, even though it is in the lower zone (area of "mother"), because it is where the letter ends up (remember, in graphological symbolism, everything starts with mother, ends with father). So, the shape of the lower loop of the *f* may tell you how the writer feels about her father.

The letter f.

Emphasis on planning

Emphasis on doing

Fluid thinking

Keeps it simple

Fatalism

Missing father

Family pride

Father rejection

Altruism

The *x*-Files

The letter *x* has an important place in history. Those who couldn't write their name could at least make their mark, their *x*, to sign a legal document.

To analyze the *x*, determine whether the cross bars are straight or bowed, and whether the pressure is heavier on one side or the other. Even its placement in the check box on a form will reveal information about the writer. Is it on the left side of the box or the right side? That will tell you something about how the writer feels about the past and the future. If she makes only one diagonal line without a cross-bar, consider it carelessness. You can also check the pressure. For such a simple structure there is an amazing number of forms of the letter *x*.

Tales from the Quill

Richard Kokochak, who specializes in jury screening using handwriting analysis, has turned analyzing the letter *x* into a science on its own merits. Richard analyzes the direction the cross bars are made, where they are placed on the jury questionnaire, the pressure, style, and several other aspects of this deceptively simple letter. He helped select more than 50 juries in just over 2 years using handwriting analysis.

The Letter *k* Is Okay

The small letter *k* looks like a person. The stem is the spine, and the cross bars are like the arms. That opens up several possibilities.

A warm, affectionate person who loves to hug and hold her partner close frequently wraps the arms of the cross bar around the stem in a loop. One whose cross bars don't touch the stem is less comfortable with physical contact.

Rebellious

Angry

Standoffish

The letter k.

The *k* with cross bars that slash *through* the stem suggests some hostility, which may be directed at the self, since the movement is toward the left. Then there's the *k* with a "buckle" instead of a cross bar, which is actually closer to copybook style. The trait graphologists call a large buckled *k* the "defiant *k*" or the "rebellious *k*," presumably because it bursts out above the middle zone and makes its presence known.

mmm mmm Good

The *m*'s and *n*'s are used by the trait school to determine the writer's thinking style. The theory is that rounded tops on these letters signify "cumulative" thinking. Since the rounded top is an arcade form, it follows that cumulative in this context means successively building one idea on top of another. So, a cumulative thinker would be one who remembers and uses what she has learned in the past. She "accumulates" ideas.

Sharply pointed tops are a sign of the "investigative" thinker who wants to know the reasons why for everything.

Fine Points

Here's an intriguing bit of information: The copybook *m* has three humps, which signify (from left to right) me, you, and the world at large. If the first hump is the higher, the writer is self-confident and relies on her own opinions. If the second or third hump is higher, other people's opinions are more important than her own.

Sharply pointed bottoms are made by the "analytical" thinker. Analytical means to analyze, so the pointed *m* and *n* writer digs for facts and then carefully examines them.

The *m* and *n* with a thready, wavy top is called the "superficial" thinker. Her mind skims along the surface, picking up what it needs along the way and discarding the rest.

You'll probably find an assortment of *m*'s and *n*'s in most handwritings because we use all the different types of thinking for different purposes. However, one will be dominant.

Mind Your *p*'s and *q*'s

Okay, forget the *q*'s, but the letter *p* has some interesting messages attached to it. As a mostly lower-zone letter, the *p* is often referred to as the "physical *p*." Thus, a long loop on the *p* would show an interest in physical activity. However, the reverse is not necessarily true. Someone with short *p*'s could be the captain of the football team.

The "peaceful *p*" has a rounded top. Actually, this applies to any letter that is rounded because the writer who shies away from angles is more of a peace lover.

The "argumentative *p*" is the copybook form, which requires a tall, straight stroke that moves high into the upper zone. The writer loves to engage others in a debate, if not a downright argument just for fun.

The "bluffing *p*" has a large lower loop and may be used by flirtatious women who don't back up their implicit sexual promises. It may also appear in the handwritings of sales people.

The letter p.

Bluffer

Easily influenced

Argumentative

r You Still with Me?

For some reason, the small letter *r* is connected to the writer's dress sense. An *r* that looks like a backwards 3 is said to be a sign of the natty dresser, someone who pays special attention to her appearance and the image she projects. Maybe it's because it takes more time and effort to make this letter form?

The letter r.

Mechanical

Sharp thinker

Dress-conscious

The "flat-top *r*" is made by those who work well with their hands and enjoy using tools. The theory behind this interpretation may be that the flat top is an arcade, which is favored by people who are interested in building.

The "needle point *r*" has a sharp top and is used by those who live by their intellect. They're very sharp-minded and curious about learning new facts. The rounded top *r* is a sign of someone who is more susceptible to outside influence.

The printed *r* or any printed letter in a generally cursive writing is often a sign of creativity. The printed *r* is also called the "parochial *r*," because it is taught in Catholic schools.

Oh, My Dear! Signs of Culture

The so-called "signs of culture" in handwriting include the Greek *E*. Even though this is actually a capital letter, it is sometimes used in the lowercase. The trait school defines it as someone who has an interest in literature and likes to read.

> **Tales from the Quill**
>
> The trait-stroke schools like to talk about "cultural letters," but it's a fascinating fact that many highly cultured people, including brilliant scholars and literary giants, make no cultural letters in their scripts at all. Moreover, the Greek *E* is seen fairly frequently in the handwritings of prison inmates!

The "lyrical *d*," another Greek letter, is also said to indicate cultural leanings. Some graphologists believe it is mostly adopted by poets. Interestingly, you won't find it in the writings of Dickinson, Milay, or Whitman.

Finally, the figure-eight *g* is considered a sign of literary talent. It is made in one smooth, fluid stroke that presumes a quick, facile mind. Add to that a philosophical bent and a sense of humor, according to Huntington Hartford *You Are What You Write* (Macmillan, 1973). You'll find these forms in the next figure.

Cultural letters.

Lyrical d

appreciates and

Greek e

Nine

Greek g

Change

L. A. Confidential: The Communication Letters

The middle zone, as the area of daily life and relationships, is where we communicate. Therefore, the middle zone letters are where we look to find out *how* the writer communicates. Although the middle zone encompasses all the vowel letters and the parts of other letters that don't rise above or sink below the middle ones, the round letters, *o* and *a*, lend themselves especially well for the purpose.

Think of *o*'s and *a*'s as little mouths. How many of those little mouths are open and how many are closed? If all the *o*'s and *a*'s are closed, it suggests someone who is close-mouthed and careful in what she reveals. It doesn't mean she doesn't like to talk. Maybe she talks a lot without saying much. Look for a balance of open and closed forms. If the writing is crowded, with lots of words covering the paper, you can bet that she is quite chatty. When the *o*'s and *a*'s are wide open at the top, she has loose lips. Gossip is her favorite sport.

The lowercase *a* that looks like this typographical letter *a*, with a covering stroke over the top, is often made by those who have something they'd rather not discuss. In many cases there is childhood sexual abuse in their background. However, please note that this is a creative form of the letter *a*, and many artistic types use it.

The type of *a* or *o* for which the writer makes a full circle before actually forming the letter is a sign of "talking around" a subject, never directly addressing family problems. This is often the case in families where alcohol abuse is a problem.

Intrusions

Clear communication calls for direct, simple speech. One who proliferates an overabundance of technical jargon or multifarious, meandering discourse ends up only obfuscating the essential underlying connotation. See what I mean?

Anything beyond the plain facts is fluff or shows intent to distract and distort the information. Extra strokes in communication letters effectively tamper with clear communication. One way to interfere with the free flow of information in handwriting is to add extra loops to the *o*'s and *a*'s.

Chicken Scratch

Intruded ovals often are made by victims of sexual abuse. When hooks, loops, or black marks appear inside middle-zone letters, check for other signs of abuse.

Extra loops are the equivalent of zipping your mouth shut and locking it. A loop on the left side of the letter, since the left side represents the self, suggests a form of denial or, in effect, keeping secrets from yourself. When the loop is on the right side, the secrets are kept from others. Some writers make loops on both sides of the letter. That can mean a real Sneaky Pete. But she's probably only fooling herself. When extra loops or hooks appear inside o's, a's, or other round letters, they are called "contaminated ovals."

Secrets and Lies

Tiny loops that hang down inside o's and a's are a fairly uncommon phenomenon, but they show up often enough to mention. Loops are containers for emotion, so extra loops inside the o's and a's indicate unreleased emotion about some experience or event. We don't know what it was, but these loops usually stand for something unpleasant. The writer might desperately want to talk about what's troubling her, but just can't get the words out.

Hooks inside o's and a's are a bad sign. Some graphologists call them "stingers," as they represent sneaky, nasty ways of communicating. Others say it is the sign of one who speaks with a forked tongue. One author goes so far as to call it the indisputable sign of a pathological liar! That may or may not be true, but be sure to check on the facts before believing anything such a writer tells you.

e Is for Ear

Part of communication is listening, as well as speaking. The trait school uses the small letter *e* to determine whether a writer is a good listener or not. Think of the *e* as an ear. If the letter *e* is wide open, it would signify someone who listens well. If the letter *e* is squeezed shut, the writer has her hands over her ears. She isn't a good listener. Of course, this could be extrapolated to any other letter!

I'll Believe Anything You Say

When left open wide, the small letter *b* is akin to a mouth naïvely hanging open with the writer ready to believe anything you tell her. Innocent or just plain clueless? The overall writing will reveal the writer's level of maturity.

The Least You Need to Know

♦ Some individual letter forms can help you interpret personality. Use them judiciously in the context of the whole picture.

♦ The small *t* relates to goals. Check the stem height, cross-bar length and placement, and overall pressure. Beware of bizarre *t*-crosses.

♦ Communication letters are like little mouths. Check to see if they're open, closed, or have a forked tongue!

♦ Extra loops, hooks, or other intrusions into the oval letters are known as "contaminated ovals," and can mean problems in communication.

♦ Greek letters are viewed by some as a sign of culture.

Waving the Red Flag: Danger Signs

In This Chapter

- The problem of honesty
- The red flags of dishonesty
- The red flags of violence
- Mixing drugs and handwriting

No person is all bad, nor all good either. I believe there is truth in the saying, *there's a little bit of larceny in us all*. In fact, the human animal is a conglomeration of attributes, mannerisms, and characteristics that run the gamut from almost totally, 100 percent honest to dirty rotten scoundrel. Conscience is buffered by many shades of gray along the honesty/dishonesty continuum.

What one person views as lacking integrity or honesty may be perfectly acceptable to another. How about the employee who makes personal photocopies on the company copy machine? Or spends hours on the Internet at work, e-mailing jokes to friends?

For the scrupulously honest individual, taking even a paperclip home would be unthinkable. Someone else might feel justified in handling his personal business on company time, with an attitude that says "the company can afford it," or "they owe me!" And few people, if they hit the jackpot at the corner phone booth, would walk away and leave the pile of change for the next guy. Yet, that money obviously belongs to the phone company.

In every chapter so far, we've covered the positive and negative aspects of each element of handwriting, using "natural and spontaneous" as a benchmark. Now, however, we're going to go beyond plain old negative behavior and move into the realm of pathology. Before we get into this important topic, however, please take note: *there is no such thing as a "criminal handwriting."* When identifying signs of potential for dishonesty or violence in handwriting, as in everything else, the key word is "potential."

Fine Points

One red flag appearing a few times shows a tendency. When present consistently, the behavior is part of the overall personality pattern.

This subject really demands an entire book, but what follows is merely an introduction to some of the more noticeable and significant red flags that can be found in handwriting.

One True Thing: Honesty and Integrity

There are two basic problems in determining dishonesty and *integrity* in handwriting. First, *honesty* is subjective, and the writer's view of dishonesty will affect how it appears in his writing. Even when someone's behavior positively stinks, it may not clearly show up in his handwriting if he doesn't feel guilty about it.

Second, handwriting reveals only attitudes and potential. We aren't using a crystal ball, so predicting whether the writer will act on his potential or not should be left up to the psychics. Thus, one whose handwriting is filled with signs of dishonesty may or may not act on his potential for bad behavior, which doesn't make it any less useful to know that the potential is present.

def•i•ni•tion

Honesty, the way I see it, is never deceiving, stealing, or taking advantage of the trust of others, and integrity means staying true to your own set of principles and beliefs.

Dishonesty runs the gamut, from deliberate lying to concealing information to bending the truth slightly to save someone's feelings. Even those little white lies are a form of dishonesty that some feel are necessary and important in our society.

Graphologists generally look for groups of four or more graphological red flags before reaching a conclusion of probable dishonesty, but the overall pattern is, as always, the most important clue. Just one characteristic may be enough in a particular sample; it depends largely upon the quality of the rhythm.

Dishonest acts may be either spontaneous or premeditated. Some people suffer no qualms about stealing, lying, or cheating on a daily basis. Then there are those who, in normal circumstances, would be horrified at the thought of committing a dishonest act. Yet, under pressure, when opportunity presents itself, they might cave in and behave in a manner that is out of character. Is the impoverished parent who sneaks a carton of milk to feed her baby in the same category as the teenager who shoplifts an iPod? Both stole, but with very different psychological motivations. The signs in handwriting will be different for both types. As Pulver points out, it's our job to interpret, not to judge.

Read the Road Signs

Some of the following red flags for dishonest behavior have been covered in previous chapters because they are part of the range of normal behaviors. However, outside the context of their "normal" meaning, and when combined with other negative traits, they take on a more menacing significance.

- ◆ *Cover stroke.* This is a stroke that literally covers over another stroke, making it look like a single line. To produce a cover stroke, the writer makes a sudden change of direction. An inappropriate change of direction in handwriting symbolizes a change of direction in the writer's thinking. He has second thoughts about revealing something.

   When the cover stroke is in the lower zone, which is less common, the writer may have something embarrassing to hide about his sex life. A cover stroke on a circular letter in the middle zone, such as *a* or *o*, is more difficult to execute than on a straight letter. It often indicates avoidance or denial of the truth. Again, embarrassment may be a factor.

Cover strokes and extreme t-*bars: the handwriting of convicted serial killer Bobby Joe Long.*

- *Slow arcade.* Often made by the hypocrite, the slow arcade writer is highly aware of the way things look. He is image-conscious and has a "do as I say, not as I do" attitude. An arcade at the end of a word which curls back to the left suggests a deliberate concealing of the truth, perhaps by evasion. Thus, it may not be an overt lie, but a sin of omission.

- *Secondary thread.* The writer is evasive in another way. Determined to avoid taking sides or committing to a specific course of action, he is opportunistic, manipulating and exploiting any situation he can to suit his own needs. In the worst case, the writer is a con artist who uses all kinds of chicanery and deception. He bends the truth the way he bends the middle zone. By remaining ambiguous, he dodges responsibility. If he can't be pinned down to a particular statement, he can't be blamed for the outcome.

- *Extremely wavy baseline.* This is less a sign of direct dishonesty than one of plain old unreliability. The writer may tell you he'll do something, but it never gets done because he is easily sidetracked. He'll say he's going to be somewhere, but never shows up. His passive-aggressive behavior keeps on edge anyone who is counting on him.

- *Counterstrokes.* These are strokes that turn in the direction opposite to what is normal and expected. One example is an ending stroke that should move to the right, but instead returns to the left. It's another form of evasiveness and covering up.

Counterstrokes: serial killer Westley Dodd, whose counterstrokes appear in the upper-zone letters, which bend in the wrong direction.

> There is a chance that through your work, you can believe you can, I'm not sure. On the other hand, I could harm a child. Thus, I am willing to continue I still have some doubts. I'll finish this letter in have a small sample of that.

- *Extremely long t-bars.* When the *t*-bars cover entire words, in combination with signs of rigidity (many angles, heavy pressure, cover strokes, etc.), they suggest a highly controlling nature.

- *Fragmented strokes.* Bent, or broken and patched-up, or *soldered* strokes suggest the writer wants to make himself look better than he is. Usually, however, he just ends up looking worse.

def•i•ni•tion

Strokes may be **soldered,** or patched up, by laying one stroke over the other. The difference between soldering and covering is that cover strokes are made in one movement, while soldered strokes are made separately.

◆ *Coiled forms.* Strokes that curl into shapes like a snail's shell are a sign of extreme self-centeredness. The coiled stroke goes into the center in a leftward motion, bringing everything back to the self. This is a form of elaboration that suggests vanity and a need to protect the ego. The writer draws attention to himself, but when things go wrong he makes excuses and will say anything to make himself look good.

Coiled forms: Marcus Wesson, incestuous father convicted of killing nine of his children.

◆ *Excessively complicated strokes.* These strokes reduce clarity and can come from a need to cover up information with excessive secrecy or to draw attention away from the truth. When the complications involve many circular strokes, it suggests a trap that the writer uses to lure and ensnare the unwary—a graphological "roach motel," with the roach on the outside.

◆ *Exaggerations.* Exaggerations of any sort draw the eye and obstruct the simple truth. You can expect self-aggrandizement, trickery, and bluffing from this writer. His need to push himself forward through these outlandish forms is a sign of insincerity and misrepresentation.

◆ *Double-looped ovals.* When made inside the communication letters (*a, o*), double loops slow things down and render clear communication difficult. The extra loops are, in effect, like trying to hear someone over the phone when his hand is covering the mouthpiece. The message comes through muffled at best.

Chicken Scratch

Oval letters that open at the bottom are called "embezzler's ovals," a major red flag. Many who write them commit heinous crimes far beyond embezzlement.

Embezzler's oval: bottoms of the letter a *in the handwriting of former Enron CEO Kenneth Lay.*

♦ *Letters are omitted.* In a slow handwriting where some letters are omitted, we conclude that the writer deliberately leaves out important information. Certain facts that might be detrimental to him if known are conveniently eliminated or swept under the rug. The same is true when ending strokes are suspended in midair, rather than returning to the baseline (called "trait suspendu"). Information is dropped; the writer is not telling the whole truth.

♦ *Letters made to look like other letters.* Similar to omitted letters, these represent a deliberate attempt to distort a situation and make it appear other than it is. A test of legibility is to take the word out of context and see if you can still read it.

♦ *Signature does not match the text.* This tells us that the writer is not what he seems. The form of the text tells the truth.

Felon's Claw or Cat's Paw

The so-called "felon's claw" (also known as "cat's paw") is included here because of its name. It actually has little to do with felons, and nothing at all to do with cats. The felon's claw is a counterstroke, made claw-shaped by its cramped arcade form, and is located in the middle and lower zones.

The person who chooses the claw shape has been made to feel guilty all his life. As an adult he repeatedly sets himself up for punishment by creating situations that result in the familiar feeling of shame. Deep down, the felon's-claw writer believes he is worthless and engages in behavior that validates that belief.

In the lower zone, the claw form is associated with guilt of a sexual nature. In most cases, the writer experienced sexual abuse in childhood and feels guilty about it, blaming himself rather than the perpetrator. Some graphologists have reported that felon's claws appearing in the middle zone, combined with contaminated oval letters (ovals with double loops or hooks inside them), are a sure sign of a thief!

He was found to be hyperintensive over a year ago, with loss of weight and

Felon's Claw: Dr. Harold Shipman, convicted of killing 15 of his elderly patients and a suspect in hundreds more deaths.

get out of my CpR

(1) Coiled form, (2) counterstroke/shark's tooth, (3) letter a that looks like something other than a.

No Evil *d* Goes Unpunished

The "maniac *d*": in a handwriting that is moving along normally, the small letter *d* (actually, it can be any upper-zone letter) suddenly flops over to the far right. We saw an example in the Zodiac Killer's writing earlier. It signifies sudden uncontrolled explosive behavior in someone who otherwise may appear as mild-mannered as a mouse. After he has acted out his rage, the writer returns to his normal behavior.

Mack the Knife

The "shark's tooth," so-named for its resemblance to the eating apparatus of the Great White, is a particularly unpleasant handwriting feature. It combines a counter-stroke with an inappropriately curved form and is easiest to see in the small letters *r*, *s*, *w*, *m*, and *n*. The final stroke of these letters bows opposite the direction it was intended to go and looks like a shark's tooth. This letter form exposes the cunning person who appears loyal and pats you on the back with one hand, while holding a knife he'll stab you with in the other. The writer tells you what he thinks you want to hear as he secretly furthers his own interests.

Unloving Spoonful

Graphologists seem to like giving silly names to oddly shaped strokes. The next one is called the "spoon-*e*." This fairly uncommon structure is a combination curve/angle where an angle doesn't belong, and is another example of a counterstroke.

The standard lowercase letter *e* begins at the center and makes a smooth outward motion that ends to the right. A spoon-*e*, on the other hand, starts with a straight stroke that is hidden by the curve. The movement requires a stop-and-turn motion, which puts a brake on the forward motion and results in the counterstroke.

The spoon-*e* writer is calculating and cautious under the guise of correctness. Strong self-control is indicated, not in the positive sense, but as in *premeditated* behavior. The writer doesn't show how he really feels, but acts in a way that he believes will produce the desired results. Evasive, cagey, and shrewd, he hides his true motives behind a pleasant face. The victim never sees it coming.

*Spoon-*e *(left), shark's tooth (right) , elliptical* g *(below).*

Spoon-*e*   Shark's tooth *r*

Elliptical *g*

The Awful Oval

As we run the gamut of unpleasant behavior, the elliptical *g* deserves a mention. The middle-zone portion of the letter, rather than being a smooth, round form, is squeezed into an ovoid shape diagonal to the baseline. The downstroke, which is supposed to go straight down, below the baseline, instead moves upward before descending with a rightward curve that looks like a backward *c*.

The writer is sly and devious, hiding his true intentions, which are to deceive and mislead. Those he deals with may not be able to quite put their finger on what's wrong because "he seems so nice!" They know only that they don't quite trust him. His motivations are self-centered, and he works to get what he wants, even at others' expense. He may be a braggart who boasts and puffs himself up. He wants to give the impression that he is far more than what he really is.

Stabbed oval: Dr. George Hodel, believed by his son Steve Hodel to be the infamous "Black Dahlia" killer. Note the stabbed oval, wide space between the message and the signature, and the strange G in his name, which obscures the message.

Stabbing strokes in the middle of oval letters (notably, *o, a, d*) indicate communication problems. One high-profile graphologist calls these the signs of the pathological liar.

Tales from the Quill

Ellen worked as a secretary for MediMart Pharmaceuticals for 7 years, smiling on the outside, but hating every moment of her job. One day she quit without notice. Before she left, Ellen secretly sabotaged the computer system, programming complicated passwords into the most important files and deleting dozens of others that were needed on a daily basis. She also left realistic-looking plastic bugs in the desk drawers of her former boss. Her otherwise copybook handwriting featured the elliptical *g*.

Downhill Racer: Signs of Violence

Strong variability in slant, baseline, size, and other aspects of a handwriting always adds to the negative interpretation of the red flags. Although the big picture is always more important than the small details, don't ignore the fine points. If you see any of the following red flags in a handwriting (especially when there are two or more of them), pay very close attention.

- *Extremely heavy pressure.* The writer is suffering from a buildup of excess frustration. He doesn't appropriately release his strong feelings, and may resort to drugs and alcohol which, in turn, may lead to violent behavior.

- *Variable pressure.* The writer of variable pressure is unpredictable, unreliable, and inconsistent. He blows hot and cold, and you never know when he'll fly into a rage. Variable pressure is often seen in the handwritings of convicted criminals.

- *Muddiness.* Muddy writing is a result of unrelieved pressure and exposes extreme tension in the writer. The writer lacks the intellect or the interest in trying to finesse his way through a situation. He simply blurts out whatever comes to mind, regardless of how unlikely the story. In combination with other negative traits, such as dot grinding, the writer may be sadistic. *Be careful how you interpret muddy writing, as there may be a physiological cause.*

- *Extreme right slant.* When combined with extremely heavy pressure, this is a dangerous combination—Molotov-cocktail dangerous. When this writer erupts, everyone in the immediate vicinity had better duck for cover, as he goes ballistic without warning.

- *Bizarre t-crosses.* Often seen in the handwritings of convicted criminals, these strange forms signify the writer's willingness to go to whatever ends are necessary to achieve his goals. The behavior is usually the most grossly violent type and may include torture.

- *Clubbed strokes.* When pressure suddenly thickens on the ends of letters or words, it signifies an outburst of emotion. If the thickened pressure looks like a club in the middle zone, you can be sure that the writer uses his words to bludgeon.

Clubbed strokes: former Green Beret doctor Jeffrey MacDonald, convicted of killing his pregnant wife and children.

- *Stabbing or slashing strokes.* Here's the opposite of the club stroke. This stroke starts out heavy on the left side and thins to a nasty-looking point that is made in a downward, slashing motion. The writer has a bad temper and a cruel tongue that slashes his victims. Watch out for sharp knives when he's angry.

Stabbing or slashing strokes: Erik Menendez of the Menendez brothers, who killed their parents.

- *Dot grinding.* When punctuation is extremely heavy and actually ground into the paper, it's called dot grinding. Kathy Urbiha, a registered nurse and graphologist who works with prison inmates, reports that she frequently sees dot grinding, particularly with compulsive-type sexual offenders. Inner tension and a habit of ruminating on or reliving the offending behavior is behind this characteristic.

- *Black spots.* The "black spot" is different from dot grinding, which presses heavily into the paper. The black spot is a filling in of a loop or circle with ink. Klara Roman identified it in people who suffer from guilt and feel that they have a "black spot" in their past that they need to hide. Interestingly, it's been seen in the handwritings of several attorneys!

Black spots: Carol Bundy (no relation to Ted Bundy) helped her serial killer boyfriend by putting makeup on his victims after death.

◆ *Harpoons.* These are extremely long, hooked strokes coming from below the baseline. These initial strokes, as seen in serial-killer Ted Bundy's handwriting, expose hidden aggressive behavior that is compulsively acted out.

Harpoons: serial killer Ted Bundy's long, hooked initial strokes.

◆ *Extreme angularity.* Handwriting in which the angle is the dominant connective form shows aggression. When combined with narrow forms and heavy pressure, the personality behind the writing is basically antisocial, having a need to dominate in relationships.

◆ *Disturbed rhythm.* When rhythm is either extremely brittle or extremely slack, the inner personality lacks harmony and the behavior shows it. The writer of brittle rhythm snaps at the least provocation. The writer of slack writing gives in to every impulse. Disturbed rhythm in combination with other red flags often indicates pathology.

◆ *Jump-up letters.* These are letters that pop up out of the middle zone and jump into the upper zone where they don't belong. Alone, they signify someone who is normally calm and passive, but occasionally rears up over others and asserts himself. They are a red flag when combined with other negative indicators.

◆ *Capitals in cursive.* When capital letters appear midword in cursive writing, the writer behaves inappropriately to get attention, like blurting out rude remarks or generally acting like a jerk.

◆ *Changing styles.* Writing that changes from cursive to printing, or to some other style in a relatively short period of time (from one paragraph to the next, for example) is an indication of unpredictable behavior. You never know how he's going to act.

Don't Drink and Write: Drugs and Alcohol

Substance abuse involves physiological as well as psychological changes. The handwriting indicators in the early stages of drug or alcohol abuse may be somewhat different from those found later. Research shows that a low level of alcohol in the blood has relatively little effect on handwriting. The writing tends to become slightly more irregular and may increase in size.

Once the writer is inebriated, his coordination is affected and motor disturbances appear in the handwriting. The letters grow in size, breaks between letters increase, and legibility is reduced. Finally, when the blood alcohol level rises to around .3, the person becomes incapable of writing at all, and will probably lose consciousness.

Even with short-term alcohol use, motor activities can become impaired. If you've ever been with someone who'd had "one too many," you couldn't help but notice his slurred speech, unsteady walk, and clumsy movements. The motor system was affected by the alcohol and it shows up in the handwriting.

Hallucinogens, such as marijuana and LSD, affect the liver, spleen, gall bladder, lungs, and nerve centers of the brain. Used over a period of time, some types of recreational drug use can result in tremor that carries over to handwriting. Tremor shows up as a very shaky-looking writing line. LSD use is characterized by bizarre forms of letters. Overwriting is sometimes seen in the handwriting of heroin users. Overwriting is a matter of the writer literally tracing the letters over and over again.

The Least You Need to Know

- Honesty is hard to determine for certain in handwriting.
- There are some definite red flags that can help you determine the level of potential for bad behavior.
- The red flags signify potential only. We do not know whether the writer will act on that potential.
- Drugs and alcohol impair handwriting.

Part 6

The Last Word

Before wrapping up your study of handwriting analysis, you'll need to know how to report what you've found. That's what we'll do in this part. We'll also deal with some practical matters, such as how to turn all this knowledge into a paying business, and how to keep yourself and your clients out of court.

Is graphology the career for you? Whether you decide to go forward full-bore or use what you've learned just for your own personal enlightenment, you'll now have a good foundation for understanding yourself and others in a way you never thought possible.

Chapter 20

And They Lived Happily Ever After

In This Chapter

- ◆ Compatibility isn't enough
- ◆ Essential ingredients
- ◆ Similar drives help
- ◆ Relationship nightmares

Have you ever begun a relationship that seemed absolutely wonderful, only to have it turn out perfectly awful? That guy you just knew was Mr. Right couldn't have been more wrong? Or the woman you adored suddenly transmuted into a totally alien screaming meemie?

It's easy to be on our best behavior on the first date when everything about the new guy or gal is electrifying, sensational, and all those other superlatives that rarely survive the first blush of romance. But once the humdrum rhythm of daily life sets in and the shiny newness begins to wear off, those annoying little foibles start showing up.

Handwriting supplies much of the information you need to bring out the best and understand the worst in a relationship. Appreciating your partner's motivations and needs *before* entering the relationship could help you to avoid a lot of needless heartache.

Not that graphology can fix up a bad match or stop you from falling into a victim role, if that's what you do. Other important factors also enter into the equation, such as chemistry and goodwill. What an analysis will do, however, is equip you to recognize negative patterns that you may be guilty of perpetuating so that you can begin to break out of them.

Goodwill Hunting

So you've met this guy. He's got everything on your list: tall, dark, handsome, great personality, good job, nice car, and his own home. And he's not married. What more could a girl ask for? Try goodwill. Without it, a relationship is doomed. Goodwill is an attitude that overrides circumstances that might otherwise cause the relationship to fail. Goodwill implies willingness to overlook the other partner's imperfections and weaknesses, and to show unconditional love. I couldn't say it any better than the Bible: *Love believes all things, hopes all things, endures all things. Love never fails.* (I Corinthians 13:7)

This isn't to suggest that either party should compromise to the point of being a pushover, a doormat, or accepting abuse. The goodwill has to flow in both directions. If only one person is showing goodwill toward the other, the relationship becomes like a car with a flat tire. It may limp along for a while, but eventually, the tire will fall off the wheel, resulting in major damage.

It would be great if goodwill could be seen in handwriting, but all we can do as graphologists is point out areas of strength that the couple can build on, and those nasty old potential trouble spots that need work.

The Happy Couple

So, what makes for a happy couple? Two people may have everything it takes for a compatible relationship, but it doesn't work out. On the other side of the coin, a couple may seem so different that they are totally incompatible, but if both want to make the relationship work, it will. Chemistry is the magic ingredient. Like goodwill, chemistry is not something you'll find in handwriting, so we'll have to start with what we *can* find.

I asked the members of the Vanguard Forum Online (an online handwriting analysis discussion group) what they felt were the most important elements of a good relationship. Sex was cited only a couple of times. The top three, mentioned by nearly all who responded, were the following qualities:

- Good communicator

- Sense of humor

- Sensitivity

> ### Tales from the Quill
>
> I especially liked Vanguard member Alice Konkel's response to "What do you look for in a mate?" She said, "I would look for someone who can really get their arms around life, easy to laugh, especially at himself, cries from the soul and smiles big and with his eyes. He needs to be smart enough to be interesting. He needs to have enough passion to take a stand on important things, but they don't need to be my things."

Driving Miss Daisy Crazy

Although opposites attract in some ways, there are a couple of areas where it is important for both parties to be at least in the same ballpark. Physical drive is one of them, intelligence is the other.

There are times when life can be so filled with problems that sex is the only fun thing you've got going for you. A partner who shares the same drives and intimate interests can make everything look a little brighter; for a couple whose drives are very different, a rough road may lie ahead.

If you have low energy, it's not very pleasant to be browbeaten by your high-energy partner into visiting friends after a long day of work, when all you want to do is curl up in bed with a whodunit. Neither does it feel good to the energetic person if he's forced into being a couch potato, just because his low-energy mate doesn't feel like going out. Clearly, couples with similar physical drives are likely to be more content with each other than couples whose drives are very different.

Like everything else in handwriting, drive is determined by looking at a cluster of factors. Look at the whole page of writing: is the energy "moving"? Or is it stagnant, sitting rooted to the page, going nowhere? That's the first clue. Pressure and pastosity are also important factors. Thicker, heavier-pressured writing, while not an indicator of physical strength, does reveal stronger drives.

Check the length and width of the lower loops. The longer and wider they are, the greater the drive, but only to a point. Extreme length and width, however, may be interpreted quite differently (we'll discuss that a bit later). Here are some typical characteristics of different drives:

Low drive

- Writing looks static, with little rightward movement
- Light pressure
- Short, cramped lower zone
- Sharp ductus (stroke edge is clean and thin)

Moderate drive

- Moderate movement to the right
- Medium pressure
- Lower zone is copybook length and width
- Medium ductus (stroke edge is neither thin and sharp nor thick and fuzzy)

Strong drive

- Strong left-to-right overall movement
- Medium to heavy pressure
- Moderately long and full lower zone
- Pastose ductus (thick stroke)

Excessive drive

- Extreme rightward movement
- Very heavy pressure
- Extremely long and/or full lower zone
- Muddy ductus (messy ink flow, blobs)

Letter about Odd Thomas. Sorry to have taken so long to reply, but I was working 90 and more hours a week to finish Velocity and dropped the ball on all correspondence.

Strong drive: novelist Dean Koontz's vigorous writing reveals drive, stamina, and enthusiasm for life.

When I left my home on Tuesday, October 25, I was very emotionally distraught. I didn't want to live anymore! I felt like things could never get any worse. When I left home, I was going to ride around a little while and then go to my mom's. As I rode

Weak drive: "Killer Mom" Susan Smith's writing just sits on the page, unsure and depressed.

Intelligence

The other factor that should be fairly equal is intelligence. It's easier to share your mate's interests when you understand them. That doesn't mean you have to play golf or go to the opera if you hate it, but at least you can relate on some level to what the other person enjoys, and you can discuss it. Intelligence in handwriting is seen in the organization, positive departures from copybook, and expressiveness.

Fine Points

IQ can be accurately determined from handwriting. There's a formula that scores five characteristics (organization, simplification, expressiveness, rhythm, and originality) in handwriting. The resulting score is usually within about five points of the Stanford-Binet test score.

Divorce Court

It's a fascinating fact that what first attracts one person to another frequently is the same thing that ends up turning them off. The man who enjoys his girlfriend's independence and ability to be self-supporting may end up resenting the fact that she doesn't need him to take care of her. Or, the woman who is attracted to a man because he is sensitive to her feelings may later become angry with him for being a wimp.

Every relationship has its good and bad points; no one is 100 percent at fault for what goes wrong. We choose each other for a reason, but sometimes one person outgrows that reason and it may be time to move on. Besides, some relationships were never meant to be.

In this section, we'll discuss some relationships you will probably want to avoid. On the other hand, if you are looking to be neglected, criticized, or outright abused, there's someone for everyone. All types can apply to both sexes.

Tales from the Quill

Sally's husband, Mark, started working the night shift. When he arrived home in the morning, Sally was getting ready for her day. They hardly had time for a quick kiss hello and goodbye, let alone sex. Sally didn't want to give up the morning hours to stay in bed with Mark, and he resented it. However, a handwriting analysis revealed more fundamental problems in their relationship than the sexual frustration caused by their schedules.

Romancing the Stone

Outgoing Ellen saw Bruce as the strong, silent type, which she thought meant he was powerful and protective. But shortly after the wedding, when he sat silent in front of the television night after night, rebuffing her attempts at conversation, she felt she had hit a stone wall.

The Stone Wall doesn't relate well to others, except in the early stages of courtship, when he's pretending to be someone he's not. He doesn't need or want much social interaction. In fact, he's much happier on his own or with someone who will leave him alone in his own world. He's withholding and emotionally cold. Because he doesn't understand personal relationships, he expends his energy developing his intellectual side instead.

The Stone Wall type

- Very wide overall spacing, particularly word spacing, and very wide right margin
- Very small size
- Extremely simplified forms
- Cramped lower zone
- Sharp, pointed strokes
- Linear, not curved style

I admire what you are doing to help those who have had

The Stone Wall type: Dr. Jonas Salk's writing suggests someone caught up in his intellect to the exclusion of social interaction, although he could be charming when the situation warranted.

Flirt Alert

The Flirt is a social butterfly who's happiest when she's center stage. She won't sit on the sidelines, waiting to be introduced, but claims the spotlight. She seeks intense, passionate relationships; just don't count on her for long-term commitment. She doesn't want to deal with anything unpleasant, and if you get sad or sick, she won't be around for long.

The Flirt demands lots of attention, affection, and approval. Without it, she'll soon be in the arms of someone else. If you want fun and excitement with no strings attached, the Flirt may be what you are looking for. However, if what you seek is a nurturing life partner, you're in for a rocky ride.

Thanks for everything !

Theresa Russell

The Flirt type: actress Theresa Russell's large, showy writing indicates someone who is comfortable in the limelight.

The Flirt

- Loose rhythm

- Showy, elaborate capitals

- Elaborate writing with swirls and decorations

- Lots of rightward movement

- Narrow right margin

- Wavy baseline

- Large lower zone

Mission Impossible

Those who feel compelled to brag about their sexual prowess frequently don't perform when it comes down to the nitty-gritty. There are several possibilities. *Extreme* width in the lower zone suggests someone who spends a lot more time fantasizing about sex than acting out her fantasies. Someone who is sexually frustrated, perhaps due to impotence, may make a downstroke that ends in a tic instead of a loop. Whether the impotence is physically or emotionally based is for a doctor to decide.

Extremely long loops are another sign of frustration. The energy stays in the lower zone, unreleased. Such individuals may use sex more as a tranquilizer than as a means of emotional, as well as physical, intimacy. They flit from partner to partner, seeking as much sex as they can get, yet never feeling satisfied. The sexual addict would fall under this category.

Women Who Love Men Who Walk All Over Them

Some people call her the Earth Mother, others, the Caretaker. And then there are those who tell it like it is: she's the professional Doormat.

Loving someone means treating that person kindly and caring about his needs. This type of person goes far beyond that. She lives to help others, and puts her own needs last, if she considers them at all. Her biggest fear is of not being seen as loving and helpful. It's easy to take advantage of this type. She won't say no even when it's in her best interests.

The Doormat type is attracted to bad boys: drug addicts, alcoholics, criminals, or just plain creeps. She is sure she can rescue them, but what usually happens to rescuers is that they eventually resent it that their efforts at "helping" are not appreciated. They then shift into the abuser role as they begin nagging, "after all I've done for you ...." This losing *victim-rescuer-abuser triad* sounds like Alice's tea party with the Mad Hatter, where everyone would periodically get up and move around to the next seat.

def•i•ni•tion

The **victim-rescuer-abuser triad** is a common occurrence in unhealthy relationships. Eventually, both partners take turns playing all of the roles.

The Doormat

- Small-medium overall size
- Garland forms
- PPI is especially curved on the downstroke
- Bowed *t*-bars
- Light pressure
- Slight downhill slant to the baseline
- Close word spacing

The Doormat type: Nicole Brown Simpson's overly rounded writing reveals the need for attention, affection, and approval.

Men Who Love Women Who Let Them Walk All Over Them

The Doormat usually gets walked on by the type of partner who acts like a T-rex. He's aggressive, critical, and a Perfectionist. He knows everything, and you are nothing in his eyes. Everything must be done the Perfectionist's way, or else. The "or else" might include yelling, name calling, or even physical violence.

The Perfectionist

- Very heavy pressure

- Either muddy or very sharp writing

- Strong right slant

- Compressed, narrow writing

- Tall upper zone

The Perfectionist type: aviator Charles Lindbergh's handwriting contains several characteristics of the Perfectionist.

Call Me Irresponsible

Loving a Peter Pan type may be fun for some, but it can also be emotionally draining. You never know whether he will show up on time, or even show up at all. Is he telling the truth or not? It's anyone's guess. The boy who never grew up doesn't stick to social conventions. He makes up his own rules as he goes along. This type is a con artist who will say or do whatever it takes to get him what he wants.

The Peter Pan

- Secondary thread forms combined with angle forms

- Light pressure

- Complications in the middle zone

- Loose, slack, or disturbed rhythm

- Strong right slant

abused + runaway children is an excellent one. I plan on doing the same thing. Don't lose sight of that goal. The

The Peter Pan type: Lyle Menendez, convicted of helping his brother kill their parents, has the slack rhythm of the Peter Pan.

Attila and His Hun

The Attila is an extreme personality type, but one that is insidious enough and found frequently enough to mention. Former FBI profiler Roy Hazelwood interviewed a group of women who had all had relationships with men who, it turned out, were sexual sadists. These women (Hazelwood calls them the Compliant Victim types) were not poor, innocent young girls who were ignorant about men and relationships. In fact, Hazelwood described them as well-groomed, articulate, and intelligent. They ranged across a wide spectrum of education and careers, from a fire systems engineer, to an insurance broker, secretary, nurse, and loan officer. Yet, they shared several personality traits:

- Low self-esteem

- An all-encompassing fear of abandonment

- Inability to deal with criticism

- Distrust of others

- Difficulty making decisions

- Fear of emotional withdrawal by their partner

- Inability to show their emotions

Fine Points

The main difference between the handwriting of a Compliant Victim and that of an ordinary "nice" person is the rhythm. The Compliant Victim type's rhythm is droopy and slack, while the just-plain-nice person's rhythm looks stronger, more elastic.

Every woman interviewed said that the man she became involved with was charming and that nothing stood out about him as unusual or threatening. Eventually, though, the abuser revealed himself as extremely possessive. He set up rules for his partner's behavior and refused to allow her even to go to the store alone or without permission. He isolated her from friends and family until she was entirely dependent upon him for everything. He cut her off from everything she used to care about as an individual.

The Compliant Victim

♦ Excessive roundedness

♦ Medium-large overall size

♦ Crowded spacing

♦ PPI rounded and lying on its back

The Compliant Victim type: Carol Bundy, a nurse who helped her serial killer boy-friend, has perfect Compliant Victim handwriting.

Sadistic Attila men have a strong need to be in control, and often have friendships where they dominate the other person. They usually have stable jobs. Because their schtick involves dominating an unwilling partner, they tend to prey on conventional, loving women.

The Attila Type

♦ Long, heavy *t*-bars

♦ Extremely heavy punctuation

♦ Very heavy pressure

♦ Muddy ductus

♦ Strong degree of narrowness, retracing

♦ Extremely long, narrow lower zone

♦ Very rigid overall

The Attila type: convicted wife-killer Herbert Brenk's writing contains the heavy, slashing strokes of an angry man.

Dump That Chump

You may know an abuser whose handwriting doesn't fall into one of these categories. Those listed here are very general types, intended just to give you an idea of what to look for. If the abuser has no remorse, his or her handwriting may not show some of the characteristics that would otherwise appear.

The important thing to understand is, abuse doesn't have to be physical. A partner's words can beat as painfully on their victim as fists. If someone mistreats you, regardless of what his handwriting shows, do something about it. Get help from a therapist, support group, or minister. Don't allow yourself to be abused. *It almost certainly won't get better.*

Handwriting analysis should never be the sole deciding factor in whether you should or shouldn't marry someone, but it can arm you with what you need to know about each other's temperament, needs, and motivations. By identifying potential problem areas and learning how to build on strengths, your chances of a happy, satisfying relationship will be greatly improved.

> **Chicken Scratch**
>
> One major red flag for the sadistic type is extremely heavy pressure, which shows unrelenting frustration and anger. When combined with a strong right slant or large, block-printed writing, very dark punctuation, and pressure so strong that it leaves deep ridges on the other side of the paper, these warning signals should not be ignored.

The Least You Need to Know

- ◆ It's not the graphologist's responsibility to determine whether a couple is compatible, but only to show areas of strength and potential problems.

- ◆ Relationships are often happiest when both partners have matching physical drives.

- ◆ Couples with similar intellectual development and interests can develop a deeper level of sharing.

- ◆ Handwriting usually gives clues to abusive behavior, but they may be so subtle that you won't recognize them. Pay attention to the behavior.

21

Writing the Analysis

In This Chapter

- ◆ What do you do, now that you know what you know?
- ◆ Putting it in the blender
- ◆ The mini-analysis
- ◆ Going more in-depth

So, you've got all this wonderful knowledge about handwriting. Now, what do you do with it? As you've discovered, no one particular element of the writing can be interpreted out of context. Knowing that the writing is right-slanted might tell you that the writer is moderately emotional, but you need more information to get a good "fix" on the personality. For instance, along with the slant, the pressure will reveal how long the emotions stay with the writer. Then you need to add information about the margins to know whether the writer's emotions are holding him back; and all the other pieces of the puzzle that play a part in making the writer who he really is.

This chapter will help you put all those discrete pieces together into a coherent whole. You'll learn how to synthesize your findings and to see that the whole is always greater than the sum of its parts—that's the gestalt.

Putting It All Together: The First Impression

When you first look at a handwriting sample it can seem like a jigsaw puzzle of a thousand pieces, all in the same color. Even though you've learned the basic principles of handwriting analysis, you may not yet have achieved that "aha!" flash of insight that gives you the key to understanding the essence of the writer's personality.

Making up a "laundry list" of traits is easy. Anyone can pick out "resentment strokes," "yieldingness strokes," "vanity strokes." Many handwriting analysts never move beyond this stage, not understanding the need to evaluate each trait against the others. A report that speaks to the writer's heart takes more than just a superficial dusting on the surface of his personality. It means having a thorough understanding of the writer's motivations and needs.

Don't be discouraged; there are no tricks and you don't have to be psychic. The ability to look at a handwriting and quickly grasp the core personality can be learned. Using some specific techniques that will help you synthesize and fit together all those things you know, you'll master it before you can say "graphogobbldygook."

Finding the Guiding Image

Synthesis means making a series of deductions to arrive at the desired end—an accurate picture of the writer's personality. There are several methods of synthesis that apply graphological theories or principles. Trial and error will tell what works best for you.

def•i•ni•tion

Guiding image is the writer's core personality. It's the underlying character of the writer, which you can find in the two major opposing forces in the handwriting you are examining.

One method is to find the *guiding image*. Everyone has personality conflicts or contradictions of some type, and the guiding image is made up of the two major opposing forces in the personality. For instance, let's say the writing has a strong right slant, showing a need to move out toward others, but at the same time, the spaces between the words are very wide, which indicates a need for the writer to separate himself from others.

He needs to move toward others and also has a need for space? Sounds like a contradiction, doesn't it? These are the opposing forces or the basic conflict in the writer's personality. Examining the surrounding factors in the writing will explain the apparent inconsistency. Perhaps the writer *wants* to reach out to others but is afraid to (that's what a narrow middle zone would show).

Once you are able to identify the opposing forces, you'll have a basis for writing the analysis. The following checklist will help to get you started by giving you some specific traits to look for in the writing. I've included some hints in parentheses so you'll know where to look in the writing. You can photocopy the list and check off each appropriate item on your copy.

Handwriting Analysis Checklist

__ Emotionally responsive (right slant)

__ Emotionally reserved (upright slant)

__ Retains past emotional experiences (strong pressure)

__ Quickly forgets emotional experiences (light pressure)

__ Detail-oriented (careful *i*-dots and *t*-crosses)

__ Prefers the big picture more than small details (*i*-dots and *t*-crosses high and to the right)

__ Sensitive to criticism (big loops)

__ Criticism has little effect (no loops)

__ Enjoys verbal communication (large middle zone)

__ Tends to be secretive (small middle zone)

__ Relies on intuition to make decisions (smooth breaks)

__ Logical thinker (strong connectedness)

__ Enjoys physical activity (large lower zone)

__ Sedentary type (small lower zone)

__ Well organized (balanced overall arrangement)

__ Needs help getting organized (messy overall arrangement)

Using statements from the checklist, write on a new sheet of paper a couple of sentences describing the writer's personality. For instance, take "logical thinker." You could say something like this: "John is a logical thinker. That means he is more comfortable having all the facts and figures before making a decision, and is less likely to listen to his intuition."

See how easy that is? Do that for each item and you'll quickly have a one-page analysis. Once you're comfortable with doing these quickie profiles, you'll be ready to go on to a more detailed analysis.

> ### Tales from the Quill
>
> You are welcome to copy the handwriting checklist and make it into a trait chart to give friends when you're practicing your skills, or you can make your own. Just leave out the notes in parentheses and check off the items that apply to their handwriting. With practically no effort at all, you've given them a mini-analysis! Believe me, they'll be impressed!

How Do You Do? Asking the Writing Questions

Asking the writing questions helps you get deeper into the writer's personality. Just be ready to listen to the answers. How can you ask a writing question? Will it answer you? Following are some examples and clues on how to find the answers in the writing:

1. Is the writer reactive or proactive?

   Reactive: Variable slant, baseline, middle zone height; small or poorly formed capital letters.

   Proactive: Good rhythm, direction, speed; zonal balance.

2. Is the writer resilient or not?

   Resilient: Strong left to right movement, fluidity, rhythm.

   Not Resilient: Variable baseline, dished *t*-bars, slack ductus.

3. Does the writer have initiative or not?

   Has initiative: Simplification, lack of beginning strokes, speed, stick PPI.

   Lacks initiative: Long beginning strokes, slowness, school type, elaboration.

4. Does the writer acknowledge his mistakes and learn from them or not?

   Learns from mistakes: Zonal balance, upper zone not too tall, lower zone returns to baseline.

   Justifies and rationalizes mistakes: Upper zone too tall and narrow, copybook style, complicated ovals.

5. Does the writer keep his feelings to himself or act them out?

   Inhibits feelings: poorly formed lower zone, narrowness, wide right margin, narrow left margin, sharp ductus.

   Acts out feelings: right slant, elaborate capitals, moderate to large size, heavy pressure, pastosity.

6. Does the writer keep commitments?

   Reliability: Good rhythm, left to right movement, balance, harmony, clear middle zone, clear line spacing, no zonal interference.

   Impulsive: Wavy baseline, variable pressure, slackness, muddiness.

7. Does the writer use his imagination and willpower for goal setting?

   Goal-setting: Well formed upper zone, strong horizontal movement, good pressure.

8. Does the writer feel secure within himself?

   Sense of security: Good rhythm, well-formed capitals (especially the PPI), good pressure.

9. Does the writer have a clear perspective on life?

   Perspective: Good zonal balance, overall clear spacing, good margins.

10. Does the writer make and keep commitments to himself and others? A function of self-discipline and will power.

    Integrity: Good rhythm, simplification of form, fluidity, moderate pressure, clear ovals, balance.

11. Does the writer have goals, a mission in life?

    Goal-directed: Strong left to right movement, pressure, balanced margins, moderately straight baseline.

12. What motivates the writer?

    Approval: Rounded writing, strong garlands, long lead-in strokes, bowed *t*-bars, variable baseline.

    Money and material possessions: Heavy pressure, overblown lower zone, pastosity.

    Pleasure and comfort: Large middle and lower zones, pastosity, loose rhythm, ending strokes return to the left, extra large capitals, narrow right margin, narrow line spacing.

    Recognition: Moderately strong pressure, large capitals, good rhythm.

Other Questions You Could Ask

You might not want to use these in the analysis, but it helps to imagine the writer in different life situations. Ask yourself how the writer would …

- React in a traffic jam?

- Handle an irate customer?

- Deal with a child having a tantrum in public?

- Act at a party?

- Perform in bed?

- Ask the boss for a raise?

- Break off a bad relationship?

Using the Gestalt Method to Analyze a Handwriting

Let's analyze a handwriting for practice. The writing of the following sample is that of former first lady Senator Hillary Rodham Clinton.

How Does It Look?

Using the gestalt method, we start with how the writing looks overall:

- *General impression:* The handwriting is lively and active, with an emphasis on movement. The organization is pretty good, although it could be improved by a little more space between the lines (the paper size may have affected the spatial arrangement, if she wanted to fit her message onto one page).

- *Form level (form level is a combination of many factors, but it basically means "does the writing look well balanced and harmonious or not"):* Good form level with simplified, original forms. The signature is congruent with the text of the sample.

- *Space/form/movement:* In the overall picture of space, form, and movement, there is good balance.

- *Picture of space:* Moderately good distribution of space between words, lines, letters, and well-balanced margins. The left margin is a little narrow, but again, that may be a factor of paper size.

Handwriting sample: Hillary Rodham Clinton.

Dear Mr. Klein,

    I did a double take when I looked at the photo you made of Eleanor Roosevelt and me, wondering what I was wearing at the time it was taken because my clothes were not immediately recognizable to me. Then it dawned on me I was looking at another miracle of modern times! What a high compliment the article and photo are — even to be compared with Mrs. Roosevelt. I will try to be worthy of that.

    With best wishes,

      Hillary Rodham Clinton

- *Picture of form:* Simplified, original forms with some irregularity.

- *Picture of movement:* Rapid progression from left to right with moderate rhythmical pressure. Some of the return strokes in lower zone letters are stunted by hooks.

What is the conclusion? This is an original writing with a medium-size middle zone, largely connected, with interesting letter combinations. Garlands and arcades predominate with a mixture of curved and linear forms that are disproportionately short in the lower zone.

The Synthesis

In putting our overall impressions together, it helps to give them a context. Let's break them up into four areas: intellect, social skills, drives, and controls. This will give you a place to start and will provide a good overview of the personality.

- *Intellect:* Original, rhythmic, quick, simplified, connected. Hillary is a quick thinker who doesn't suffer fools gladly. She has the ability to come up with her own unique ways of doing things, rather than relying on the old tried and true methods that worked in the past.

- *Social skills:* Strong movement, right slant, good pressure pattern, stunted lower zone, some irregularity. She is sensitive and understands complex people-problems. Her strong intuition and flexibility allows her to deal with many personality types on their own level.

- *Drives:* Good pressure, somewhat stunted lower zone, irregularity. She's an intellectually lively, active individual whose enthusiasm is quickly aroused and discharged. Good stamina and vitality help her get through a long day.

- *Controls:* Tension, irregularity, connectedness, good organization. Hillary is spontaneous and may be impulsive at times, but with generally good self-discipline. She adapts well on a surface level, but is unlikely to change her value system, even under pressure.

- *Self-image:* Modest PPI and other capitals, medium-size middle zone, strong left-to-right, good upper zone movement. The writer is independent, with the ability to project her needs onto the world. She's not afraid to reach out for what she wants on the surface, but she may neglect some of her deeper needs.

Typecasting: Using Typologies

Using typologies can help speed up the process of analysis by as much as 75 percent. Typologies categorize personality types into groups and are used by many psychologists. The Myers-Briggs Type Indicator, based on Jung's two attitudes and four functions, is widely used.

Jung described two attitudes—extrovert and introvert—and four ways of functioning—thinking, feeling, sensing, and intuiting. Although one function is used primarily, everyone uses all the functions to some degree or another.

Think of how much information you would already have if you could look at a handwriting sample and immediately decide whether the writer was an introvert or an extrovert. That's pretty easy, isn't it? Identifying thinking or feeling, sensing or intuiting, is nearly as easy and supplies a tremendous amount of information about the person. You can apply what you know about the general type, and personalize it to fit the writing you are analyzing.

Besides Jung's, some of the other typologies I've found helpful include Freud's neurotic types: Depressive, Schizoid, Obsessional, and Histrionic; Fromm's Receptive, Exploitive, Hoarding, Marketing types; Adler's Comfort, Pleasing, Superiority, and Control types; Maslow's hierarchy of needs; and the Enneagram with its nine types.

My favorite book on Freud's types is *The Art of Psychotherapy* (Methuen, 1979, 1980) by Anthony Storr. If you're interested in learning about the Enneagram, try *The Enneagram Made Easy* (HarperCollins, 1994) by Elizabeth Wagele and Renee Baron. Felix Klein wrote monographs describing Fromm's, Maslow's, and Adler's types and their handwriting equivalents.

> **Fine Points**
>
> There are numerous books in print on the Myers-Briggs types, such as *Please Understand Me*, by Kiersey & Bates (www.keirsey.com), and *Type Talk*, by Kroeger & Thuesen (www.typetalk.com). Several handwriting analysts (including yours truly) have also written monographs applying Jung's and other types to handwriting.

Saying What You See—Writing the Report

The report you provide speaks for you. Always edit your work carefully. Typographical errors, misspellings, and poor grammar detract from the message. Long, run-on sentences tend to be confusing and obfuscate the meaning. Try to figure out what this analyst is trying to say:

> The writer has a desire to distinguish himself from others, at the same time enjoying the approval of others, although he is self-reliant and at ease with people, evaluating and appraising others in a critical, fault-finding way.

Huh? This sentence was taken from an actual analysis that someone paid good money for. Let's try rearranging and rewording it:

> While the writer enjoys the approval of other people, he wants to distinguish himself from the crowd. Once he becomes comfortable in a group, however, he tends to be critical and fault-finding.

Fine Points

Keep a style and grammar manual handy. Strunk & White's *The Elements of Style* and *The Elements of Grammar* (Allyn & Bacon, 1995) are excellent, but *Woe is I* (G.P. Putnam's Sons, 1996) by Patricia T. O'Connor is also a lot of fun to read.

Some sentences should be short and to the point, connected by slightly longer, explanatory ones. Read the analysis out loud. If anything sounds blurred or confusing to you, it certainly won't be clear to the client. Rewrite or cut out any sentence that doesn't read well.

Use easily understood language, not graphological or psychological jargon. And never make psychological or medical diagnoses unless you are legally qualified to do so. If you stick to describing behavior, you'll be doing your job.

The Mechanics

Make sure you know what question is to be answered by the analysis. Is it a profile that needs only to cover the high points of the personality? Or a comprehensive analysis that will discuss the more in-depth issues, such as childhood development? Or, is the report meant to determine whether the writer's personality is suitable for a job?

The profile analysis is usually about 350 to 700 words long. That's one to two typed pages. It should be an overview of the writer's strengths and weaknesses, and isn't the place to discuss early childhood trauma. A comprehensive report is usually several pages long and is often accompanied by various charts or graphs. This is where it's appropriate to thoroughly discuss all aspects of the writer's background and show how it helped to mold his temperament.

There are three parts common to all analyses—a beginning, a middle, and an end. What's important is to make everything in each of those parts accurate and beneficial to the client. An introductory paragraph outlining what handwriting analysis is and what the client can expect isn't a bad idea. Then, make a statement about the purpose of the analysis.

Be upbeat. You have the power to wound with your words, and no one is all bad. Even the lowest form-level (worst-looking!) writing has something you can comment on in a complimentary way. Analyses should always begin and end on a positive note. You want to provide self-knowledge, not a reason for self-immolation. Dealing with someone's psyche is a tremendous responsibility, and your analysis can have a favorable effect if you present it well. Any negatives should be sandwiched somewhere in the middle and discussed diplomatically.

End the analysis on an encouraging note that will leave the client feeling hopeful and eager to improve his life with the information you have provided. A call to some type of action leaves the client feeling that he has benefited from the report. You might offer some suggestions for graphotherapy if you've studied that branch of graphology, or psychotherapy, if called for.

The handwriting itself will tell you how to approach the client. If the style is highly simplified, stripped of any extra strokes, you can be more direct and candid, and tell it like it is. If a writing has many loops and garlands, the client is very sensitive and needs kid-glove handling.

Chicken Scratch

Be very careful how you word negative information in a report. Put yourself in the reader's place. Would you appreciate reading, "Joe, your handwriting shows you are suicidal and were sexually abused as a child"? Instead, it probably would be more useful to say something like this: "I can see that you've endured some very painful and difficult life experiences."

Don't Try This at Home: Analysis Do's and Don'ts

There are some do's and don'ts to consider when you write your analyses:

Do:

- ◆ Answer any questions directly and accurately.
- ◆ Be sure you can back up every statement in your report.
- ◆ Couch negative comments in diplomatic language.
- ◆ Make suggestions for developing weak areas.
- ◆ Allow the client room to disagree. You may be wrong. Or you may be right and he just isn't ready to accept it right now.

Don't:

- ◆ Diagnose physical or mental illness without a license.
- ◆ Forget what it's like to be the person who is being analyzed. Remind yourself how vulnerable you felt when it was *your* writing under the magnifying glass.
- ◆ Be dogmatic.
- ◆ Be too hard on yourself if you miss something important or are just plain wrong. Every graphologist has a humiliating story to share.

Professional Is as Professional Does

You must be able to coherently report your findings or you will have wasted your time and your client's. Some analysts provide verbal reports, while others are more comfortable in writing. One advantage to a verbal report is being able to explain what you mean on the spot (sometimes a reader misunderstands what the writer meant). On the other hand, when the client has the report in hand, he can reread and review the material easily. If writing isn't your forte, consider taking a creative or business writing course. If verbalizing your opinions makes you nervous, try attending a local Toastmasters group.

A poorly prepared report full of grammatical and typographical errors detracts from the message and reflects poorly on you and on graphology as a profession. If you do your part to present a professional image, we all benefit.

The Least You Need to Know

- ◆ The analysis should be a synthesis of all the writing elements, not just a list of traits.

- ◆ A checklist will help you get started writing the analysis.

- ◆ Ask the writing questions about specific situations to help you get deeper into the personality.

- ◆ Choosing a typology will help you get lots of extra information about the writer.

Chapter 22

Making Handwriting Analysis Pay

In This Chapter

- You *can* make money as a graphologist!
- Creating a clear vision
- The computer, graphology, and you
- What's legal, what's not
- Working in the real world

How much money would you like to make, working as a handwriting analyst? Thirty thousand dollars a year? Fifty? One hundred thousand dollars? More? The good news is, there *are* graphologists who are making a good living doing what they love, and you can, too.

When I began my full-time graphology practice in 1989, I had been analyzing handwriting, first as a hobby, then part-time for more than 20 years. In 1989, I thought I was doing quite well, having prepared some 300 handwriting analysis reports for individuals. Five years later, I found myself writing more than 1,000 reports a year. That's an average of five a day, every day, which is more handwriting than I ever expected or wanted to analyze!

The point is, you *can* become a successful handwriting professional if you have the keys to unlock the door to success in the field. Like any entrepreneurial business, starting a handwriting consulting practice takes commitment, hard work, and, unless you're independently wealthy, a leap of faith. But in this field there's an additional challenge that you'll have to overcome.

Doctors, lawyers, and other consultants don't need to explain what their work is to the people they are hoping will turn into clients. Handwriting analysis, on the other hand, often meets with skepticism because many people have never heard of it, and others believe it's akin to fortune-telling. So along with selling our services, we sometimes have to educate prospective clients about what we do.

Be Committed

The first step to success in any endeavor is setting an intention, a goal; make a commitment, then create a workable plan to accomplish it. Start the process by asking yourself some serious questions:

♦ Am I willing to give up time with my family while I build a graphology practice? And will my family cooperate?

♦ Am I willing to work very long hours and do what it takes?

♦ Am I willing to cut some of the fun things out of the budget so the money will be available for the business?

Only you can decide whether you have what it takes to create a successful handwriting analysis business:

♦ A real love of handwriting and of the people it represents.

♦ A desire to help others, not just to build your own ego by entertaining friends with what you know about someone's personality from their handwriting.

♦ The wherewithal either to market yourself, or to hire someone to do it for you.

Knowing your limits and your capacity to achieve will be part of the answer. And what's the best way to do a reality check and find out if you've got what it takes to be an entrepreneur? Have your handwriting analyzed, of course!

Don't Miss the Train(ing)

It may seem obvious, but before you get ready to hang out your shingle, be sure to spend time acquiring good training and a firm foundation in graphological principles. Studying this book and following its advice provide an excellent start. Beyond that, there are correspondence courses, including my own self-study program (there's a list of recommended courses in Appendix B). And very importantly, analyze as many handwritings as you can lay your hands on.

The well-educated graphologist knows that a knowledge of handwriting is not enough by itself. A basic understanding of personality development and abnormal psychology are just as important, if not more so. And if you plan to venture into personnel screening, you'll also need to know about employment laws. A good book on organizational behavior would help, too.

> **Tales from the Quill**
>
> A business owner saw a newspaper article featuring a graphologist in her town. The article claimed this woman was the "top graphologist in the country." Wanting to hire a new receptionist, the business owner decided to contact her. On close questioning, this so-called "top graphologist" admitted that her only training was an online class that claimed it would make her a handwriting analyst in 10 minutes.

Raising the Standard

Everyone has a personal set of ethics and standards, and no one has the right to tell anyone else what to do or not to do. Unless, that is, what they are doing is outright unethical and harmful to their clients or to the practice of graphology. We are dealing with people's lives, and we need to be responsible and ethical in the way we present ourselves. Please read the graphologist's Global Code of Ethics posted on my website (www.sheilalowe.com).

Chicken Scratch

Inflating one's credentials is unethical. When a professional is called upon to testify in court and is unable to substantiate his claims about the supposed degrees and courses he has taken, he looks bad. Even worse, he opens himself up to charges of perjury and possible jail time. And what one graphologist does reflects on all.

Is It Legal?

There are many applications for handwriting analysis, such as working with individuals to gain greater self-knowledge with couples in relationship compatibility, or helping someone make vocational choices. Probably the widest use, however, is pre-employment screening.

Many employers recognize handwriting analysis as an important tool in personnel selection and employee management. At the same time, they want to protect themselves from lawsuit-happy applicants and employees, and are concerned about the legality of using someone's handwriting this way.

Here's where I should probably insert some legal mumbo jumbo, to the effect that what follows should not be construed as legal advice and that state laws vary, so you may want to check with your attorney. The information that follows applies generally to all handwriting professionals practicing in the United States, so if you live elsewhere, talk to an employment lawyer in your own area.

Is It an Invasion of Privacy?

One of the biggest concerns employers raise is whether a handwriting analysis invades an applicant's privacy. Some people believe that their handwriting is private and shouldn't be used to reveal anything about them. Where do they, and the employer, stand legally?

In cases related to other personal matters, such as your likeness (photograph), the courts have decided that generally, you have no right to privacy. Just ask the paparazzi! The same is true of your voice. Barring illegal wiretaps, if someone records your voice, it's not an invasion of privacy. That is, unless the situation where you were recorded was intended to be private.

Did you know that if you have a large bay window in the front of your house and you leave the curtains open, that legally, you have no expectation of privacy if someone looks in? You'd have to pull the drapes and the peeper would have to go to extreme measures to see in before your right to privacy would be violated. Makes you want to draw the shades, doesn't it!

> **Tales from the Quill**
>
> A handwriting professional was sued by a woman who was refused employment. She claimed that she had not given permission for the analysis, and that it was an invasion of her privacy. At trial, the graphologist was able to show that the applicant had signed a waiver, giving permission for her handwriting to be analyzed. The case was dismissed.

The law says that if a person doesn't take "reasonable steps" to protect his privacy, *there is no expectation of privacy.* We can apply this principle to handwriting analysis. When the applicant fills out the employment application form in his handwriting, he knows the employer and others are going to read it and consider the information he has written there; therefore, there is no expectation of privacy. Having said that, it's not a bad idea to use a waiver, even if it seems like overkill.

A Potential Problem

Now, here's where a potential problem could arise. Let's say that Mr. Jones at XYZ Company, a manufacturing company, retains a handwriting analyst to prepare a report on an applicant he's considering for the sales manager position. The analyst blithely faxes over the report, assuming that Mr. Jones or his secretary will be there to receive the fax.

Instead, the receptionist picks up the fax, reads the report, and picks up on some comments about the applicant that could be construed as negative. In water-cooler conversation, she repeats what she read to her friend, coloring it slightly with her own take on it. Her friend repeats the remark to someone in the receiving room, coloring it a bit more with her own viewpoint, and so on, and so on. You get the picture. It's like that old "telephone" game, where one person whispers something to the next, and by the time it gets around the room, the original message is completely distorted.

These days, virtually everyone in business has e-mail, so this is less of a problem than it used to be, as reports can be e-mailed directly to the person with the need to know. But we also have to be careful with what we say in e-mail. Remember Enron? When the company folded, about a million company e-mails, many of them highly personal, were posted on the Internet by the government. *Never put in writing something that you wouldn't want to come back and haunt you.* Some handwriting analysts prefer to give only oral reports.

Fine Points

If you feel alone in the world of graphology, apply to join the Vanguard2 Forum Online discussion list. This wonderful group has members on all levels of expertise around the world. It's a place to network, learn, and make new friends. Anything pertaining to human behavior is fair game. The only rule: no personal attacks allowed. E-mail your request to join to sheila@ sheilalowe.com.

Sex, Drugs, and Rock 'n' Roll for $100, Alex

And the answer is: Talking about sexuality and substance abuse when the handwriting sample shows a potential problem in these areas is tricky. Before you put yourself in jeopardy, know the question is: what should or should not be included in the handwriting analysis report?

To be smart and legally sound, you should prepare your reports with a specific question in mind. For instance, "Does this person have the personality requirements for the job?" or "Why is this writer having problems keeping a relationship together?" or "What is a good field for the writer to look for work?"

Once you know the question, your report should address the answer directly and specifically, relating your comments to the job at hand. That means, unless the applicant's sexual functioning has some direct effect on the job, it is inappropriate to discuss it. The applicant's sexual preferences or sex drive is usually not the employer's or your business.

Fine Points

In the case of an applicant seeking a position as a schoolteacher or caregiver where red flags for inappropriate sexual behavior or substance abuse appear, the graphologist would be justified in discussing them with the client.

To know what is appropriate and fair game for discussion, ask for a good job description along with the handwriting sample. Besides knowing the type of duties the employee will be handling, you'll need some information about the environment she'll be working in. For instance, will she be in a private office on her own with employees reporting to her? Or does the job require interaction with a team? Will her duties keep her tied to a desk, or will she be driving around in her car much of the time? Who will she report to?

With the answers to these questions, you'll be much better equipped to provide a report that will be helpful to your client, the employer. Without knowing what the questions are, all you can give is a mishmash of personality traits, kind of like vegetable soup—good, unless you wanted navy bean. You have to know what the client is looking for.

The job description will provide clues about whether the successful candidate needs to be independent or subordinate; whether she needs to handle many routine tasks or is required to make quick changes; whether the job calls for a more sedentary or a more active person; whether an outgoing personality is important; and numerous other traits of concern to the employer.

Anyway, back to the original point. Don't discuss personal aspects that have no bearing on the job. There is one caveat to that rule: If you see danger signs—red flags—you are obligated to report them to your client. But it may be better to do so in person or over the phone, rather than in writing. This would include signs of possible substance abuse.

> **Chicken Scratch**
>
> Discussing sexual issues or substance abuse with an employer is definitely not an area for a beginning graphologist. If you think there may be a problem, ask an experienced handwriting analyst for help.

Point of Impact

The Equal Employment Opportunity Commission (EEOC) deals, among other things, with job application testing procedures. They want to know whether a test discriminates against a prospective employee. If the answer is yes, the test violates Title 7 of the Civil Rights Act. It's called *Disparate Impact.*

A test would be discriminatory if it centered on race, age, gender, ethnicity, or religious affiliation. Add to that the Americans with Disabilities Act (ADA), which forbids discrimination against persons with mental or physical disabilities.

def•i•ni•tion

> **Disparate Impact** occurs when an employment policy indirectly discriminates against one or more protected classes of individuals, or when similar standards have different consequences. Protected classes include gender, race, age, religion, and national origin.

Handwriting analysis does not conclusively reveal age, gender, race, or religion, and most of the time, the analyst never meets or even sees the applicant. Thus, it is one of the most nondiscriminatory tests available.

People who have contacted the EEOC to find out whether there was any reason why an employer shouldn't use handwriting analysis were told, "We are not aware of any evidence or cases which suggest that graphology has an adverse impact on a protected class." As long as you know the laws and stay within their confines, you should be fine.

When you instruct your client on how to obtain a legally sound handwriting sample, you may want to suggest that he ask the applicant to write answers to questions such as the following:

- What interests you most about this position?

- What motivates you to do your best in a job?

- What is the biggest mistake you've made and what have you done about it?

Telling It Like It Is: Ethics and the Handwriting Analyst

Don't make hiring recommendations; that's not your job. Along with your analysis, the employer has his impressions from the interview, background check, and skills testing. He is the one with all the facts, and he is responsible for deciding whether to hire an applicant or not. All you have is one piece of the puzzle, the handwriting, and that does not equip you to tell the employer that he should or should not hire someone. What you *can* do is provide an objective analysis of the applicant's personality based on the requirements for the job.

What They Don't Know Can Hurt Them

As a handwriting professional, you have a responsibility to teach your clients what you expect from them, as well as what they can expect from you. Prepare an information sheet explaining what you will provide, what it will cost, and what information they can and cannot expect from the analysis. Let the client know how to avoid potential problems from lawsuits over handwriting analyses. Rita Risser's book, *Stay Out Of Court*, boils it down to three essential points:

- Request a handwriting sample of all applicants, whether or not their handwriting is going to be analyzed.

- Focus the analysis strictly on personality characteristics necessary for successful job performance.

- Supply the report only to those with a direct need to know the results (e.g., hiring committee, employer, supervisor).

Whenever possible, examine original samples of at least one page in length (see Chapter 1 on what constitutes a good sample). When an inadequate sample (such as a photocopy, fax copy, or just a few lines) is supplied, include a disclaimer stating that your findings are subject to later verification if you are provided with the original writing.

Ask Not What Your Client Can Do for You

The client/employer needs to be able to expect certain things from you, the hand-writing analyst. Let's call it the Client's Bill of Rights:

- ◆ The client has the right to expect competent services.

- ◆ The client has the right to receive timely results.

- ◆ The client has the right to expect an accurate analysis.

- ◆ The client has the right to have his questions answered about the applicant's personality.

Because there is no state or federal licensure for handwriting analysts, a prospective client may not know how to properly select a competent practitioner. The most important thing for him to know is that any graphologist who prepares handwriting analysis reports for money should be certified by a reputable educational handwriting analysis organization (not just the school where they studied, which has a profit motive in promoting them).

Aside from personal references from a happy user, the prospective client would be wise to contact one of the nonprofit organizations, such as the American Handwriting Analysis Foundation (AHAF) or the American Association of Handwriting Analysts (AAHA). You'll find contact information about several such organizations in Appendix B.

We Have Rights, Too!

The client isn't the only one with rights. Here's my Graphologist's Bill of Rights:

- ◆ The analyst has the right to expect an adequate handwriting sample to analyze.

- ◆ The analyst has the right to qualify his or her opinion when the sample is less than adequate.

- ◆ The analyst has the right to expect appropriate fees, paid in a timely manner.

- ◆ The analyst has the right to refuse an analysis if the client does not offer proof of a reasonable "need to know," such as for employment or relationship compatibility.

Computer + Graphology = Strange Bedfellows?

In the mid-1990s, I was approached by a software company asking me to work with them to develop a computer program that would analyze handwriting. Although my first husband and I had developed a rudimentary program back in 1977 for my personal use, I balked at the idea. I didn't see how untrained users would be able to get an accurate report.

Many meetings with the software engineers ensued, where they convinced me that between us, we could put together a program that would take the drudgery out of the analysis process, provide reports for people who weren't so comfortable writing them, and get the word out about graphology.

After hundreds of hours of testing and research, Sheila Lowe's Handwriting Analyzer™ was born and quickly grew into a tool that is used internationally by businesses, governments, law enforcement agencies, psychologists, graphologists, and individuals. The feedback has been phenomenal.

Fine Points

RI Software, developer of the Handwriting Analyzer, has made it possible to do analyses right from their website, www.writinganalysis.com, without purchasing the software package. You can do a short analysis for free, or a full analysis for a nominal fee.

The Handwriting Analyzer software comes in two versions. The Professional version is designed for employers and graphologists doing both employment and personal analysis. It provides a variety of personal and business reports, charts, and graphs. The Job Ranking graph allows you to view the scores of several applicants next to each other and see how they rate. Or, you can compare one applicant to several job descriptions to see which he is best suited to. The Personal version focuses solely on personal reports, which cover some different areas from the business reports. I call it the Handwriting Analyzer Lite.

Sheila Lowe's Handwriting Analyzer—a sample screen showing the category list and some of the margin category choices.

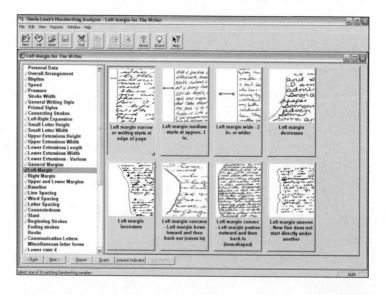

How'd They Do That?

The Handwriting Analyzer software uses the same principles of gestalt graphology that you've learned from this book: spatial arrangement, writing form, and writing movement. Some of the individual strokes and letters are also listed, but they are given less weight when the software computes the results.

The question I am most often asked is, "Do I need a scanner?" The answer is no. The computer can handle only the measurable aspects of handwriting. The analysis still requires human input. The second question is, "Then how does it work?"

Easy! Compare the handwriting sample you want to analyze to a series of on-screen illustrations. Inside the Analyzer, you'll find a list of categories of handwriting elements, such as "Organization," "Writing Style," "Rhythm," and so on.

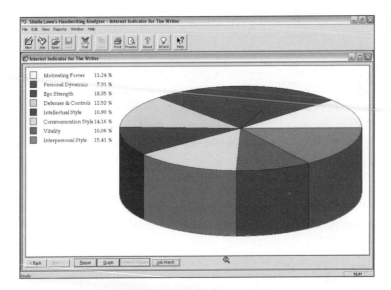

Interest Indicator Chart.

Next to each general category is a series of pictures of handwriting. Let's say you selected the category "Slant." Seven types of slant are illustrated, from "Upright" to "Variable." Simply click your mouse on the picture where the slant looks most like the handwriting sample you are analyzing (descriptions on the illustrations and "Q-Cards" tell you what to look for). After you've matched the handwriting in at least 10 major categories, generate a report by clicking on the "Report" button.

Job Ranking and Job Matching Graphs

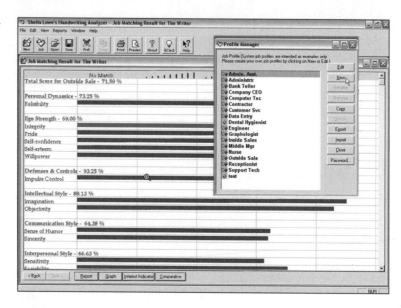

CliffsNotes for Graphologists

The Handwriting Analyzer software can be a helpful teaching tool for people studying graphology. Students prepare an analysis and compare their results to the computer report. They can test themselves by trying to find where in the handwriting the various statements came from.

By the way, I don't mean to brag (yeah, right), but Sheila Lowe's Handwriting Analyzer won the Ziff-Davis Five Star Editor's Pick Award, and has been featured in *Entrepreneur* magazine, *PC World*, and many other prestigious places.

The Last Word—Really!

If you're feeling brain-dead by now, don't worry. Just relax and let it all simmer. One day soon, you'll look at a handwriting sample and get that big "aha!" moment, where the personality behind the handwriting suddenly becomes clear.

The most important lesson that I hope you have learned from these pages is that no element of handwriting means anything standing on its own. Always, *always*, look at the whole picture and interpret every sign or feature according to the context in which it appears.

Finally, no matter how many handwriting samples you analyze, please remember: behind every handwriting is a human being with tender feelings, just like yours. As the great graphologist and fine human being Felix Klein reminded fellow graphologists in a letter shortly before his death in 1994, *"Be kind. Everyone is fighting a hard battle."*

Happy Analyzing!

The Least You Need to Know

- There are important steps to follow along the path to success as a graphologist.
- You have to decide what sacrifices you are willing to make in order to be in business for yourself.
- To create a successful business, you can't just be a good graphologist—you also have to be good at sales and marketing.
- There are many different applications for graphology. Working with human resource managers is the most popular.
- Ethical practice means being transparent about your background and credentials, not inflating them.

Glossary

airstroke   The movement of the pen as it is raised from the paper and continues in the same direction in the air.

angular forms   Sharp, straight strokes that are made by stopping the pen and changing direction before continuing.

arcade forms   Forms that look like arches, rounded on the top and open at the bottom. Fast arcades have a more positive connotation than slow arcades.

baseline   The invisible line upon which writing "rests."

connectedness   The degree to which one letter attaches to another.

connective forms   The shape of the connections between letters. The primary connective forms are garland, arcade, angular, and thread.

copybook   The standard of handwriting instruction taught in a particular school. The most common copybook standards in the United States are D'Nealian and Palmer.

covering stroke   A stroke that unnecessarily covers over another stroke in a concealing action.

cursive writing   Writing in which one letter is joined to the next.

double curve   An indefinite connective form that combines the arcade and the garland. Also called a "double s link," due to its resemblance to the letter *s*.

downstroke   The movement of the pen toward the writer. The backbone of handwriting, without which the writing becomes completely illegible.

figure and ground   The dark space (ink) and white space (paper). In the handwriting gestalt, it refers to the balance between the ink and the paper.

final   The ending stroke on a letter when it is at the end of a word.

form   The writer's chosen writing style. The way the writing looks, whether it is copybook, elaborated, simplified, or printed.

fullness   The width of letters compared to their height. The ratio of height to width in the copybook model is 1:1 in the middle zone and 1:.5 in the upper and lower zones. Full writing is wider than copybook.

garland forms   A cuplike connective form that is open at the top and rounded on the bottom.

gestalt   The German word that means "complete" or "whole." A good gestalt needs nothing added or taken away to make it "look right." Also, a school of handwriting analysis that looks at handwriting as a whole picture.

initial   An added stroke at the beginning of a letter as it moves into the word.

knots   Extra loops that appear as if tied in a knot.

letter space   The amount of space left between letters.

ligature   The connections that tie one letter to another.

line direction   Movement of the baseline. May slant up, down, or straight across the page.

line space   The amount of space left between lines.

margins   The amount of space left around the writing on all four sides.

movement   Writing in four dimensions: across the page, up and down as it goes from left to right, into the paper, and above the paper (airstroke).

narrowness   The width of upper- and lower-zone letters, which is less than half the middle-zone height in the copybook model. See also *fullness*.

natural handwriting   The writing of someone who has reached graphic maturity and no longer needs to stop and consciously think about what he is writing.

pen hold   The place where the writer grasps the barrel of the pen and the angle at which he holds it.

personal pronoun I (PPI)   The capital letter *I*, the one single letter in the English language that represents the writer.

pressure   There are several types of pressure: grip pressure refers to how tightly the writer holds the pen; primary pressure is the degree to which the pen digs into the paper; secondary pressure is the rhythm of light/dark strokes produced by movement on the paper.

printed writing   Disconnected writing.

printscript   A creative combination of printing and cursive writing.

psychogram   A circular graph devised by Dr. Klara Roman in the 1930s to provide a visual measurement of personality.

rhythm   Periodicity, alternation of movement.

school model   Same as copybook—the style of writing taught in school.

simplification   Eliminating extra or superfluous strokes from the copybook model.

size   May refer to the overall size of the writing or the proportions between zones.

slant   The angle between the up- and downstrokes in relation to the baseline.

space   The overall pattern of spatial arrangement on the paper. Includes the width of margins and letter, word, and line spacing.

speed   The personal pace at which the writer's pen moves across the paper.

supported strokes   Upstrokes partially covering the previous downstrokes. Originally taught in European schools.

tension   The degree of force exerted on the pen compared to the degree of relaxation.

thready forms   An indefinite connective form that looks flat and wavy.

trait stroke   A school of handwriting analysis that assigns personality trait names to individual writing strokes.

tremor   Shakiness along the writing stroke produced by poor physical health, anxiety, or external causes.

upstroke   Movement of the pen away from the writer.

variability   The degree to which the writing varies from the copybook model.

word space   The amount of space left between words.

writing impulse   The result of the pen touching down on the paper and moving across the page, until it is raised from the paper.

writing zones   The three distinct areas of writing: upper, middle, and lower zones. Each represents a specific area of personality functioning, but all work together to produce the whole person.

Recommended Handwriting Analysis Organizations and Schools

Recommended Schools of Handwriting Analysis

Sheila Lowe's Self-Study Course in Gestalt Graphology

A companion to *The Complete Idiot's Guide to Handwriting Analysis, Second Edition*, this series of lessons builds on and amplifies topics introduced in the book. Although it is designed as a self-study program, students are welcome to e-mail or call with questions. Lessons may be purchased separately, or in a group at a discount.

Contact: www.sheilalowe.com/gestalt.html
Phone: 805-658-0109

Felix Klein's Courses

The Felix Klein gestalt graphology courses, personally taught by Janice Klein, consist of three levels: elementary, intermediate, and advanced. Each level has 10 lessons and may be paid for on a lesson-by-lesson basis (no contract to sign). The elementary course includes trend, connections, slant, pressure, style evaluation, and so forth.

Contact: Janice Klein, 250 W. 57th St., Suite 1228A, New York, NY 10108.
Phone: 212-265-1148

The Insyte Challenge

This course, taught by Sister June Canoles, combines holistic and trait-stroke methods. Students must *evaluate* from day one in lesson one. It includes 20 lessons of approximately 26 pages each with practice exercises in each lesson, final tests, super sheets, flash cards, scrapbook work, and enrichment cassettes.

Contact: http://insytegraphology.com
Phone: 408-252-9696

Step-by-Step System of Handwriting Analysis

The SSS course is a comprehensive course taught by Erika Karohs, for the serious student who wants to become a truly professional analyst. Prior knowledge of handwriting analysis is desirable but not a prerequisite.

Contact: www.karohs.net
Phone: 831-624-8151

Academy of Handwriting Sciences

The comprehensive training includes step-by-step lessons, hundreds of handwriting illustrations, flash cards, review questions, examinations, complex charts, extensive report writing, recommended reading, and more. The academy provides a personalized and thorough review of the student's lessons and questions.

Contact: http://iwhome.com/spectrum/academy.htm
Phone: 520-529-8531

Recommended Organizations

The Vanguard Network for Handwriting Professionals and Serious Students

The Vanguard is not a formal organization. It is a network of ethical handwriting professionals and serious students actively pursuing a career in handwriting analysis. Members of the network are committed to maintaining ethical professional standards and cultivating their analytical abilities and competency. The Vanguard also offers a quarterly newsletter, available by subscription, and Vanguard2 Forum Online is a private Internet discussion list.

Information about events, a certification syllabus, and a free copy of the Vanguard newsletter are available for downloading from www.sheilalowe.com.

Contact: Sheila@sheilalowe.com
Phone: 805-658-0109

Nonprofit Handwriting Analysis Organizations in the United States

The following are nonprofit education organizations that welcome anyone interested in handwriting. Most offer newsletters, conferences, and certification testing.

American Handwriting Analysis Foundation
www.handwritingfoundation.org

American Association of Handwriting Analysts
www.handwriting.org

National Society for Graphology
www.nationalsocietyforgraphology.com

American Society of Professional Graphologists
www.aspghandwriting.org

Handwriting Analysis Research Library
www.handwritinganalysisresearchlibrary.org
413-774-4667

Overseas Handwriting Analysis Organizations

UNITED KINGDOM

The British Academy of Graphology
www.graphology.co.uk

British Institute of Graphology
www.britishgraphology.org

International Graphology Association
www.graphology.org.uk

BELGIUM

Association Belge de Graphologie
www.graphologie-asso.be

CANADA

International Graphological Colloquium
www.igc-grapho.net

GERMANY

Deutsche Graphologische Vereinigung
www.schriftpsychologie.org

ISRAEL

Israel Society for Scientific Graphology
www.graphology.org.il

ITALY-FRANCE

Associazione Italo-Francese di Grafologia
www.agif-grafologia.it

For many other graphological associations around the world:
www.graphology.ws/2162-graphology-organisations.htm

Index